MASS COMMUNICATION IN PREVENTION AND CONTROL OF AIDS

About the Author

Archana Rakesh Singh (nee Shukla) is a faculty in mass communication at Panjab University, Chandigarh. Earlier, she taught at the Gwalior study centre of Makhan Lal Chaturvedi National Journalism University, Bhopal.

Dr. Singh gained her Bachelor and Master degrees in Journalism from Rani Durgavati Vishwavidyalaya, Jabalpur and the Banaras Hindu University, Varanasi, respectively and topped both. After clearing the University Grant Commission's National Entrance Test, she was accepted as Junior Research Fellow at AJKMCRC New Delhi, where she completed her Ph.D. She has been involved with the subject of AIDS communication since the mid-1990s. She was a part of the investigating team from MCRC, Jamia Millia Islamia for conducting AIDS awareness and Media search Survey amongst adolescents in Chennai.

MASS COMMUNICATION IN PREVENTION AND CONTROL OF AIDS

Strategies for Adolescents

Archana Rakesh Singh

CONCEPT PUBLISHING COMPANY, NEW DELHI-110059

Cataloging in Publication Data—DK
Courtesy: D.K. Agencies (P) Ltd. <docinfo@dkagencies.com>

Singh, Archana Rakesh, 1966-
Mass communication in prevention and control on AIDS : strategies for adolescents / Archana Rakesh Singh.
p. cm.
Includes bibliographical references (p.)
Includes index.
ISBN 8180692698

1. AIDS (Disease) and mass media—India. 2. AIDS (Disease)—India—Prevention. I. Title.

DDC 070.449 362 196 979 2 22

ISBN-81-8069-269-8

First Published 2006

Published and Printed by
Ashok Kumar Mittal
Concept Publishing Company
A/15-16, Commercial Block. Mohan Garden
New Delhi-110059 (INDIA)

Phones : 25351460, 25351794
Fax : 091-11-25357103
Email : publishing@conceptpub.com

Dedication

This work is dedicated to the memory of
Late Mr. Anwar Jamaal Kidwai

My first guide, who showed me the direction and urged me to move on

Acknowledgements

As one ventures to take up an enormous task such as this one, one is confident that there is a support system that will ensure a successful completion of the task. Without this support system, anyone desirous of conducting research, will have to work twice as hard.

For this study, not only teachers, friends and family have helped, but absolute strangers have extended a helping hand whenever the need arose. All the teachers, staff and students of sample schools, all participants of FGDs, staff of different libraries that I have visited, members of various government and non-government organizations working for the cause of AIDS, my thanks to them all. It would not be possible to thank all of them by name but their cooperation is appreciated.

At the very outset, I would like to express my deep felt gratitude, to Late Prof. A.J. Kidwai Sahib. This work is dedicated to his memory. Had he not been a source of encouragement and guidance to me, I would not have taken up a subject as sensitive as AIDS. It was his confidence in me that helped me face all challenges. I shall always remain grateful to him.

My sincere thanks to my supervisors, Dr. Gita Bamezai of the National Institute of Health and Family Welfare, New Delhi and Professor H.R. Kidwai, former Chairman, AJK Mass Communication Research Centre, Jamia Millia Islamia, New Delhi.

Dr. Bamezai always gave me a patient hearing, solved the puzzles of methodologies and sampling, introduced me to the subject of research from a practical standpoint. She always helped me to stay updated on the latest developments in the field. She took personal interest in my work and offered unending support and guidance. I am grateful for her strict supervision and demand for perfection. She always helped me improve myself and this is one lesson that I have learnt for life. My sincere thanks to her.

Prof. Habib Kidwai took over where A.J. Kidwai Sahib had left. With same faith in my abilities he urged me to move on. He has always been supportive and always took time off from his busy schedule to listen to my problems. With his characteristic calmness he solved all the problems that I faced. I am thankful for his constant encouragement, support and guidance, without which it would not have been possible to complete this work.

My sincere thanks to the teachers and staff of Mass Communication Research Centre Jamia Millia Islamia and the National Institute of Health and Family Welfare, who helped me at all times. Mr. Y. Nigam, Mr. Fahim Khan, Ms. Poornima Bradoo from MCRC, my deep thanks to them all. Special thanks to the staff of the statistics department of NIHFW, who worked with me for days helping me finalise my questionnaire. The entire designing and coding of the questionnaire was completed at NIHFW and I remain grateful to them.

A special mention has to be made of Dr. Bhashini Rao, Enisha Sarin, Dr. Shankar Chowdhary, Ms. Anjali Gopalan, Ms. Vijaylaxmi Bose and Ms. Ruhi Tabassum Khan for involving me in AIDS related projects, which helped me to get a deeper insight into the subject.

I am grateful to my sister, Ms. Shilpa Singh and to my brother in law, Mr. Dhiraj Singh, who spent days and nights, helping me to enter the data of 443 questionnaires into the computer. It was a repetitive and tiring job and would not have been possible single-handedly.

Mr. Naresh and Niti Sachdeva deserve a special mention for the help they extended in arranging school permissions in Ghaziabad. They also arranged for my stay in Ghaziabad while I was there for the survey. My thanks to them.

I would also like to acknowledge the contribution of Dr. Kiron Bansal of IGNOU, who offered friendly advice and gave useful tips for report writing. Thanks to Dr. Charanjeev Singh and Mr. Swaran Singh of Panjab University who solved the mystery of SPSS for data analysis. Special thanks to Professor B. K. Kuthiala, Dean, Faculty of Media Studies Guru Jambheshwar University, Hisar, for useful guidance which has improved this project remarkably. My special thanks to Ms. Suneet Khetarpal for designing the cover.

This is also an opportunity to thank my parents Major B.K. Shukla and Mrs. Sudha Shukla, who have always been my pillars of strength. The confidence of my father and the unflinching support of my mother makes me strive harder to excel myself. They have taken care of my children, managed my home and offered all help that I ever needed. Their contribution to this work cannot be measured. Merely thanking them would not be enough, but all the same I want them to know that I feel deeply grateful for all they have done for me.

This is also the time to thank a few dear people, who tolerated my absent mindedness, my bad moods and preoccupations. My daughters Sowmya, and Pallavi, learnt early in life the significance of education. My deep felt thanks to them for giving me a peaceful home and patient understanding. God bless them both.

Last but not the least, my heartfelt thanks to my husband Mr. Rakesh Singh, who invested so many years of his life in my education. His contribution to this work is very much the same as mine. He helped me with tables and graphs, burned the midnight oil to help me finish the collation and compilation of the final report and managed home and hearth with élan whenever I was out of town. Despite his demanding work schedule he always spared time for my work as he was my sole adviser and critic. Without his support, I would not have been where I am today. My thanks to him.

I want to once again thank all the people whose names are mentioned above and also all the people whose names are not here but they are always in my memory.Thank you one and all.

Archana Rakesh Singh

Contents

1

Introduction

Communication and development are the major domains of human endeavour which are intimately linked with each other.The process of development calls for a strategy of communication which is aimed at altering the targeted persons from mere recipients of information to seekers of information. This is achieved by the design of communication systems, as per the needs and purposes of the targeted persons. The Triple M theory of the emergence of mass society, mass culture and mass communication links, mass communication to the formation of nations and societies as a result of geographical, social and psychic mobility.

Many people have defined communication in different ways. Aristotle defined the study of communication as a search for all available means of persuasion. According to Berlo, the sole purpose of communication is to influence. Schramm described the purpose of communication as immediate reward and delayed reward. According to Lee Thayer, the basic purposes of communication are, the Information function, Command or Instructive function, Influence or persuasive function and the Integrative function. In order to fulfil these varieties of functions mass media uses various approaches. These approaches range from intra personal to mass approaches, with each approach contributing to the fulfilment of the various functions in its own way. (Kaliyaperumal, 1992).

Mass communication can best serve in the process of change, if it is treated as a science, art and indeed as subject matter. It is much more than editing, reporting, broadcasting or telecasting. The word communication is derived from Latin origin, 'communis' which means— to make common, to share information, idea or attitude, to impart, to transmit. All meaningful social interactions are called communication. The main function or purpose of communication is to change or guide other people's behaviour. (Mcquail Denis, 1994) People vary so widely in their socio-economic conditions, traditions, attitudes, beliefs and levels of knowledge that a uniform communication approach may not be suitable. Communicators have to develop an understanding of the mass audiences. In such instances, audiences are usually grouped according to various characteristics—for example, language, art, culture, economic class, educational level and so on. Understanding of these audiences is usually built up over time through research and experience. There is always a need to study the role that was being played by the mass media in the process of development in general and in various aspects of development such as, agriculture, housing, education, trade, commerce, science and technology, defence, health etc. in particular.

Diffusion researchers pioneered the 'Two step flow' dimension of mass media where in diffusion stresses the acceptance and adaptation of innovations, and two step flow model emphasizes on transfer of information. The adapters of innovations range from innovators, early adapters, early majority, late majority to laggards. (Katz and Lazarsfeld, 1955) The concept of ethnodevelopment contradicts the diffusion theories (Rogers, 1976) and suggests that projects must be designed by the people rather than for the people. 'Basic needs model' is proposed for self-management and self-organisation of the poor. Whatever the strategy, communication is an integral part of any attempt at development. Media persons and media organisations are in the centre of development communication. Development cannot be measured in terms of economic growth alone. Social, political, cultural, growth is imperative for overall development. Technology transfer and economic communications are necessary for economic development but these are not sufficient for social development. Cognitive, affective and connative dimensions of values which foster social development for balancing the contributive and distributive justice of economic growth for a harmonious social life, would warrant affecting changes in the opinions, attitudes, values and value orientations of public through appropriate communication policy. The communication patterns in modern societies tend to be one sided as denoted by the popular definition as 'who says what to whom and with what effect'. The concept of communication geared towards the transmitter, with access to sophisticated tools of mass media is incomplete unless the last part of the definition is given due importance. Trying to control the behaviours of people by disseminating messages widely and quickly is expecting too much from the communicators without the proper study of the receivers.

Theory of media and communications has many variants, but most support the modern (that is, secular, materialistic, western, individualist etc.) ways and individual motivation as the key to change. People need to want to 'get on' (Mclelland, 1961). The contribution of mass media can take several forms. They can help promote the diffusion and adoption of many technological innovations which are essential to modernization (Rogers, 1962,1976). They can encourage a state of mind favourable to modernity (Lerner, 1958). In societies that are moving towards development, communication policies have to be designed for every sector. Apart from having development communication policies for agriculture, industry, education, housing, trade and commerce, rural and urban areas, science and technology, defence, youth, and women etc. one major area which offsets development planning is health communication. The present development communication programmes seem to address themselves to symptoms rather than to the causes of underdevelopment (Trakroo and Jagatdeb,1992).

Health and family welfare are an integral part of development programmes, but the use of mass media has not succeeded in persuading people to adopt certain measures. The main factors identified are paucity of resources, vastness of Indian traditional ethos, low education and literacy profile, diversity of languages and dialects, lack of coordination between communicators and policy planners and the overall resistance to change. Trakroo and Jagatdeb suggest that the overall health communication should be such that it not only empowers people but also enables them to make informed decisions on personal and delicate questions. Concrete relationships have been drawn between, socio-economic development and health communication as they are found to be complimentary to each other. Health communication contributes to actions and organizations in the development process. Further health development is important in mobilizing people's efforts in social and economic life. Communication in that sense is the product of the society and also the moulder of society (Hiramani and Sharma, 1992).

For the purpose of this study, only the mass approach of communication has been studied. This media reaches a large audience in a short time. Uniformity in message is maintained. Although selective perception and retention are hurdles in the effectiveness of this method but mass media certainly has proven value in spreading information. However, mere spreading of information is not sufficient unless it is followed by its effectiveness in changing attitudes and practices. The wide gap that exists between awareness of family planning and the adoption of contraception also shows the inability of mass media by themselves to produce behaviour changes, and there is consequently a strong tendency to integrate mass media with other channels of communication.

Mass media can create an environment, make issues out of topics, help to create a favourable social climate, counter hostile propaganda, dispel rumours and clarify doubts and misunderstandings.

For the purpose of spreading messages about AIDS and related subjects, and in order to reach out to different target groups one or more media has to be adopted. A judicious combination of methods and media will depend upon the target audience and the contents of the message. While selecting the methods and the media, one has to consider the background of the target audience, their communication patterns, power structure of their society, culture etc. Methods of communication could range from individual contacts, group discussions demonstrations and campaign methods to mass communication. Mass media although does not directly change behaviour, but it provides the right atmosphere, the ambiance for behaviour modification. Mass media can make a topic popular, fashionable or noteworthy of attention. A message when picked up by a few opinion leaders can be spread around and become a way of life.

The Issue of AIDS

Developing countries the world over are facing several deadly diseases, chief among them is Acquired Immune Deficiency Syndrome or AIDS. This acronym evokes a response of familiarity today. Two and a half decades ago it was not so. In the summer of 1981, the Centre for Disease Control in the United States of America reported that five previously healthy homosexual men in Los Angeles were suffering from an unusual type of pneumonia caused by Pneumocystis carinii, a parasite which is mostly harmless to humans. CDC also reported that 26 previously healthy homosexual men in New York and Los Angeles had developed a rare form of skin cancer called Kaposi's Sarcoma. These reports signalled the arrival of a mysterious acquired disorder of the human immune system which disabled the body's defences. This was the beginning of one of the biggest public health and developmental problems of this century, which started from mere smoke signals and swept across the globe like wildfire. By, early 1989, more than 140000 AIDS cases had been officially reported to WHO from around the world. By May 1997, this figure skyrocketed to 544067 cases (AIDS: No time for complacency, 1997). By the year 2000 more than 40 million people have been infected. More than 7000 people are getting infected everyday.

AIDS is now the fourth leading cause of death globally (*Newsweek*, June 11, 2001). The first reported case in Asia was in Thailand in 1984. By 1997, over 65000 cases of AIDS have been reported from this region. By the year 2000 nearly 10 million people have been infected in this region. Thailand and India have reported the largest number of cases (95%). The alarming rise in the Sexually Transmitted Diseases has put our country at top position in AIDS cases in the South Asian sub-continent. In India the HIV epidemic has reached an advanced stage with Maharashtra and Manipur continuing to have the highest rate of infection (NACO, 1994). India has more than 20 million HIV infected people, the largest number in any country. It appears that India is sitting on a time bomb which has already begun exploding. It will not be long before the predicted 6000 to 12500 people begin to die everyday (Mundal, M., Gilada, I., 1993).

Nearly two decades after AIDS was first identified, scientists worldwide are still grappling with the human immunodeficiency virus in a race to find a vaccine and a cure. According to latest research a new virus strain has been discovered which will require new type of treatment. Scientists are worried that this new virus found in South Korea has already been transmitted worldwide. Vaccines have to be developed to deal with various types of HIV (News report, *The Indian Express*, 2001). Drugs for treating AIDS have been developed, but they are expensive and can alleviate the condition only for some time. As most of the men and women afflicted are in the prime of their life, the epidemic will devastate the world especially in areas that are least able to cope. In order to win this grim battle against the epidemic it is imperative that prevention and control measures are taken at all levels—local, national, international.

HIV is a challenge that requires each of us to reconsider our traditions, morals and values and to respond positively to the pandemic. It is easy to be complacent about one's community and society, turning a blind eye to the truth. The myth of Indian morality lies shattered as more and more Indians are found to be HIV positive. Going by the present trend one in every three Indians is going to be HIV positive by the year 2006. The statistics are mind boggling. The situation seems more serious because Indians are still in the denial stage of the pandemic where they do not want to believe that they are as susceptible to the disease like anyone else.

The literature in health education/disease prevention, as well as the experience with AIDS suggests that community based AIDS prevention campaigns are most effective in bringing about rapid, large scale risk behaviour change. This is also true because there is a critical social dimension to AIDS risk behaviours. Individuals identify within a variety of groups: friends, family, profession, or ethnic groups. What they perceive to be socially acceptable within these groups has an impact on their attitudes and behaviour. There is an intimate relationship between group acceptance and individual conformity. In their false norm theory Asch and Crutchfield explain that naive subjects look to the group for some kind of confirmation of their interpretation of their environment. Non-conformity evokes a feeling of discomfort (Henry Clay Lindgren, 1986).

One example of this is the family planning effort. The idea of a small family has been sold to a generation of people and slowly as the majority of educated class chose to plan their family, the two children family became a norm. As the example was set by the educated class its effects are visible in the attitude shift of the uneducated class as well. Although the exercise took its time, and it is yet far from achieving its complete success, it can be said that consistant messages both through the mass and the interpersonal medium can lead to behaviour modification in the long run. The different steps towards sustained behaviour change through persuasive and constant communication have been outlined as:

Unaware-Aware-Knowledgeable-Ready to change-change in behaviour-sustained behaviour change

One can see that the family planning effort mentioned above has followed the same pattern. The communication aimed at a result similar to one mentioned above should follow a multi-pronged strategy, the messages coming not only through the mass media but also from the interpersonal and traditional means. However, even before a strategy has been designed to clear the misconceptions about AIDS in the minds of the people, it is important to find out what these misconceptions are and how far the people are aware of the disease and its implications and which are the areas where they lack information. It is, therefore, important to have information and education programmes aimed at all men and women including adolescents. Besides, it has been found that information campaigns often do not have budgets sufficient to ensure adequate exposure, and planners may not have sufficient understanding of target audiences to create relevant and understandable messages (Mendelsohn Harold, 1981).

It is important to recognize that AIDS is not just a health problem. It has major social and economic consequences. It also has political and ethical implications. Prevention and control of this deadly pandemic which has very serious medical, social, behavioural, economic and developmental implications has now become imperative.

Use of Mass Media for Communicating About AIDS

The mass media represents the most readily available and potentially most economical means of imparting information about HIV/AIDS. Along with other forms of communication the mass media can effectively raise public awareness and concern about HIV/AIDS. However, efforts to curb the HIV/AIDS epidemic cannot rely on news media to do it on their own (Poitor, Meyer and Zulu,1992). Communication experts have called for the mass education of the general public, and argued that this large scale education has the potential for not only correcting misinformation, but also for creating and maintaining a more favourable environment for AIDS prevention (Hornik R., Romer D., 1991).

Media has been involved in the coverage of AIDS issue since the very beginning and hence it cannot remain emotionally immune to this epidemic. The earliest press coverage of the disease was when it first surfaced as a gay disease. Over the years the nature of press coverage of the disease has changed dramatically. Initially the press coverage could be called crude and insensitive as it emphasized on the sex lives of a certain group and only reflected the public opinion at that time. As the society matured in its attitude the press too grew. By 1983, the press had taken on a responsible role and stressed the real risks and tried to calm down public hysteria over the disease (Garret, 1994). An expert group concluded at their meeting at the WHO (1993) that mass media campaigns 'have promoted widespread AIDS awareness, safer sex, and condom use'. In fact, an analysis of 10 major social marketing programmes concluded that mass advertising has contributed more to increased condom sales than any other factor, including price, cultural attitudes towards family planning and the level of national socio-economic development (Boone, M.S., Farley, J.U., Samuel, S.J., 1985). Evaluation studies have shown that there have been positive changes in condom use following AIDS prevention campaigns in the Netherlands,

Switzerland, the United Kingdom and the USA. For example, the Swiss campaign resulted in an over 50 per cent increase in the use of condoms, with over 70 per cent among those between 17-20 years of age (Romers, Hornik, 1991).

Reporting in the media can have far reaching effects amongst the public. According to the agenda setting hypothesis, of McCombs and Shaw, mass media are the directors of our perceptions. They acquaint the masses with a certain portion of reality, and through this familiarisation, agenda setting is done. Rogers and Dearing came down on the simplistic formula of McCombs and Shaw. Real life indicators of the issue should also be there for any agenda to be set at all. As is common knowledge that selective perception and cognitive dissonance helps the audience to chose the messages of their liking. Thus, the messages given by the media must find reinforcement in personal life and experiences to be accepted. This is where mass media efforts have to be supported with interpersonal and group efforts to fight the ignorance about this situation. It is convenient to think about communication from the communicators point of view but it is interesting to note the receivers viewpoint. Whilst the communicator might create the *message*, it is receiver who creates the *meaning*. Messages do not enter the receiver's head exactly as the communicator desires—messages are interpreted and analysed intellectually and meaning is constructed by the receiver. Mass media must be careful not to sensationalize news about AIDS, which can cause undue panic. According to the London based UK NGO Consortium for the third world, media reporting can be misleading due to:

- Inaccuracies, or careless use of language.
- Indiscriminate reporting of scientific information, or unbalanced selection of scientific stories.
- Misinterpretation or sensationalization of information.
- Personal attitude of reporters and editors which have influenced their reporting.
- Repeating information which though accurate at the time, has later been proved wrong.
- Failure to keep pace with rapidly changing information.
- Unfortunate use of quotes which seem to give credence to inaccurate and sometimes damaging misinformation.

Although meaning can never be conveyed absolutely, it is possible to build up meaning over time—through interaction at personal level—or through the use of a combination of multimedia and interactive approaches when dealing with larger audiences.

Although the HIV infection is a serious issue, it is important to treat it delicately and not to cause unnecessary panic among the public. Strategies have to be devised by which public is made aware and not alarmed. What is needed, therefore, is not just planned campaigns, as opposed to regular media programming, but *well planned* campaigns which utilize the full potential of mass media and entertainment. The technology and methodology for planning and implementing such campaigns do exist. Research has established that mass media are most likely to change behaviour when the information is targeted at specific audiences, comes from a credible source, provides a personally relevant and engaging message. Effective use of mass media requires careful planning, audience research, message development, pre-testing, dissemination strategy, evaluation, coordination with existing services, and linking mass media with interpersonal communication (Brown, W.J., Singhal, A., Rogers, E.M., 1989). It is important for the audience to recognise the salience of the issue, or its usefulness in their lives even if it clashes with their value system. Attitudes consists of direction, intensity and salience (Lemert, James B., 1981). Of the three components Lemert suggests, it would be easier to establish the salience of the issue in the minds of the people than other two. If people are convinced that the issues or problems are salient to them, they may be able to overcome their aversion to them enough to absorb some more information about the issue.

The Government of India has undertaken several programmes for the prevention of HIV and for dissemination of information about the epidemic. These programmes have been undertaken at national level and are directly or indirectly assisted by international agencies. One such programme, National AIDS Control Programme (NACP) was launched by Indian government in 1987. The World Bank assistance for this was US $ 84 million. This programme functions through its agency the National AIDS Control Organisation (NACO). NACO involves multiple AIDS related activities concerned with AIDS control programmes. At the central level NACO is involved in the planning, consulting, implementing, monitoring and assisting various steps undertaken by the AIDS control cells operating from various states and Union Territories. NACO also aims at essential areas like blood safety, control of sexually transmitted diseases, setting up of surveillance centres for testing of HIV virus of which more than 62 centres are already operating in the country.

Many other agencies conduct exploratory research in the field, including KABP surveys amongst different target groups and evolve guidelines for future campaigns suitable for different groups. Voluntary Health Association of India, USAID, Universities talk AIDS programme of the National Service Scheme, Department of Sports and many other government as well as non-government organisations conduct independent studies to evolve strategies for increasing awareness about the disease. Today, a special challenge in health care is taking on early comprehensive and concentrated AIDS prevention action before a major epidemic goes underway. For this, a combination of planned strategy and adequate financial and technical resource is required. Appropriate information through the mass media highlighting the adverse effects of AIDS and its impact on the society seems to be the top priority.

The mass media should help set an agenda for the country to fight the AIDS pandemic in coordination with the government, the medical professionals and the voluntary agencies. So far, the media in India have treated AIDS more as news than as a growing menace and scourge threatening both human lives and dignity (Norms for journalistic conduct: Press Council of India, 1998).

An exploratory content analysis study conducted by the Operations Research Group during 1989-90 revealed the inadequacy of print media coverage of AIDS in India. The coverage of prominent urban dailies focused more on clinical diagnostic research on AIDS in western countries, and little on the AIDS problem in India and its social implications. There are very few independent reports on AIDS and the sources of most of the stories are international agencies. Further, most stories were located in inside pages or in supplements and contentwise were superficial in nature. Newspapers are to quote experts reactive 'rather than proactive'. Instead of taking the initiative to write about the disease with the point of view of educating the public, the mass media tend to only cover the events related to AIDS and very rarely come up with analytical and thought provoking stories. However, for the benefit of the newspaper organisations and to maintain a certain decorum in the reporting of AIDS related news the Press Council of India has laid down some guidelines for the coverage of AIDS related news items by Indian newspapers.

From sporadic news, AIDS must become a campaign target for our mass media with the following Do's and Dont's:

- Media must inform and educate the people, not alarm or scare them. The emphasis must be on the HIV can be prevented from going into unaffected humans.
- Media must hammer home the point that AIDS through sexual transmission or blood infection can be prevented. Minimum precaution of use of condoms in sex, and sterilization of skin piercing instruments and their prompt disposal after use.
- Media must report every case pertaining to AIDS be it positive or negative. There must be constant liaison between the media and the medical profession to report on the latest developments and research findings.
- Media must highlight and crusade against such practices as quarantine, isolation and ostracism of AIDS patients. Besides being an affront to human dignity, these practices will not minimize AIDS infection, and are injurious to public health as: they give a false sense of security to the people outside the stigmatised group that the threat of infection has been removed and the need of precaution minimised. Also such patients will drive the AIDS problem underground and make the campaign against the scourge more difficult.

Community education, using all the latest expertise of mass educators, behavioural scientists and media experts, has to play a crucial role in spreading the message about prevention of this deadly disease. Option builders of society (political and religious leaders, movie and sports personalities etc.) must take leadership in educating the public about AIDS and how to avoid contacting this infection. Innovative and positive use of media will go a long way in making AIDS awareness campaign a success. Bringing about behaviour change, or providing a framework of support for existing appropriate behaviours, requires effective communication and the provision of resources. Mainly the requirements include: Awareness, motivation, ability, environment. A communication backdrop uses mass media to create 'top of the mind' awareness and help those working at the ground level to legitimise their activities. For instance, the red ribbon has come to symbolise the international struggle around HIV/AIDS, but this meaning has only developed through continued association with HIV/AIDS messages. The red ribbon thus acts as a trigger or reminder that links to an individual's deeper perceptions and understanding of HIV/AIDS. Mass media can be used to provide backdrop communication to HIV/AIDS activities on the ground, to reiterate key messages and concepts, and to achieve clear objectives. It can link people to the resources, it can promote vital messages and break down myths, it can promote new information and so on. Mass media can follow the following suggestions for effective AIDS prevention messaging:

- Media must force the authorities to impose rigorous blood testing norms on prostitutes and issue periodical warning to the public about areas where incidence of AIDS is high.
- Media must help the authorities in eliminating commercial blood collection and ensure pre-testing of all the blood donors for HIV and other diseases.
- Media must respect the right to privacy of AIDS patients and must not subject them to needless exposure and social stigma.
- Every mass medium must observe the terms of the final document of the international consultation of AIDS and human rights, and promptly report the violation of such rights protecting the basic human rights to life and liberty, privacy and freedom of movement.

Obstacles to Media and Communication Campaigns

Finally, a legitimate question can be raised at this point: if there is so much evidence that proves that mass media can effectively help in raising awareness, why not all countries implement well planned mass media and entertainment campaigns for AIDS prevention ?

Political Commitment

This is almost the first step. Policy makers have generally been reluctant to air prevention messages on the mass media which constitute a major obstacle (Piotrow, P., Meyer, R.C., Zulu, B.A., 1992). Carefully designed communication materials have not been released because of the opposition from politicians, broadcasters or other gatekeepers afraid of arousing religious or other resistance (Piotrow, P:, Meyer, R.C., Zulu, B.A., 1992).

Higher Start Ups

When given the choice, many policy makers tend to hesitate in choosing well planned media campaigns because of their higher start up costs, despite the fact that mass media may be the cheapest approach to use, on the basis of per capita costs. Mass media approach has been found to be most cost effective in the long run (Piotrow, P., Meyer, R.C., Zulu, B.A.,1992). A meeting in WHO on effective approaches to AIDS prevention concluded that although mass education is often expensive, it may be cost effective in terms of costs per person reached (Global programme on AIDS, 1993).

Lack of Technical Expertise

An in depth analysis, of the mass communication component, of medium term plans of national AIDS programmes, of a sample of seven countries revealed that the plans lacked definitions of appropriate 'media mix' or audience segmentation. They did not seem to be based on good knowledge of media habits and preferences of the various segments of the target groups in different regions of the countries, and among different socio-economic groups and different age groups (Elkamel, M.F., 1986).

What emerges from the foregoing discussion is that, with respect to AIDS prevention, although there is a clear opportunity for effective mass education of the general public, unplanned media coverage and entertainment material will not be appropriate or sufficient. Actions taken now will strengthen national capacities to undertake successful media campaigns. This study was designed keeping in view the need for more research on audience segmentation. The particular segment chosen for this study was school going adolescents in Delhi and Ghaziabad.

The Purpose of this Study

This study aims at finding out the role played by mass communication in AIDS prevention and control. Different research methods have been used to fulfil this aim:

- Content analysis of print media to find out the AIDS related news content in Indian newspapers.
- Study of AIDS related messages on audio visual media.
- AIDS awareness and mass media reach survey of a selected target group.
- Focus Group Discussion with the sample used for the survey.

- The impact of the disease on the social and economic scenario has been discussed at the very outset, it was felt that the implications of the mass media's involvement with the control of the disease could be studied only if the social and economic implications of the disease had been understood thoroughly.

Adolescence: Period of High Information Needs

As early as in 1992, it was estimated that about 20-25 per cent of all the HIV infections occur among young persons. Recent studies have shown that maximum people with AIDS are young adults who are in the most productive age group. This would imply that they have acquired the disease in their teenage years considering the time span of about 10 years required for the AIDS related complexes to turn into full blown disease. The infection rates in young people appear to be increasing everywhere (Faustin K. Yao, 1992). Further, in many countries it is likely that the rates will increase faster amongst girls than the boys because of cultural and social norms which subject girls to sexual experience at an earlier age. Several factors bring to the fore the urgency of dealing with the issue of young people facing the prospect of HIV and AIDS:

- AIDS can be considered to be essentially a sexually transmitted disease.
- Everywhere, with very few cultural differences, young people are becoming sexually active at an even younger age.
- HIV transmission *via* sexual activity and incest is a real possibility even though a taboo topic in many societies.
- Given the long incubation period of the disease, we can safely assume that many HIV positive adults were probably infected during their teenage years.
- The opposition of political and religious leaders (not to mention the parents and teachers) to open and objective discussions on AIDS education for young people makes implementation of innovative and potentially effective interventions on AIDS difficult.
- Even if many young people are sexually active it is also true that many are not. They have not yet acquired behaviours which can put them at risk of HIV infection. It is, therefore, much easier to teach them positive behaviours now than to try to change the negative ones that are firmly established.

The recent government decision on the inclusion of sex education in schools has met with some opposition from certain members of the public, who believe that sex education will lead to increased sexual activity. The biological readiness for sex begins with puberty but its social acceptance is delayed with late marriages. Adolescence is a period of curiosity and this makes the adolescent oscillate between peer and porn to bridge the information gap (Quraishi, S.Y., 1995). Young men and women are faced with various developmental tasks which they must come to terms, in order to achieve necessary biological and psychological progress. Adolescence is a crucial time of life, not only for health education and health promotion in general but also for HIV prevention and AIDS education specifically. Four facets of these development demands have been demonstrated which bear significant relationship to HIV prevention:

1. *Body*: Mastering the physical changes which accompany puberty and learning to accept one's own physical appearance.
2. *Sexuality*: Acquiring sexual experience and engaging in intimate relationships: Coping with social and gender role expectations.
3. *Risk Taking*: Handling individual willingness and social pressures to take various health risks.
4. *Peers*: Building up social relations and a circle of friends outside the family, becoming more and more independent of parents (Mussen, P.H., 1970).

A large number of adolescents gather their initial and subsequent experiences without condom protection. Children and adolescents are regarded as one of the most relevant target groups for prevention and education since short term sexual encounters, changing partners or drug use often seem to be common elements in the development process (Sahani Ashok, Xirasagar Sudha, 1992).

A study conducted by this researcher in 1993, amongst school going and slum adolescents of Ghaziabad district proved that AIDS awareness levels were distinctly related to economic background, parental education, and mass media exposure. Factors associated with high level awareness were found to be:

School Education + Good Media Exposure + Educated parents = High level of awareness

Factors associated with low level awareness

Illiteracy + Limited exposure to media + Low parental education = Low level of awareness

(A study of AIDS awareness amongst school going adolescents in Ghaziabad. Paper presented at the Conference on Adolescent health, AIIMS, 1993.)

Adolescents fall readily under peer pressure. This weakness can be converted into strength by creating opinion leaders amongst the peer group itself. In the Dominican Republic, teenagers have been trained as peer sex educators since 1985 and AIDS education was incorporated into this programme in 1988 (Health Administrator Vol. 3, 1989). Stimulated by the information given by the peer educators the teenagers wanted them to repeat the talk to their parents.

A similar phenomenon was observed by the team of APAC-MCRC in Madras. the teenagers are not only curious to learn about AIDS, STDs and sex and sexuality but also want their parents to be better educated in these matters in order to facilitate free exchange of ideas and opinions at home. It was also learnt that young people who wish to learn about these issues do not know where to turn to for information. Media messages go down well with them (APAC-MCRC Study, 1994).

In order to explore the readiness of the students to learn about sex, sexuality, AIDS, it is important to conduct both qualitative as well as quantitative research. It is important to find out the appropriate message format and the medium to be used. AIDS affects in terms of social and psychological development, the most vital segment of the population, the young adults. This study, therefore, concentrates on the target group of adolescents between the ages 13 years and 17 years.

Objectives of this Study

General Objective

To review the role of mass media in AIDS prevention and control by assessing the AIDS awareness levels and media exposure amongst the target group of school going adolescents.

Specific Objectives

1. Study the socio-economic and psychological aspects of the disease.
2. Review the use of mass media for AIDS communication.
3. To ascertain the awareness of the target groups towards the implications of AIDS.
4. Survey media habits and preferences of the target group.
5. To find the appropriate media which is preferred by the target group for the dissemination of AIDS related messages.
6. To conduct qualitative research with the target group in order to substantiate the findings of the survey.

In the light of the above objectives the study will be able to find the most suitable medium and method for AIDS awareness messages for the target group of adolescents.

The Present Study: An Overview

Mass media has been reporting AIDS cases and discussing other issues related to AIDS since the very beginning. Just as it took some time for the society to understand the implications of AIDS, mass media also took its time to conceive media strategies free of bias. In the review of literature the various studies conducted on the performance of media towards the awareness generation in case of AIDS have been included. The threat of AIDS is not confined to the high risk behaviour groups but to the entire population. Considering the seriousness of the issue it is imperative that the public should be aware of the implications of the infection and the precautions to be taken in order to avoid the infection should be common knowledge. The most vulnerable group that needs awareness about AIDS is the adolescents. Studies that have been made with adolescents as the target group have also been included in the review.

The review of literature revealed that the implications of AIDS were so many, it being an issue of medical, social, economic, health, education and even communication concern. The review reflects the objectives of the study.

The study begins with an effort to understand the psycho-social and the economic implications of the disease. The psycho-social motivators of behaviour and emotional distress as they occur for patients and their loved ones and the broader social response to AIDS have been discussed. According to Micheal Merson, "All sectors of life are threatened so is the development process itself" (Panos Media Briefing, 1992). Economic impact of AIDS on developing countries will be baffling as AIDS both feeds off and contributes to poverty. Nearly every sector of the economy may be affected, in ways not always predictable or obvious. In this chapter various economic aspects have also been highlighted.

In the Indian context particularly, the HIV infected person strongly fears the social denial. Self-esteem is undermined by social targeting and blame placing along with the physical effects of a serious ailment. The psycho-social problems are faced not only by the people with AIDS but also by their carers, societies and countries at large because this is a problem with serious psychological, social and economic repercussions. Serious losses threaten agriculture, medicine, industry and nearly every sector of the economy.

The cost of treatment is a relatively small, visible slice of a rapidly growing bill. The Asian Development Bank's list of indirect costs includes loss of output from disability and premature deaths and by people not themselves infected but who spend time caring for others; a possible increase in wage costs as a result of labour shortages, and damaged tourist industry.

The overriding reason for the rapid spread of HIV has been the high correlation that exists between poverty and vulnerability to the virus, a correlation that has led to high rates of infection in the most economically deprived populations. Poor communities have less access to health care, inadequate health care means that sexually transmitted diseases often flourish, hence a greater risk of HIV infection. Lack of education, limits the awareness about AIDS. For people struggling to meet their immediate needs for food and shelter avoiding a disease which might not materialize for years can be low on the priority list. A detailed study of the psycho-social and economic implications of AIDS has been conducted. This study was important to make because only after one understands the seriousness of the issue can conduct further research with dedication and conviction. Enumerating the psychological, social or economic problems faced by the people with AIDS and by their carers would be discussing only one side of the coin. The efforts which can be made through the use of IEC to help in the cause of AIDS had to be studied too. Communicating about AIDS stresses on behaviour modification. Creating changes in behaviour is, however, a difficult process. In the case of AIDS, the task is further complicated by the sensitive and personal nature of the issues, dealing as they largely do with sex and sexuality. The task of IEC, in this situation, is primarily to create a climate conducive to behaviour change and help individuals develop necessary skills for prevention. Various strategies used in the field of health and AIDS are also discussed. The process by which IEC can make a person aware of the problem, then motivate him to act towards betterment and change his behaviour, has been described step by step. Formative research is a part of IEC as it helps in formulating interventions for awareness generation. The present awareness levels decide whether the message should be more informative or motivating. The choice of the medium for the message will depend on the extent of access that the target group has to the medium.

In order to study the role of print medium and audio visual medium on AIDS awareness two different studies were carried.

A content analysis was conducted to review the role played by the Indian print media in disseminating information about AIDS. The main objectives of this content analysis were:

1. To identify and analyze the AIDS related content in the prominent Indian national daily English language newspapers.
2. To measure the content quantitatively as well as qualitatively.

A gradual increase in AIDS reporting has been seen in the content analysis, that can be attributed to growing awareness and serious concern about the subject. The media has acquired a more open stance in discussing sensitive issues such as sex, sexuality, sexually transmitted diseases and AIDS. The maximum number of articles appeared in *The Times of India* followed by *The Hindu* and *The Hindustan Times*. The articles were mostly news reports and news analysis in the form of editorials. *The Hindu* published more analysis and discussions. *The Times of India* published the only article related to the economic aspect of AIDS. Maximum number of public health messages appeared in the *Indian Express*, some of them covered the entire page of the newspaper. Maximum number of human interest stories appeared in the *Statesman*. The main findings of the study revealed that initially there was a spurt of concern for the subject which gradually changed into a more meaningful understanding.

Since, press coverage is not the only mass communication method by which the issue of AIDS can be tackled, consistent and clear messages from all channels of mass media, traditional and interpersonal media, need to work together. In the next section of this chapter, a study has been made on the use of the audio visual media for AIDS communication in India.

Popular public service messages were designed by the National AIDS Control Organisation. Most of them had the underlying theme of celebrity recommendations. There are spots with Shabana Azmi, Shah Rukh Khan, Madhuri Dixit, Aparna Sen, Kabir Bedi, Sarika, Jaspal Bhatti and many more. Many of these spots are reviewed in this study. The National AIDS Control Organisation has produced a number of audio spots designed by the DAVP for broadcast during popular film song programmes like Jaimala and Chhayageet. Besides the NACO, State AIDS Cells operate at state level, with their own managerial bodies under the state administration. The radio spots are mostly of one minute duration and provide all the information about the spread, the precaution and also the seriousness of the disease. Many of them have voice-overs in the voices similar to popular film stars in order to attract the general public. Celebrity endorsements are used in radio jingles as well. This section tries to review the most common radio jingles.

The impact of media coverage of any subject depends on the interaction of several factors. These include the previous knowledge of the readers or the audiences, the content of the message, the credibility or otherwise of the journalist, the reaction of the people with whom the reader or viewer goes on to discuss what they believe they have read, seen or heard. For the purpose of a complete overview, a survey was carried out amongst school going adolescents of Delhi and Ghaziabad. This study found the mass media reach and exposure amongst the target group and the AIDS awareness levels of this group. It also found if the students are interested in sex education or whether they have already been given formal education about sex, AIDS, and STD. This study will be helpful in creating interventions for this group, planning mass media strategies, choosing the most appropriate media and the most appropriate time of telecast/broadcast of the messages. In case of interpersonal communication, it can be decided who should be the most suitable person to impart this knowledge to the students.

The Focus Group Discussions conducted among the students from the same sample revealed a marked difference in the reactions to AIDS among the students from various schools and locations. The discussions also revealed that girls in the metropolitan city are far more outspoken as compared to the satellite town. These findings are based on observation method.

The study makes a modest attempt at finding out the treatment meted out to the subject of AIDS by the mass media and the information expectations of the target group.

2

Role of Media: Theoretical Dimension

Ever since the recognition of Acquired Immune Deficiency Syndrome (AIDS) in 1981, much concern has been voiced on the actual and potential impact of the disease. This concern is amplified in the developing countries where there are myriad issues of concern and AIDS only adds to the problems. It has been nearly two decades since the first AIDS case was diagnosed in the country in 1986. Since then, the number of people with AIDS is constantly on the rise. Considering the implications of the disease, public awareness is of prime importance.

Mass media has been reporting AIDS cases and discussing other issues related to AIDS since the very beginning. Just as it took some time for the society to understand the implications of AIDS, mass media also took its time to conceive media strategies free of bias. As one looks back at the history of the press reports related to AIDS, one can see that the nature of press coverage has undergone a dramatic change. Past experience with public health campaigns suggests that mass media in isolation have little effect on health related behaviour and have to be combined with other elements for a campaign to be successful. They can, however, be useful in increasing public awareness.

Since 1986, AIDS campaigns have run gamut from hard sell dramatic techniques, such as those in Australia and UK, to the soft sell, even light hearted approach in some Scandinavian countries. Many of the initial AIDS awareness campaigns in a number of countries were evaluated in 1988. The general outcome of those campaigns has been an increase in the public awareness of the AIDS problem, but failed to change AIDS related lifestyles other than in certain communities with high risk behaviour where the campaigning has been intensive and carefully concentrated. Studies indicated that, when seeking to increase the knowledge of AIDS without adequately catering for effects on fear and tolerance, educational strategies may be directly responsible for psychological 'boomerang' effects, opposite to those intended (WHO). In the United Kingdom, for instance injecting drug users, the intended target of a campaign using posters and television spots did not even perceive that the messages were aimed at them (Long, 1991). The slogan 'zero grazing' which was used in the Ugandan campaign to mean 'stay with one partner' was not even understood by the target audience, and another frequently repeated spot using drum beats to spread a sense of fear, did not appeal to young people who interpreted the drums as an appeal for abstinence (Piotrow, Meyer and Zulu, 1992). Just as sensational news coverage can set back AIDS prevention efforts, poorly planned mass media campaign can do the same. In Nigeria, frightening and confusing mass media material has resulted in negative attitude towards people with AIDS and unfounded fears aroused by the Australian campaign which used death visuals, was apparently so great that those at high risk practiced denial and did not respond (Piotrow, Meyer and Zulu, 1992).

Role of Mass Media: Theoretical Perspective

The mass media represent the most readily available and potentially most economical means of imparting information about HIV/AIDS. Along with other forms of communication, the mass media can effectively raise public awareness. According to Lazarusfeld and Merton, the media have the ability to 'canalize' behaviour, directing persons who already accept one idea or product to accept a similar one (Agee *et al.*, 1985). On the subject as sensitive as AIDS and in the view of a largely illiterate population, the 'Two step flow' dimension of mass media can be used. Opinion leaders, who imbibe the message from the media with the least 'noise' are homopholous with the target audience and can thus pass the message more effectively.

Whenever new ideas are floated in the society some individuals act as the trendsetters, some as change agents, who are able to provide resources and information to bring about sustained attitudinal change. According to Rogers, mass media can promote the diffusion and adoption of many technical and social innovations (Rogers, 1962). Lerner described the Western inspired media as mobility multipliers (Pye, 1963). Most informed observers are now vary of single factor explanations of social change and do not really believe in the direct mechanistic effects from new technology. Social movements that have evolved around AIDS in other countries have grown along different lines, drawing in specific groups of people at different levels. Many of these movements are organic, routed in generalized sense of urgency around a particular issue, and growing over time. Changes can happen only if they have the support of maximum number of people who believe that their lives will improve through and as a result of the process of change. Social changes those are possible only through flow of messages between people.

Actual changes in behaviour are more likely to be the result of a range of communication and education systems. The media form only a part of the total system. There is a close link between learning and communication and, therefore, between the systems of communication and education. The aim of media education in modern society is to reveal how the media may influence ways of thinking and understanding. At present many new media forms coexist with the 'old' media, none of which has disappeared. At the same time the media are converging and linking. It is hard to escape from the deterministic element in much current thinking about the new media with societal effects again being attributed to intrinsic features of technology. Rogers, views technology along with other factors, as cause of social change (Rogers, 1986). As technology evolved over the years, researchers have found an element of bias in form, imagery and content (Barthes, 1967). Thus various audiences relate to different media based on their perception. In the present times one can observe the phenomenon of multimedia convergence—or media mix—any medium in which two or more forms of communication are integrated. The status of various media is changing with new media overtaking the old in terms of accessibility and reach, the old media are adapting to the changes by way of improving their content and presentation styles. History of mass media is a history of change, however, lately the change has been too rapid leading to an overdose of messages in the public mind. This change also creates many avenues for message dissemination for a variety of audience groups. Media have come to interpose between us and any experience of the world beyond our direct sense observations. They also provide a continuous line of contact with the main institutions of the society in which we live. In a secular society, in matters of value and ideas, the mass media tend to take over from the early influencers of school, parents, religion, siblings and companions. We are consequently very dependent on the media for the large part of our wider 'symbolic environment' (the pictures in our head) (Mcquail Denis, 1987). An essentially functionalist theory of media dependency formulated by DeFluer and

Ball Rokeach (1989) treats the relative dependency of the audiences on the mass media source (compared to other information sources). The theory posits that the more an audience is reliant on the mass media for information and the more the society is in a state of crisis or instability, then the more power the media are likely to have (Bal Rokeach, S.J. and De Fluer, M.L., 1989). In present scenario though the AIDS situation may not be treated as a crisis situation but it is no less than one. It will not be long before the AIDS bomb begins to explode and then the functionalist theory will be largely applicable.

The mass media are linked directly with the society. These linkages have been explained by the normative theories of media, which deal with ideas of how media ought to, or are expected to operate. From the 17th century onwards the newspaper was seen as the tool of political liberation and socio-economic progress, or a legitimate means of opposition to the established order of power. It was in 1947, the United States Commission on Freedom of Press, added the notion of social responsibility to the principles of freedom (Blanchard, 1977). Thus the notion of news media to be truthful, accurate, fair and objective is being adhered to. In the present scenario, when the media is turning into a market driven business proposition, the social responsibility theory, especially in the case of public health related news items seems almost necessary.

In order for the message to have an impact on a society the media will have to concentrate on not just the message but also on the society for which it is intended. Basically, this will correspond with the existing social grouping such as community, religious or ethnic minority etc. It also exemplifies the audience as a public in the sense of an active, interactive and relatively autonomous social group. There are likely to be normative ties between the audience and media source and between the audience members themselves. These ties help the audience to learn, not just from the mass media but from sundry other sources. Bandura studied the learning behaviour of people in a society and disagreed with most reinforcement theorists.

Albert Bandura and Richard H. Walters (1963) explain the appearance of behaviour that is already in the repertory of the learner but state that the operant learning theory (Skinner, 1963) does not explain the appearance of novel behaviour. In Bandura's theory the anticipated reinforcement is considered to be facilitative rather than necessary condition, because there are other factors than response consequences that influence what individuals do (Bandura 1971). Audience research continually uncovers that there is a value system which informally regulates the media use and audience behaviour (Mcquail Denis, 1987) Forerunners of what was called the 'Uses and Gratification Approach' (Berelson, 1949) sought to interpret the motives for content choice and the satisfactions looked for and derived from media in terms of everyday social circumstances and needs. The extent of effects that mass media has on its audiences has always been a subject of debate. Particular effects are occurring all the time without being able to see or predict the aggregate outcome. There can be many effects without pattern or direction. That is why need is being felt for professional media planning. Efforts to curb the HIV/AIDS epidemic cannot rely on news media to do it on their own (Piotrow, Meyer and Zulu, 1992).

Interpersonal Communication

The media are only a part of the total system of communication in every society. There is a close link between learning and communication and, therefore, between systems of education and systems of communication. Besides mass media, there are other means of communication, such as interpersonal communication and face to face communication. These can also be used effectively in disseminating the message of AIDS. Interpersonal communication methods such as specially organised workshops, plays, puppet shows or slide shows designed specifically for a particular target audience are sometimes more effective than the mass media in reaching the target group physically as well as psychologically. In a homogenous group it is easier for the message to penetrate as the symbols and semantics are specific for the target audience. In face to face communication methods, such as counselling, the matter can be explained in detail and the point of view of the target obtained. However, in order for communication to occur in such a setting there should be a certain amount of credibility to the communicator. He should in a way act as an opinion leader, teacher or counsellor. Such a person should not only be sound in knowledge but also not judgemental of the target's situation. A great amount of empathy is required from the communicator in order to build trust with the target.

Concerned by the rapid spread of AIDS, affecting people in all the regions of the world, the Fortieth Health Assembly in May, 1987, urged all the member states to establish or strengthen effective programmes to combat the disease. Global programme on AIDS has developed a global strategy for the prevention and control of AIDS. Member states receive support in monitoring their own national AIDS programme through the appropriate WHO office. In the book, WHO AIDS series-4; Monitoring of National AIDS Prevention and Control Programmes; WHO Geneva 1989 some of the practical aspects are set out in monitoring AIDS prevention and control programmes. This book emphasizes that the burden of AIDS prevention should not fall on one individual or a single central body; to be effective, a decentralised system suited for the country and its infrastructure should be devised. Three main objectives are outlined in this book: Identify population groups, Strengthen Health education units at all levels to provide information and Education to the public and to promote the use of condoms.

The book further provides the guidelines to monitor an activity plan per strategy. For the mass media the book recommends that first of all mass media should be screened to see whether messages are being broadcast or published. Whether the radio and newspaper messages are readily understandable. Whether the posters are being distributed, videotapes shown to the target groups. In short the book emphasises the close monitoring of all mass media messages, their frequency and availability.

> Similarly WHO series-6; prevention of sexual transmission of HIV; WHO Geneva 1990 emphasises on education in the absence of cure. Such education should be aimed at people whose behaviour places them at risk. Education should go along with interpersonal training skills. Some salient points of discussion are: Health care providers should be educated, high risk behaviour groups should be targeted, condoms-education and availability at low price, voluntary HIV testing and counselling services should be made available.

These guidelines cover the important aspect of the Sexually Transmitted Diseases (STD) as an important source of risk for HIV infection. Management of STDs is important to interrupt the spread of HIV infection through sexual transmission. This calls for a behaviour change in order to prevent the exposure to HIV. In the book IEC: Keys to progress in behaviour change, IEC programmes are cited as the best tools available to prevent the spread of HIV infection. IEC programmes have helped to decrease the incidence of STDs, smoking, heart disease and drinking while driving. In the developing world IEC programmes have promoted personal hygiene, maternal and reproductive health, use of oral rehydration therapy.

The behaviours to be modified are deeply ingrained, highly personal, and largely beyond the reach of direct government action. Developing countries face still more problems: limited access to mass communication media outside major urban areas, illiteracy, multiplicity of languages and culture within the country, insufficient number of health care workers, limited infrastructure and insufficient resources. IEC activities usually begin with a public information campaign that uses a variety of media and communication techniques to reach as many people as possible with broad messages about AIDS. Depending on emotional, psychological and social environment individuals hear and react to messages about AIDS in different ways.

Manual Carbello and Ronald Bayer (1990), stress that nowhere, and at no time, has the need to encourage and foster the cooperation and active participation of broad sectors of population been so evident as in the case of HIV/AIDS. Understanding human behaviour in order to modify it for the sake of health has become the global challenge. Biomedical approaches to preventing HIV/AIDS are currently beyond reach and may be so for many years. AIDS pandemic has given rise to social experiments that have demonstrated the viability of behaviour change at both an individual and group level. Manual Carbello and Ronald Bayer (1990) define the behaviours involved in HIV transmission as "covert, stigmatized, illegal or socially proscribed" and for this reason special research methods and techniques are required in order to elicit reliable, valid, sociologically sophisticated information in these areas. A number of important psycho-social factors are related to high risk behaviour and these too call for systematic study in themselves. In the context of HIV infection, the contribution of the behavioural science is not only crucial but complimentary to clinical research.

One of the most vulnerable groups in India is the commercial sex-worker. The average CSW neither has the ability to insist on the use of condoms nor does she have the abilty to take care of herself after being infected. The Psycho Social Research Unit, National AIDS Reference Surveillance Centre, CMC Hospital, Vellore engages in behavioural research from time to time. Jacob, K.S., Jayakumari, Harriot, John K. Jacob, John Jacobs T. conducted this study with the support of ICMR (1992).

Sex workers attending a custodial care institution for sex workers and all the patients attending a clinic for STD at the district hospital during one week were interviewed. 231 out of 250 patients attending the OPD at CMC were also interviewed over two days. Awareness of

AIDS and socio-economic and demographic details were assessed. Most subjects in all three groups were ignorant of AIDS (OPD–58%, STD–77%, Sex Workers–96%). Among OPD, women were largely ignorant, rural areas, illiteracy and lower socio-economic state. Newspapers and radio were cited as the commonest channels of information but even these had reached only about quarter of the sample. Subjects who knew about sexual mode of transmission of HIV, seriousness of AIDS, lack of treatment and preventive measures formed a minority. Most of the Indian population living in the rural areas does not have an access to most channels of mass communication. Rapid increase in HIV seroprevalence have been reported in India, particularly among injecting drug users in the North Eastern states and among the sex workers in major cities. Seroprevalence rates among female prostitutes in major cities and towns rose from less than 1 per cent to 30-60 per cent between 1986 and 1991 while HIV prevalence in their male clients reached 3-10 per cent. These figures are quoted from *HIV and AIDS in Asia: AIDS Care*, Vol. 4, No. 4, 1992; Carfax Publishing Company. The paper also talks of interventions. A pilot HIV/AIDS prevention project has been launched in Bombay's red light district to promote safer sexual behaviour among prostitutes. Discussions with sex workers about health issues and the promotion of condom use and distribution. Awareness of HIV prevention and the number of condom sales points in the targetted neighbourhood has apparently increased.

Among other categories that have been studied extensively is the truck drivers. A survey among the truck drivers in Madras revealed high levels of STDs, a history of multiple sex partners and low use of condoms. Furthermore, AIDS was not seen as a personal concern. Providing a free supply of condoms and dissemination of information were seen as the key areas of interventions. A health education booth was set up at a check post, where drivers could pick up condoms and health education pamphlets, and be treated for STDs. Providing the truck drivers a place to rest, drink tea and talk to each other as well as to counsellors was seen as a key to furthering communication (ARFI, 1992).

Strategies to interrupt the epidemic of HIV must comprise many different elements. There is increasing evidence that control programmes targeted at STD transmitter core groups can be highly effective in reducing HIV transmission. Truck drivers form one such group, others are sex workers, their clients, professional blood donors etc. According to Moses Stephen, Plummer A. Francis, Ngugi Nelizabeth, Nagelkerke J.D. Nico, Anzala O. Aggrey, Netinya Achola, O. Jachomiah efforts to control sexual transmission of HIV in Africa have consisted largely of information and education programmes directed at the general public. Few programmes focus on the role of what have been termed high frequency STD transmitter core group. Because of their central role in STD transmission, intensive efforts to reduce HIV infection, transmission in such a group will have considerable effect in slowing the spread of the HIV epidemic.

Another group which deserves mention amongst the high risk behaviour groups are the male sex workers. They may not be as readily available as the female sex workers but can be found soliciting on streets in most of the big cities. Simon M. Patricia, Morse D. Edward, Balson M. Paul, Osofsky J. Howard, Gaumer Richard H., studied the male prostitutes (1993).

A male prostitute is a biological male who receives payments, either in money or in trade, in exchange for sexual favours and solicits on the streets. Two hundred and eleven male street prostitutes between ages of 18 and 51 years were interviewed and tested for HIV. Three lifestyle factors were found to function as barriers engaging in risk reduction behaviour. Subjects who were more economically dependent on prostitution, perceived less control over the hustling encounter and reported increased pleasure from sexual activity with their customers were more likely to engage in risk taking behaviour. Prostitutes perception of the severity of HIV infection was not significantly associated with their risk behaviour.

This was the first study on male prostitutes and their health needs. Yet, because of a propensity towards high risk taking behaviours, the male prostitute is both a likely recipient of infection, as well as an important epidemiological bridge for transmitting HIV to others. A sample of 211 adult males was recruited from New Orleans, Lousiana. Subjects scores on four HIV related risk factors (anal-genital, oral-genital, sexual orientation, syphilis serostatus) to form an HIV risk scale. Although male prostitute is able to accurately assess his own susceptibility to HIV infection, he does not use his knowledge to engage in HIV related risk reduction. They are also aware of condoms as a protection against HIV infection but never use them in any of their transactions.

The awareness levels of the female sex workers are sadly not so high. Whereas the male sex worker frequently enjoy their sexual encounters and wilfully take up this occupation the situation of the female sex worker is pathetic. Long working hours, measly income, low standard of living, invariably a strict Madame, heavy debts, and many a times, a child. These women are unable to exercise any control over the wishes of the client. If the client refuses to use a condom, these women find it impossible to make him wear one, without the support of the Madame of their house (Raman, S. Sundara, ARFI, 1992). AIDS research foundation of India (ARFI) began an intervention programme with the sex workers in Chennai. The women reported that although they were willing to use condoms, the customers were not. ARFI then turned its focus on clients using an approach based on positive re-enforcement theory: repetition of the desirability of condom use *via* various communication channels. It was found that truck drivers keep condoms in their trucks to help fix radiator hose leaks since condom rubber can help securely seal the leaks. ARFI's health educators took this into consideration during small group talks about easy availability of an effective means of risk reduction. ARFI also provides condoms easily. Condoms are available at tobacco shops at transit sites. Hence no special effort is required to buy them. Truck drivers are given key chains containing a drawer in which a condom can be kept. Since the drivers always pocket the keys when they leave the truck, this ensures that they are always carrying a condom with them.

The threat of AIDS is not confined to the high risk behaviour groups but to the entire population. Considering the seriousness of the issue it is imperative that the public should be aware of the implications of the infection and the precautions to be taken in order to avoid the infection should be common knowledge. However, the awareness surveys that have been conducted in this direction, call for increased awareness campaigns.

Vinodini, C. of the Bombay Municipal Corporation, India (1992) conducted an intervention with the commercial sex workers of Kamathipura and Khetwadi sections of Mumbai and found that the sex workers were completely dependent on the brothel keepers. STD prevalence was found to be very high while HIV rates were estimated to be 30-50 per cent. Following strategies were adopted for IEC component: Development of ethnic network for the creation of Peer group, Development of ethnic specific materials, utilization of local media to reach them and provision and distribution of good quality condoms. Besides this a close association with the Nepali Organisation of Brothel Keepers was established as many of these sex workers were from Nepal.

Initial Studies

Seroserveillance studies in India from mid-1980s revealed only sporadic cases of HIV only in the high risk groups (Simoes *et al.*, 1985; ICMR 1988); later studies showed spread (John *et al.*, 1959; Apte *et al.*, 1990; Bhave *et al.*,1990; Jayapaul *et al.*, 1990) at rates paralleled only in Africa (Jayaraman,1990). While information is available from other countries (Dab *et al.*, 1989; Foster & Furley, 1989; Lesnich & Pace, 1990), few studies have assessed the level of knowledge and attitude about AIDS amongst Indians. One survey of college students in Bombay and Pune revealed significant misconceptions about HIV and its transmission (Verma and Khorshed, 1989), Jacob *et al.* (1989) surveyed prostitutes, attendees of STD clinic and medical outpatients in Vellore and found that only 30 per cent had heard of AIDS. Other studies have also targeted only selected populations such as naval personnel (Thergaonkar *et al.*, 1991) or blood donors (Chattopadhya *et al.*, 1991). (*AIDS CARE*: *Psychological and Socio-medical aspects of AIDS/HIV*; Vol. 5, No. 2, 1993; Carfax Publishing Company.)

One of the earliest studies conducted in India was by S.B. Porter, from Stanford University, Cal USA. To assess the level of knowledge and its associated attitudes about AIDS among Indians in Calcutta, 153 English speaking adults were surveyed during April and May 1990. Sixty-five of 75 men (87%) and 77 of 78 women (99%) questioned had heard of AIDS, and majority within the past 2-3 years. Newspaper and television were mostly cited as the sources of information. Of the respondents who had heard of the disease, 95 per cent knew that AIDS was transmitted by sexual intercourse; less than half, however, also knew that AIDS could not be acquired through kissing, insect bites or by using public toilets. In general respondents had little specific knowledge regarding the symptoms of AIDS, and 29 per cent were unaware that infected persons could be asymptomatic and appear healthy. Level of education was the only variable that independently correlated with knowledge of AIDS. More than one-third of the respondents would not have dinner with or continue to work with an AIDS patient and 50 per cent believed all AIDS patients should be quarantined. In one study in Vellore, only 4 per cent of prostitutes questioned had heard of AIDS; lack of knowledge was associated with illiteracy and lower socio-economic class (Jacob *et al.*, 1989). Informal surveys among Calcutta prostitutes have also revealed high rates of ignorance about AIDS (Ukil and Dasgupta, 1990). Approximately 50 illiterate, Non-English speaking homeless people in Calcutta were informally questioned about AIDS; none of them had heard of the disease. It is clear that passive education through the mass media mostly bypass the large risk group, and the more active outreach programmes will be needed to access such individuals. Guides to planning media campaigns are available through WHO. Step by step planning, implementation, monitoring and evaluating AIDS related programmes are all described in detail. Guide to planning Health promotion for AIDS prevention and control; WHO AIDS series 5, WHO Geneva, 1989; stresses on the use of information and education to influence the behaviour of groups and individuals so as to limit the spread of HIV.

The Elements of Planning as described in this guide are:

- Establish goals
- Initial assessment
- Target audience
- Reach objectives, targets
- Develop strategies
- Communication channels
- Support services
- Monitor and evaluate
- Establish schedule and budget
- Reassessment

The book also provides samples of KABP surveys and need for initial assessment before planning a campaign are stressed:

- Local epidemiology—which group needs to be addressed
- KABP of general public
- KABP of target audience
- Communication channels

Effective AIDS health promotion needs communication through a variety of interpersonal networks. Gathering places should be used as locations for AIDS information. Mass media reach large numbers of people, legitimize discussion of public issue, reinforce new learning and new behaviour. Interpersonal media on the other hand inform or remind people, provide detailed information than mass media. Then there is the little media which support programme activities, through announcements, provide aids for training. These media come in the form of pamphlets, flyers, posters, slides, exhibitions, slogans, T shirts, scarves match boxes etc. Such media can be used in counselling sessions, promotion of condoms, training etc.

Since AIDS ls a highly sensitive issue, the little media play a big role as they are the ones who have the maximum ability to influence the target audience. This importance is stressed by Rae, N., Scechter, K., Kumaresan, G., Nataraj, S., Solomon, W. They suggest that the resources which are needed, both economic as well as social, to pick up the pieces of the pandemic the country is facing at the present, can be provided by training volunteers at different levels.The immediate concern is one of basic awareness of AIDS and related issues. The first level was of training volunteers to be health and peer educators. The next level is training them to be counsellors and service providers to primary health clinics. The volunteers who wish to work for the cause of AIDS need to have better commitment and motivation. The peer group pressure works best with young people who always want to belong to the popular group and are likely to follow the habits of that particular group. It has been seen that drug taking, smoking and even first visits to the sex workers are group activities. Once the habit is formed, it is followed.

Studies Targeting Young People

It is important to sustain effective HIV prevention programmes for the young people at or before the age at which they begin practicing behaviours that risk transmission of this deadly virus. Evidence from HIV seroprevalence studies conducted among patients admitted to 37 metropolitan hospitals during 1988-89 suggests that HIV prevalence rate is vanishingly small among 11 year olds but begin rising at the age of 12 and continues to rise throughout the teenage years (St. Louise, 1990).

John Davies targeted young people in Scotland though an innovative campaign developed by the Scottish Health Education Group. It combined the topics of AIDS and Drugs within the context of young people's broader social and health concerns. A total of 1434 young men and women aged 16-25 years, were interviewed. About half the respondents felt that the campaigns for HIV and AIDS target 'people who sleep around', 'people who are easily led'. These responses reflect the young people's perception of whom such a campaign should be trying to reach. There was little indication of shift in sexual behaviour as a result of AIDS. This research also shows that despite educational logic behind it, combining drugs and AIDS does not work. Clearer targeting of material, with messages on drugs being tailored for 13-16 year olds and those on AIDS for 16-18 years olds. Even among adults living in areas of intense HIV/AIDS infection, high risk exposure continues to be prevalent and promotion of safe sex options is imperative (Katahoire, 1992). Amongst the youth condom contribution has been shown to be successful if peer networks are used (Kelly, 1993). Research has shown that openness in discussing condoms and pictorial demonstrations as well as modelling has been shown to allay anxiety and improved used (Loibon, 1990).

The occurrence of HIV differs with gender. Just as more AIDS cases are seen among adult males than among adult females, so too there are more AIDS cases among teenage boys than among teenage girls (US Bureau of Census, 1987). On the other hand Faustin K. Yao (1992). claims that seropositivity rates increase faster among girls than boys because of cultural and social norms which subject girls to sexual experience at an early age.

In San Francisco, Declemente and others (1984) evaluated knowledge, beliefs etc. regarding personal vulnerability and perceived needs for AIDS in 1326 high school students, by adopting survey methodology. The study showed that 92.4 per cent recognized having sex with someone and 81 per cent identified sharing a needle with a drug user as modes of transmission. Only 60 per cent of the students knew that using a condom during sex could prevent AIDS.

Strunin and Hingson (1987) conducted a survey in Massachusetts on 829 adolescents using random digit dialling by anonymous telephone interviews. They found 91 per cent knew heterosexuals are at risk, while 71 per cent knew that HIV may be present in vaginal secretions. 54 per cent were not worried at all about getting AIDS and 61 per cent thought not at all likely to get AIDS in their lifetime. It was recommended by 97 per cent respondents that AIDS information should be made available in schools.

In a study of 212 college students of Kansas city, Simkins and Kushner (1986) found that 71 per cent of respondents were not concerned about contracting AIDS from their present sexual partner and 41 per cent had no concern regarding future partners.

In order to influence the young people and also to encourage more dialogue on the taboo subjects of HIV/AIDS the Department of Youth and Sports, Government of India, launched a countrywide programme called 'Universities talk AIDS'—an awareness raising campaign among the student youth in India. Prakash, B. and Larivee, C. presented a paper with the same title at the International Conference of AIDS 1992, July 19-24. The National Service Scheme, a student voluntary organization with over 1 million volunteers, launched an awareness campaign centred around a materials development contest called Universities Talk AIDS in 58 universities throughout India. State and National ceremonies honouring 8 regional winners from 2000 entries generated involvement of State and national officials, campus debate on AIDS, and extensive press coverage. Two research reports have been produced following qualitative research conducted at 4 Universities. The reports are the results of focus group discussions with students and a content analysis of the materials submitted. These studies and the information gleaned from regional trainings were used to develop a sustainable national programme aimed at students. Lessons learned from the programme include the knowledge of awareness levels of the student body, their attitude towards the implications of AIDS as they do not see it as a personal threat. Condom use was found to be rare and confusion over contraception and disease control prevails. Students were willing to discuss sexuality but the teachers were found to be resistant. The UTA was generally seen as a successful initial information gathering and awareness effort but needs to be followed up to harvest all the benefits.

Within our country only a few studies have been conducted amongst the adolescents and youth in relation to IEC strategies for AIDS Chandra *et al.* (1993) in Pune conducted a study on 400 college students in order to determine the knowledge and attitude with respect to HIV/AIDS. It was found that the students had limited information about AIDS and HIV infection. Certain misconceptions regarding transmission and prevention also existed. The study recommended need for proper health education and information at school and college level. Hiramani (1992) in his study regarding AIDS related knowledge and attitudes of 118 college students of a Aurangabad college found that majority of students obtained knowledge about AIDS from radio and newspapers. No one reported causative virus correctly. Only one-third knew about the means of transmission. Only 31 per cent knew preventive measures. Students exposure to communication channels is related with knowledge about AIDS in general. Sharma (1990) in Delhi surveyed 100 final year medical students of a medical college, regarding awareness of AIDS using questionnaires. He observed that all students knew about AIDS. Books and media were the major source of knowledge in 77 per cent students. All the students knew that there is no treatment of AIDS. 50 per cent thought it should be the combined effort of Government, World Health Organisation and public while 42 per cent thought WHO alone should have control programme (Above references from Assessment of

Knowledge, Attitude and Practices Among College Students about AIDS, MD Thesis, NIHFW, New Delhi, 1996).

In France, Cohen *et al.* (1990) studied the impact of interpersonal and mass communication on risk behaviour and AIDS knowledge amongst the general population. Mass media was reported as a source of information more than interpersonal and targeted media. Over 90 per cent mentioned television as the main source. The younger population group mentioned interpersonal sources and targeted media as compared to the older (> 24 years).

Voluntary Health Association of India conducted a Knowledge, Attitude, Belief and Behaviour (KABB) survey amongst 2000 students from 32 institutions in and around Kolkata in 1994. Median age of the target group was 21 years. 66.5 per cent students read books and magazines for acquiring health and sex related information. 82.2 per cent knew the mechanisms of human reproduction. 3.30 per cent had sexual relations with CSWs. 44.50 per cent knew the consequences of sex with unknown partner. 78.8 per cent had the knowledge of safe sex procedure. However, knowledge about precautions against the spread of AIDS/HIV was at a lower level, 18-38 per cent. 84.65 per cent had seen posters on AIDS, only 13.5 per cent attended awareness camps on STD/AIDS.

Research on adolescents has provided compelling evidence of covariation among sexual activity, drug use, and delinquency (Miller and Simon, 1974; Hayes, 1987). The early onset of sexual intercourse does not appear to be isolated behaviour, nor does drug use. R. Jessor and co-workers (1980) surmised that the co-occurrence of problem behaviours may reflect for some adolescents a choice of lifestyles rather than a choice of particular behaviours. Drug abuse and sexual activity seem to be interrelated. Ensinger and Kane (1985) found that those who drank liquor were more likely to be sexually active. Similarly, Elliot and Morse (1987) found that the reverse phenomenon was also true.

Rae, N., Sceshter, K., Kumaresan, G., Nataraj, S., Solomon, W. (1993) developed a project to provide social resources to fight the AIDS pandemic by training volunteers at different levels. The first level was training the volunteers to be peer educators and the next level was to train them to be counsellors and service providers. Volunteers came from different socio-economic backgrounds, professions and age groups. The results showed that the volunteers showed good amount of motivation in the initial stages which needs to be sustained. In the US a disproportionate share of the burden of adolescent AIDS cases is borne by the minority youth. According to the US Bureau of Census, 1987, 36 per cent of teenage cases are found among Black teenagers who make up for only 15.3 per cent of the population. One of the major difficulties in presenting a clear picture of the scope of AIDS and HIV problem among adolescents is the paucity of available data for narrowly defined target groups. Most studies club adolescents in the broad category of 12 to 19 years. This category ranges from a child at the onset of puberty to a teenager just one step away from being counted as a young adult.

Fox and Cortes, in a Brazilian study (1991) attempting an assessment of AIDS KAP among 3,600 urban adults in 4 main cities found that vast majority were aware, concerned and correctly informed. Personal risk, however, was felt to be low as few preventive measures were taken. The study recommended that scarce communication resources would be better employed if directed at specific groups in value relevant terms.

Media Related Studies

Schramme, Lyle and Parker (1960) were among the first to explore the developing patterns of newspaper reading amongst children. They found that although other media are introduced as early as age 2, the newspaper does not assume any importance on the daily basis until about the eighth grade. Intellectual ability was shown to be a major correlate of newspaper reading with the brighter children picking up the habit earlier and selecting more serious content areas.

Clarke (1965) hypothesised that young person's interest in serious newspapers content might also be influenced by parental socialisation value. He found that heavy newspaper exposure among 15 year olds corresponds with greater parental concern about curiosity traits than about good grades at school.

Benedict, Weaver and Atschull (1976) deviated somewhat from the traditional uses and gratification approach to examine the effect of the high school newspaper in training students to become sophisticated commercial newspaper users. Instructional units developed to increase awareness and educational value of the student press, as well as to elevate the level of interest in newspaper reading. According to his finding, students who received the instruction exhibited a significantly greater understanding of the structure of the newspaper.

Participation of the mass media in the AIDS prevention programme was studied by Mundul, J. and Gilada, I. of the Indian Health

Organisation (1993) Analysis of Mumbai based news clippings from 1985 to 1992 highlighting viewpoints and their choices of topics, emphasis and its sustenance are evaluated. The study concludes that for AIDS awareness both the electronic and the print media, especially those addressing rural population need to be optimally and urgently utilized. It was found that while electronic media has neglected the issue due to taboo attached print media was found to sensationalize the issue.

A similar study of the press clippings from 35 leading newspapers and magazines of India was conducted by Pant, K.M. and Singh, K.P. of the Indira Gandhi Open University (1993). The methodology adopted was to monitor all the items related to AIDS over a period of time ranging from six weeks prior to the 2nd International Congress on AIDS in Asia and the Pacific and upto 10 weeks after. Analysis of the findings considered newsworthy and the vocabulary used by the media has been done with the help of a PC.

Disadvantaged Youth and Seropositivity: A Direct Link

A direct link between poverty and seropositivity has been observed. Uneducated, disadvantaged youth, living in close proximity in unhygienic conditions in the slums appear to be at increased risk for this health threat.

A study on AIDS awareness in rural community was conducted by the Department of Preventive and Social Medicine, Rural Medical College of Prewara, Medical Trust Loni, Ahmadnagar. The survey was conducted in 20 villages. 17.4 per cent were found to be aware of AIDS among illiterate and 52 per cent among literates. In all 29.4 per cent of the respondents got their information from the mass media while 65 per cent came to know about it from doctors.

The Mass Communication Research Centre, Jamia Millia Islamia conducted a study of AIDS awareness amongst adolescents in Chennai in which 498 respondents of age group 13 to 24 years of high, middle and lower income groups participated. As many as 94.2 per cent knew something about AIDS. While 77.3 per cent of the illiterates were aware of AIDS, as many as 96.3 per cent of high school students were aware of the disease.

A study of street children in Kerala found that they are sexually active at a very young age and only 12.3 per cent are aware of AIDS.

Dr. J. Kasamiya (Preventive and Social Medicine Department of Surat Medical College) has conducted a study of social environment and HIV seroprevalence in males in Surat. HIV seroprevalence was found to be higher in two extreme groups in relation to individual income, educational status and living conditions. In Madurai, Shanmuganandan S. and Subramanian, P.T. (1989) analysed attitudes and awareness regarding the social aspects of AIDS. They used the perception technique and tool of behavioural analysis on the origination and prevention of the disease, medical care, public awareness and psychological attributes such as guilt, anxiety, depression and stressful emotions. The findings reveal that amongst the urban population AIDS has caused a deep concern in the individual as well as society where as in the rural areas the awareness of this disease is negligible or not at all. Samkaram, S. and Samkaram, H. (1993) studied the economic impact due to AIDS. Estimates and future projects of HIV/AIDS in Tamil Nadu were calculated from primary source (through survey) and secondary source (from WHO and other published data) bring out the following data: AIDS and HIV estimates, Proportion of Industrial workers affected by AIDs, Output per worker estimated Gross loss of individual output.

Sherr *et al.* (1986) evaluated public information campaign about AIDS in London (UK). High and low risk groups were surveyed before any public information campaign, after an initial series of advertisements, and after second series. Information levels were significantly raised by the first and the second campaigns. Authors note that although knowledge was increased, misconceptions were not corrected.

For the purpose of this study only the students of classes VIII, IX, X and XI were targeted. Most of the students were in the age group of 13 to 16 years of age. In this manner an attempt has been made to narrow down the upper and the lower age limits of the target groups. In order to include respondents from all strata of society, adolescents from government and public schools were studied. The mass media reach and awareness in this target group was also studied.

As the above review has shown perceptions about AIDS and HIV are many and young people especially are still in the denial stage. The following study will attempt to find the sources of information about AIDS that the adolescents use and trust. The study will also find the level of awareness about AIDS, its transmission and prevention.

3

Psycho-Social and Economic Aspects of AIDS

"Humankind cannot bear very much reality" (Eliot, T.S.) and the reality of our situation is harsh. AIDS is one of the several problems simultaneously facing the developing world, which compete for community action. It is a mistake to view the AIDS pandemic as a purely medical phenomenon. AIDS is primarily a social phenomenon with urgent and consuming medical issues attached (Silverman, D., Perakyla, A., Bore, R.).

This chapter deals with the psycho-social motivators of behaviour and emotional distress as they occur for patients and their loved ones; broader social response to AIDS will also be discussed. According to Micheal Merson, "All sectors of life are threatened so is the development process itself" (Panos Media Briefing). Economic impact of AIDS on developing countries will be baffling as AIDS both feeds off and contributes to poverty. Nearly every sector of the economy may be affected, in ways not always predictable or obvious. In this chapter various economic aspects will also be highlighted, the use of Information, Education and Communication systems for prevention and control of AIDS has also been discussed.

Psycho-Social Aspects of HIV Infection

Common response to the diagnosis of HIV infection reflect stigma associated with drug abuse, sexual promiscuity and society's pre-conceived fears. Familiar patient reactions are shock, withdrawal, despair, acute high level anxiety, depressive reactions, anger, guilt, avoidance and denial. These are usually expected in the context of a preconceived 'death sentence' and should perhaps be characterized as manifestations of 'situational distress' or 'adjustment reactions' (Winston, J.A., 1995). In the Indian context particularly, the HIV infected person strongly fears the social denial. Other major problems faced by HIV patients in India are:

- Identity crisis,
- Denial of health care,
- Low self-esteem,
- Guilt feeling,
- Family disintegration (Gracious Thomas, 1994). Psychological disturbance seen in the period after the 'bad news' about HIV is delivered will reflect twin prominent faces of patient concern,
- Fear for the future and actual course of the disease, and
- Fear of the reaction of others.

Tables 3.1 and 3.2 depict the acute psycho-social phenomenon associated with HIV infection and disease and common AIDS related patient anxieties.

Table 3.1: Acute Psycho-Social Phenomena Associated with HIV Infection and Disease

Shock

- Of diagnosis and possible death
- Over loss of hopes for good news

Fear and Anxiety

- Uncertain prognosis and course of illness
- Of disfigurement and disability
- Effects of medication and treatment
- Of isolation and abandonment and social/sexual rejection
- Of infecting others and being infected by them
- Of lover's ability to cope and their possible illness
- Of loss of cognitive, physical, social and work abilities

Depression

- Over inability to overcome the virus
- Over new and involuntary health /lifestyle restrictions
- At being 'caught out' and the uncertainty of the future

Guilt

- Over past 'misdemeanours' resulting in illness 'punishment'
- Over possibly having infected others
- Over being homosexual or drug user

Obsessive Disorders

- Relentless searching for new diagnostic evidence on body
- Faddism over health and diet
- Preoccupation with death and decline and avoidance of new infections

Table 3.2: Common AIDS Related Patient Anxieties

- Prognosis in the short and the long term
- Infection risk to and from other people
- Social, occupational, domestic and sexual hostility and rejection
- Abandonment, isolation and physical pain
- Inability to alter circumstances
- How to maximise future health
- Ability of lover/family/partner to cope
- Availability of appropriate medical/dental treatment
- Being identified as homosexual/drug abuse/prostitute etc.
- Loss of privacy/confidentiality
- Future social and sexual unacceptability
- Declining ability to cope
- Loss of physical and financial independence

Each of these issues identified in Table 3.2 is significant for the pervasive distress they may create and in terms of their being manageable to some extent by sensitive and relevant provision of information and psycho social intervention. Despite the negative connotations of a definitive diagnosis of AIDS, patients reactions may always not be so gloomy. A number of patients, particularly those who have been chronically ill but not easily classifiable or manageable, may greet such news with an unexpected sense of relief: they have at least something concrete to fight.

In addition to those discussed earlier, identification of HIV generates further complicating psychological issues that may take considerable time to adjust to and manage. These include the more nebulous issues of control and self-esteem. HIV undermines patients' confidence in their ability to remain self-determining in most spheres of life. Many also feel that their life is irrevocably focused on their infection/disease and its association with death. Self-esteem is further undermined by social targeting and blame placing along with the physical effects of a serious ailment. Intensity of psychological distress and the likelihood of the emergence of psychiatric disturbance, is also significantly related to the stage of the infection. Those with AIDS related complexes may develop greater psychological morbidity than those who are asymptomatic and those with frank AIDS (Miller David, 1988).

The development of relationship dynamics in the development of patient distress is widely accepted. Patients for whom the constancy of the disease may lead to feelings of guilt, of being a burden or a bore, will often find themselves cast in the role of 'protector' of loved ones. They may attempt to submerge their own distress in order to shield loved ones from the necessary emotional or domestic role changes and in doing so, they may suffer greater emotional, psychological, psychiatric and even physical distress.

The social milieu from which the patients presents is also of critical importance. If friends or loved ones have already developed AIDS or died, the patients fears may become intensified, leading to trauma. The psycho-social problems are faced not only by the people with AIDS but also by their carers. One study has found that chronic intense care of people with AIDS results in conspicuous psychological disturbance, including depression, chronic anxiety and functional disruption (McKusick, L., Hortsman, W., Abrams, D., Coats, T., 1987).

Most Researches on the Issue Have Demonstrated Similar Findings

- Critical cut off point for avoidance of such morbidity in spending less than 60 per cent of the working week in the context of HIV.
- If the needs of the carers are not designed into patient management protocol, both the patients and the staff will suffer (Miller David).

It is crucial to ensure that homophobia, value judgments, moralising, ignorance and fear which are as treatable as infection is preventable—are replaced with constructive determination to embrace the vital elements of prevention and treatment. How ironic that many future deaths from HIV disease should be due to social denial and avoidance rather than simply to an absence of full medical understanding.

Role of the Society

There are no recent models for a community disaster of this magnitude and universality to help one predict the effects on morale and behaviour to be expected from deaths of young adults, from urgent need to change sexual behaviour in ways which threaten self-esteem, and from stress of living with the threat of premature deaths (Piot, P., Careal, M.). There are no precedents to guide us, this epidemic will not end, like most wars, nor will it burn itself out like the outbreak of influenza; or leave unscathed communities, which might come to our rescue. Societies at large will be affected and the forces behind behaviour change will have to emerge from the society itself. Since this disease requires behaviour modification at the personal level, the general incentive for the same would manifest from social customs and family attitudes. This perspective is justified, given that the social milieu from where the HIV patient belongs plays an important role in his thought process, attitude and behaviour. Health care establishments have to adopt strategies for change keeping in mind, the social customs and traditions. The responsibility of health care personnel is not only to develop heightened awareness of personal responsibility for stopping the spread of AIDS but also of increasing public tolerance and understanding of those directly affected.

Patterns of family formations and sexual permissiveness vary widely from one country and one ethnic group to another. Moreover, as a result of acculturation, westernization, new economic networks, social mobility and population heterogeneity, cities contrast not only with rural areas but also with one another, from traditional to most cosmopolitan. Furthermore, data on sexual behaviour are very limited particularly in the quantitative aspect.

As AIDS predominantly affects young adults—people in their late twenties, thirties and forties—care taking responsibilities are often thrust upon the elderly parents in their sixties and seventies. In our culture, the usual adult role is assisting and caring for elderly parents. The necessity for this role reversal tends to create additional stress. The guilt in the situation is not only with the person who has tested seropositive but is also evident as parents blaming themselves for the situation, agonizing whether they played a role in their child's homosexuality or sexual promiscuity. There is also an assumed natural order of life, and parents do not expect their children to die before them. The personality of an individual pre-determines how he or she will respond to illness. People who are independent and grasped initiatives before becoming ill continue to strive for independence afterward.

People with AIDS are forced to make many difficult psychological and social adjustments. They are faced with painful illness and treatment, possible loss of job and income, loss of independence and a reassessment of social and personal needs. Relationships change—some become strained, others develop into deep, supportive, meaningful ties. It is essential that patients, families and friends avail themselves of the psychological and social support of the community (Lehman Virginia and Russell Noreen, 1998).

Never before, in the history of any disease, has the need to encourage and foster the cooperation and active participation of broad sectors of population been so evident as in the case of HIV/AIDS. Understanding human behaviour in order to modify it for the sake of health has become a global challenge (Carbello Manuel and Bayer Ronald, 1990). The importance of broader social attitudes, legislative action and the willingness of society to work with, as opposed to, for or against, particular groups or individuals has become all the more important.

Economic Impact of the AIDS Pandemic

As we have already discussed the impact of HIV is not only on a personal level but on the carers; societies and countries at large because this is a problem with serious psychological, social and economic repercussions. Serious losses threaten agriculture, medicine, industry and nearly every sector of the economy.The direct cost has been estimated at $ 2.6 Billion-$ 3.5 billion a year. This bill has been constantly increasing from 100,000 a year to 400,000 a year by the end of the last decade (AIDS and development; Panos Media briefing, 1992). The cost of treatment is a relatively small, visible slice of a rapidly growing bill. The Asian Development Bank's list of indirect costs includes loss of output from disability and premature deaths and by people not themselves infected but who spend time caring for others; a possible increase in wage costs as a result of labour shortages, and damaged tourist industry.

A study has been conducted in the United States of America estimating the direct and the indirect costs of AIDS through 1985 to 1991. The study presents three estimates, ranging from low to high, of the direct and the indirect costs of the epidemic in the US, based on the prevalent estimates provided by the Centre for Disease Control. The researchers calculated not just the personal medical care costs, which was estimated as $ 8.5 billion in 1991, but also non-personal costs including cost of research, screening, education and general support services. The non-personal cost in 1991 was estimated to be $ 2.3 billion. Furthermore the indirect cost attributable to loss of productivity resulting from morbidity and premature mortality are estimated at $55.6 billion (Scitovsky, A. and Rice, D.P., 1986).

Besides these a study of 28 confirmed AIDS cases shows that the transfused patients use a large amount of hospital's blood products especially platelets. For these patients the average cost of transfusion is higher than that for intensive care unit patients (Simmonneau, M., Regneer, P., Vitte Cocq, D. *et al.*, 1984). In a study of the expenditure from the first 10,000 cases of AIDS in the US, the researchers found that the patients required 1.6 million days in the hospital resulting in over

$1.4 billion in expenditure. Losses from disability and from premature deaths was estimated at $4.8 billion. The total economic burden of the AIDS epidemic will continue to rise as the number of diagnosed cases increase (Simmonneau, M., Regneer, P., Vitte, Cocq, D. *et al.*, 1984).

In a similar study in United Kingdom, the use of hospital resources by patients with AIDS and planned additional costs of clinical and preventive services for the epidemic of infection with HIV was calculated. The study was carried out by an inner London health district that has treated 18 per cent of the cases in the UK. Patients with AIDS required an average 50 days of inpatient hospital care each at an estimated current average lifetime cost of Pounds 6,800. The costs, however, underestimated the additional capital and revenue costs of planned new preventive and treatment services (Johnson, A.M., Adler, M.W. and Crown, J.M., 1986).

Smaller studies have been carried out in the various states of US. Investigation in Massachusetts suggested that the direct cost of medical care for the 24011 reported patients with AIDS was as high as $ 147,000 per patient. To evaluate the use and cost of medical services for patients with AIDS the author performed a one year cost of illness study of 45 AIDS patients. Socio-economic and demographic data as well as information on medical utilization were obtained from review of patient and hospital records. Patients with AIDS required an average of $ 46505 per patient per year (Seage, G.R., Landers, S., Barry, J., 1986).

Similarly, researchers in San Fransisco found that mean charges of patients with AIDS who received all the hospital inpatient and outpatient care at the San Fransisco General Hospital in 1984 ranged from $7026 to $ 23425 (Scitovsky, A.A., Cline, M. and Lee, P.R., 1986).

Looking at the statistics of these studies, the seriousness of the issue in our country takes on gigantic proportions. Most of these cost studies have been based on charges billed by the providers and not on analysis of the resources actually consumed by the HIV patients. The true cost of a hospital bed day is much lower in the communities with excess beds than in one where the epidemic is beginning to stress the health care system. Most patients and their families spent their own money for treatment and associated services. The nation will have to forgo considerable production because of increased morbidity and early mortality associated with AIDS. Formal estimates of income streams interrupted by the disease will have to be made:

- Data on age, education, occupation, experience and prior earnings are needed.

- Demands for acute and chronic beds, finances for physicians and other health care workers.
- The concentration of social services towards people with AIDS would be such that others would be turned away—the old, dependent, the homeless, the children and so on.
- AIDS has also been considered a threat for the financial solvency of the care providers such as health insurers (Health Policy, 1989).

The need, therefore, is to think through and resolve the theoretical problems so that we can combine knowledge and data into a deeper understanding of the HIV/AIDS epidemic, only then can we accurately project costs to the society under various possible future scenarios.

AIDS has the capacity to seriously undermine the development prospects of many nations, because those who are affected are men and women aged between 20-40 years. Its impact on development explains the World Bank's growing involvement in the AIDS funding, with projects in more than 15 countries, including India, Zaire and Brazil and several more planned. Serious losses threaten agriculture, medicine, industry and nearly every sector of economy. So far much publicity about AIDS has been focused on Africa, but as per the Asian Development Bank, by the year 2015, most of the projected 40 million HIV infections and 10 million AIDS cases worldwide will be in Asia. Countries such as India and Thailand, with high rates of HIV infections but as yet few AIDS cases face potentially very high costs in the next 5-10 years. The United Nations Children's Fund has outlined four phenomena that may undermine the social fabric of many developing countries, potentially promoting behaviours that place their citizens at increased risk of HIV infection (Lurie, Peter, Hintzen, Percy, Lowe, Robert, A., 1995).

Declining Sustain Ability of Rural Subsistence Economy

Currency devaluation, investment concessions and other efforts to promote exports disrupt rural subsistence. Small farmers and craftspeople find themselves facing stiff and sophisticated foreign competition. People in rural areas are often forced to leave their families in search of work. Ultimately these migration patterns may be linked to the spread of HIV.

Development of Transport Infrastructure

The transportational structures that have developed during the 1980s in most of the developing countries tend to support export led economy.

These networks connect outlaying areas to export centres, not other outlaying areas. Thus, they connect rural areas to urban centres with high HIV sreoprevalences. This facilitates permanent or seasonal migration by rural dwellers to large cities.

Transportational routes may also facilitate the spread of HIV. In India 64-82 per cent truck drivers frequent CSWs (Commercial Sex Workers). Almost all truck drivers on the Delhi-Mumbai route have contracted sexually transmitted disease at one time (Ahmed, S.I., 1992).

Migration and Urbanization

For developing countries as a whole urban populations are increasing 3.6 per cent per year—4.5 times faster than the urban population in industrialized countries. While some of this increase was due to natural growth in the developing country urban population size, 39 per cent of the increase was the result of migration (Harpham, T., 1986).

These migration trends have a profound implications for the patterns of sexual relations. Male migrant workers may leave a single sexual partner in the countryside for multiple casual partners in the city. The women in the rural areas remain dependent on their male partners for financial support, decreasing women's ability to negotiate for safe sex, and fostering the spread of HIV from urban to rural areas.

Reduction in Spending on Health and Social Services

Tax reductions and other concessions to foreign investors have decreased government revenue in many developing countries. Scarce government resources are frequently allocated to meet the infrastructural needs of foreign investors than the health and welfare needs of the local population. India and China have yet to face this predicament but other developing countries such as, Kenya, Zaire, Ghana, Zimbabwe have had to cut back on health care and education facilities.

The Poverty Issue

The overriding reason for the rapid spread of HIV has been the high correlation that exists between poverty and vulnerability to the virus, a correlation that has led to high rates of infection in the most economically deprived populations. Poor communities have less access to health care, inadequate health care means that sexually transmitted diseases often flourish, hence a greater risk of HIV infection. Lack of education, limits the awareness about AIDS. For people struggling to meet their immediate needs for food and shelter avoiding a disease which might not materialize for years can be low on the priority list.

In a study conducted by the US centre for Disease Control in 1988, a definite link was established between poverty and seropositivity. The researchers analysed demographic and behavioural risk factors for HIV seropositivity using data from 3601 clients of the main HIV counselling and testing clinic for high risk people in Seattle, Washington, USA. Clients with lower income were found to be more likely to be HIV seropositive, before and after controlling for other demographic and other risk factors. This result supports the hypothesis that the impoverished ~~are~~ at increased risk for HIV infection due to the physical and social circumstances in which their poverty places them. These may include poor access to risk reduction information and less support for implementation of risk reduction strategies. Action now can save millions of lives and billions of Dollars (Krueger, E. Leigh, Wood Robert, W., Diehr Paula, H., Maxwell Clare, L., 1990). One study by Thai activist Michai Veeravaidya and others suggests that $ 100 million spent on the anti-HIV/AIDS activities in Thailand in 1991-92 could eventually result in 3.5 million fewer people infected and in $ 5.1 billion saved.

Tuberculosis is the worst fallout of the HIV infection as people with AIDS contract tuberculosis very easily. So tuberculosis becomes widespread even among the people who are HIV negative. Herein lies the invisible costs of AIDS. People with AIDS and increasing number of people with TB displace other patients in hospitals which have limited number of beds. This can lead to other diseases becoming chronic and even cause death. Cost of labour and income loss due to illness and death and the task of caring for patients in addition to the direct cost of treatment of the AIDS related complexes.

Major Areas to be Affected by the AIDS Pandemic in the Developing World are:

- Loss of labour as young adults die prematurely.
- Medical supplies to be purchased from overseas resulting in scarce foreign exchange using currencies which are losing value rapidly.
- Countries with guerilla activity, terrorist movements and political unrest lose out on government and community action.

Political unrest's result in migration and more casual sex and prostitution.

- Loss of man-hours resulting in reduced industrial productivity.
- Losses in agriculture, education and skilled labour.
- Loss of education of young children due to economic constraints or death of parents due to AIDS.
- Costs of condom provision and awareness programmes.

As is clear by now that it is advisable to invest now in preventive measures than later on the cost of a widespread pandemic. AIDS has to be tackled in an overall context of development and not just a health issue.

The preceding discussion highlights the need for social and economic interventions in stemming the spread of HIV and in treating those that are infected. While biomedical scientists worldwide have risen to meet the challenges offered by the HIV pandemic, socio-economic aspects have often been ignored.

The economic policies of developing countries may be modified to reduce the spread of the disease. The priorities should be satisfaction of basic needs such as food and housing, ensure regional sufficiency and support system for marginal producers, emphasis on human resource development and formation of a truly co-operative policy rather than a top down approach. For the developing countries HIV seropositivity is a social problem, not simply a biological one. It must be understood socially, in its historically specific context, or not at all (Hunt, C.W., 1989).

Information Education and Communication: An Effective Strategy for AIDS Prevention

The efforts to control the AIDS pandemic are being made in many contexts. From the communication perspective, the main task for AIDS control, is the systematic spread of information coupled with education to make the public self-reliant and an effective means of communication to clear doubts in the public mind through free and frank discussions. The general objective of IEC (Information, Education and Communication) is to bring about appropriate changes in behaviour, especially among vulnerable populations with patterns of high risk behaviour.

Creating changes in behaviour is, however, a difficult process. In the case of AIDS, the task is further complicated by the sensitive and personal nature of the issues, dealing as they largely do with sex and sexuality. The task of IEC, in this situation, is primarily to create a climate conducive to behaviour change and help individuals develop necessary skills for prevention.

In the existing socio-cultural environment, the IEC strategy for prevention and control of AIDS cannot be only concerned with the promotion of condoms or use of sterilized needles, but go beyond to addressing issues related to such modes of behaviour which are responsible for causing the rapid transmission of this disease.

One of the earliest issues to be taken up by the IEC programmes is the behaviour modification in smokers. The following set of behaviour modification stages have been demonstrated in the case of learning to stop smoking.The first step is to create awareness about the problem, and to then provide information about its extent, magnitude and impact. Information must be given in a form that makes people personally relate to the problem, rather than lead to an impression that 'it is someone else's problem not mine' at the same time, the great deal of misinformation and misconceptions about HIV/AIDS has to be countered and corrected. People must be educated about how HIV spreads and how it does not spread, as well as what people can do and should do to protect themselves. When IEC efforts are participatory, and involve the target audiences in an active dialogue, there is a greater chance of success. Such knowledge, and continuing IEC efforts will, in collaboration with supportive services, create a climate that is conducive for behaviour change.

The role of IEC has been seen as the following:

(*a*) *To create an informed and educated public*: In order to bring about appropriate changes in behaviour. Given the geographic spread of the problem and the diversity of the groups at risk, it seems natural to use the mass media for an IEC effort. While this is necessary and can be most useful, experience indicates that more individualized, interpersonal channels of communication particularly with those with high risk behaviour is a must. Information needs keep changing at each stage, so IEC efforts must be a continuous process.

(*b*) *To educate individuals and groups with high risk/high targeted interventions*: Implementation of such approaches early in the epidemic combined with provision of services such as condoms can definitely slow the epidemic.

(*c*) *Advocacy*: IEC also has a role in advocacy. Policy and decision makers have to be persuaded to take steps and/or initiate policies and services that shall stall the spread of HIV infection. IEC efforts will have to be directed to teachers, health and health related workers and other intermediaries or influencers.

(*d*) *To make positive role models*: The creation of positive role models through IEC is extremely important. This mode too has been used with considerable success by communicators. Here the attempt will be to create—especially for the youth and adolescents—a role model for responsible behaviour; whether it is related to sexual activity such as abstinence or condom use, or to safe injecting practices.

(*e*) *To support all components of an AIDS prevention programme*: It is essential that IEC be developed in the context of an overall AIDS control programme. If the IEC campaign is urging people to seek quality STD services, then those services must be available. IEC must also work in close collaboration with counselling and with general health services.

IEC can play a number of roles. In the context of AIDS pandemic, each one of these and IEC itself takes on special importance because the only way to tackle the HIV pandemic is prevention, and the best method of prevention is behaviour change. Therefore, behaviour change through IEC and appropriate services is the best bulwark against spread of HIV.

Since communication and information has the power to change behaviour and attitude over a period of time, the objectives and goals of an IEC strategy must, therefore, necessarily have to be concerned with the wider issues such as generating a respect and understanding for the vulnerable groups, increasing male responsibility, helping the community to provide the much needed social support to the individuals and their families who are suffering from the disease, training health service providers with the knowledge and skills to cope with the disease without fear and with sensitivity to ethical norms.

The formulation of target audience specific messages is complex, influenced by socio-cultural consideration and the acceptability of the range of personal behaviour options from which an individual could chose in his/her particular situation. Messages conveyed from different agencies need to be coherent if they are to be credible to the target audience. To achieve an environment where behaviour change is possible, support services must go in tandem with the information, education and communication strategies. These include: condom programming, STD services and counselling and care services. IEC activities vary greatly from country to country and sometimes between different regions in the country itself. However some issues are common and are of interest to every region.

Talking About Sex

In the traditional cultures and societies, specially in one like ours, discussing matters related to sex and sexuality is rather difficult. In such a scenario it is important that people begin to talk about sex and sexuality and healthy discussions on such topics should not be a taboo. The reluctance to broach such topics needs to be overcome and this is possible through non-threatening and cultural specific messages. In order to be effective both mass media and interpersonal communication must be used in consonance with each other.

Complacency and Denial

Whenever a region is faced with the AIDS pandemic for the first time, there is a tendency to deny the presence of the epidemic and an attitude of 'this cannot happen to me/my family/my country'. This phenomenon has been observed in nearly all the nations that faced the epidemic. Many a times the governments and the authorities fail to recognize the importance of AIDS education as they have myriad other problems. Specially in countries where problems such as poverty, unemployment, natural disasters, terrorism, guerilla activity or political unrest abound the need of the hour is not AIDS. Besides, developing countries are faced with many number of health issues which vie with each other for attention, AIDS as a health issue lags behind. However, IEC planning should note that AIDS is not single disease, it is a syndrome which ranges from common cold to cancer to untimely death. There is no time for complacency and denial, only opportunity for action.

Combating the AIDS pandemic has been learning process for the international community and national governments. Careful planning and development of IEC approaches for target groups can maximise the use of scarce resources.

Approaches towards an effective IEC programme can be many. Each approach has a philosophy underlying it, and indicates a certain value system. Certain approaches such as promotion of positive behaviour change can be effective for any society, some others such as the fear and morality messages have not been found useful for any society. It is for each community to decide which approach suits best for it to adopt.

It has been learned that IEC alone cannot make an impact if it is not supported. An integrated approach to IEC takes into account the availability of services and commodities. An integrated approach to reaching truck drivers, for example would necessitate availability of condoms, STD services in a non-stigmatising setting and possibly counselling services.

IEC Should Lead to Action. Therefore the Means to That Action Have to be in Place

No single organisation can cover all these activities. AIDS prevention and control needs to be multi-sectoral to draw on a wide range of expertise and skills required in intervention, development and implementation. This means close collaboration between government services and NGOs conducting outreach with a particular group.

At the very beginning, it is important to review the existing situation; to conduct a thorough assessment of the programme's IEC needs; to identify the target audiences and formulate achievable objectives.

Planning

The first step is to examine and analyse national policies, especially those related to health, education and communication. For different target groups the situational analysis will vary accordingly. Next step would be to examine existing available data. There is most times no apparent need to initiate new effort to collect and analyse data. An IEC programme could draw from the large body of existing data and research in all countries, including information available with NGOs and other groups that are close to specific communities.

Before plunging into IEC programme, the situational analysis should review:

- Demographic data
- Epidemiological data
- Behavioural data
- Existing IEC material and its use

One of the most crucial steps in designing an IEC programme is the target group identification. The target groups must be carefully stratified/segmented and prioritised. In the absence of specific targeting, messages tend to be very general and incapable of generating either change or action. The targeting should be specific and tightly defined. Segmentation into target groups should be based on behaviour and vulnerable groups identified so that they can be given priority in preventive measures. For each target group, it is necessary to specify the goals of the IEC effort. These would primarily relate to the desired behaviour change. Goals and objectives achieved through IEC must be scientifically defined. Generally these should be a set of behaviour changes that are achievable. Support services play an important role in generating an impact. Influenced by the goals and objectives of the programme, the required support services come into action. This may include physical inputs and services, such as counselling. Effective implementation of any programme requires a well trained and skilled manpower. In the context of IEC, training in communication skills needs to be emphasised. Sensitization medical personnel regarding communication and dealing with HIV cases is also necessary.

Steps in IEC Materials Development Process

1. Identify problem
2. Identify target audience
3. Conduct assessment
4. Choose communication channels
5. Design prototype material
6. Pretest material
7. Revise material
8. Final pretest and production
9. Distribute material
10. Trial communication.

While designing IEC programmes cost effectiveness of the materials and the medium have to be considered. Costs are important as the resources are always scarce. It would be well to judiciously and selectively use expensive media like film and TV. The glamour of these media often results in the overemphasis on their use, even though the cost of production is very high. On the other hand traditional media and interpersonal communication tools are often neglected, though they are generally very cost effective.

Dissemination of materials produced has to be carried out carefully. Setting up a distribution network and list at the very beginning is important. Another aspect that should be built into the IEC process is monitoring and feedback. Monitoring is continuous and seeks to provide immediate inputs for corrective action. Monitoring is the ongoing process of collecting and analysing information about implementation of the programme. It helps to follow the progress of planned activities, identify problems, give feedback to staff and solve problems before they cause delays. Evaluation is the process of collecting and analysing information at regular intervals about the effectiveness and impact of the programme in whole or in parts.

IEC for Youth

A general view at developing IEC materials has already been discussed. In this section, an effort has been made to provide a target specific plan for developing IEC programmes for adolescents and youth, which also forms the target group for this research.

Planning

Herein, it is important to know the policies that exist for youth and also views on the subject of condom use and sex education in schools. Existing data and research reports can provide useful details indicating the group's habits, preferences, media habits, involvement in youth/sports organisation, effectiveness of different media etc. The target group can be further segmented in order for employing different media strategy for each segment. School students, college students, youth out of school, street children, working young people, rural areas, urban areas, metropolitan cities and so on would each need an individual study, materials and media catering only to them. An uniform decision on the philosophy for IEC needs to be made. Decisions such as sex education in school curriculum, handling discussions on sensitive topics like sexual experimentation, masturbation, condom use etc. should be clearly chalked out before starting the programme.

Role of the peer group, teachers and parents in bringing about awareness and behaviour change, as the case may be, is crucial. A well thought out and planned programme can fail if the role of these major forces in a young person's life is not clearly outlined. Behaviour goals/ objectives which are desired from the IEC programme may be listed out at the very onset.

Tentatively, the desired behavioural goals for this target group could be:

- Delay sexual initiation
- Safer intimacy options
- Increase condom use
- Discuss matters openly
- Seek information and services
- Develop healthy lifestyles
- Reduce drug injecting or emphasize sterilization and non-sharing of needles

Preparatory Activities and Material Development

As was mentioned in the previous section, close and active collaboration with other agencies and programmes is vital for the success of any IEC strategy. In the case of youth, collaboration should be established with educational authorities/institutions and with youth organisations (schools, colleges, scouts, guides etc.). Links should be established with youth clubs and sports organisations.

NGOs and voluntary organizations can play an important role because of the commitment and dedication of those involved. They are better equipped to interact with out of school youth, street children, high risk behaviour groups and so on.

Support Services

Support services play an important role in supporting behaviour change and facilitating the adoption of appropriate preventive practices and behaviours.

For this target group the support services include:

- Counselling
- Condom distribution
- STD/Health services
- Information service (hotline, through telephones, or post box)

Formative Research

Formative research will play a major role in devising the right message.

The present awareness levels decide whether the message should be more informative or motivating. The choice of the medium for the message will depend on the extent of access that the target group has to the medium. Some of the suitable media for this group are:

- *Broadcast media*: Youth programmes and popular channels like FM can effectively reach urban and semi-urban youth. Since radio is a popular medium in the rural areas also, youth from all parts of the country can benefit.
- *Books*: For the literate college going or school going youngster.
- *Street theatre*: Especially for the street children.
- *Exhibitions*: Such as the perfect health mela.
- *Peer group*: This is by far the most effective form of communication for this particular target group. During adolescence peer group acceptance and opinion matters a lot and being the part of a group that is health conscious and also considered fashionable would be the topmost priority of a young person.

A combination of these media in addition to trained teachers and counsellors for guidance should perhaps form the best media package for this group. While developing IEC material it is important to involve communicators as well as representatives of the target group in order for the message to create the right impact finally. The material produced must be within the framework of the overall approach/philosophy and the messages identified for this target group.

The dissemination of the messages requires the right medium to be used at the right time. The initial survey/research will reveal the most popular radio listening hours and TV viewing hours. Sometimes in order to save on air time, HIV related messages can be interwoven in the story line of some popular ongoing serials. One such example was the introduction of a character who is HIV +ve in the serial Tara, however, the mistake was to show him to be a person of questionable character. The impact of any communication is increased manyfold if it is discussed amongst the receivers, if their questions are answered and their doubts clarified. As it is with this particular target group, queries and questions abound. Wherever relevant, use of interpersonal communication and narrowcasting methods (which heighten the possibility of interaction between the communicator and the audience) should be encouraged.

For the target group of young persons, counselling is of special significance and relevance. Helplines, post boxes and information lines are effective because they guarantee anonymity. Although these are confined to urban areas, it is not a major constraint as the maximum number of AIDS cases are also reported from the urban areas.

Finally, monitoring and evaluation can be accomplished by baseline data on knowledge and practices. Evaluation of process and outcome is important if the results are fed back into the programme planning. Research on this target group is never ending with new media emerging everyday, the youngsters of today are exposed to a variety of messages which are haphazard in nature. The message of AIDS should be sent across in planned manner over a period of time if this target group has to be persuaded to follow certain behaviour patterns or if their behaviours have to be changed.

4

The Triangulation Method

The study has been designed keeping in mind the methodology being followed the world over in researches involving sensitive subjects. This procedure is known as Triangulation Method. Triangulation has been defined as the use of two or more methods of data collection in the study of some aspect of human behaviour (Cohen and Manion, 1989). In the recent years it has been felt that anyone method of data collection is insufficient. Objective indicators to any phenomenon are based on counting the number of occurrences of any particular phenomenon, whereas the subjective indicators to a particular phenomenon deal with the reports of the individuals about their feelings, perceptions, aspirations etc. As Carley (1981) has pointed out, neither type of research, when used alone can give us an accurate window to the world. They are best developed when used in conjunction. While quantitative research leads us to generalise on particular phenomenon, qualitative research helps us to understand the specifics.

Quantitative research would be useful to understand the behaviour of populations, while qualitative research understands the behaviour of people. It would certainly be advisable to understand the people who make the populations, not only in terms of numbers but also as human beings. Macro approaches lead us to a certain degree of generality and often suggest that more rigorous work needs to be done, a more detailed investigation is required. In such cases, a smaller scale, qualitative work can bridge the gap. It was this debate amongst researchers that has given rise to Ethnostatistics. Ethnostatistics means the study of construction, interpretation and display of statistics in quantitative research (Gephart, 1988). Qualitative results were expected from quantitative findings. Causal relationships, correlation's, significance tests became the norm. Feilding and Feilding (1986) suggested 'there are possible points of convergence' in different approaches. It has now become more acceptable in recent years to combine quantitative and qualitative research, and the process is triangulation of data to substantiate the hypotheses.

Qualitative research can help the quantitative research in many ways:

1. By providing hypotheses to be tested by quantitative method, if it is conducted before the quantitative research.
2. As a mechanism for validating survey data, as is the purpose in this research.
3. Interpreting the statistical relationships and deciphering puzzling responses.
4. Offering case study illustrations.
5. Helping to analyze complex phenomenon.
6. When an established approach gives a distorted picture.

Survey data can identify individuals for qualitative study and representative and unrepresentative cases. Using more than one method to examine the same research question enables the researcher to strengthen the validity of their findings if both are shown to provide mutual confirmation (Bryman, 1993). Since the topic of the study was sensitive and dealt with a target group that was impressionable and very young, the triangulation method was used.

This study concentrates on all the elements of communication process, such as the sender, the message, the channel and the receiver. In order to study the various elements qualitative as well as quantitative tools of data collection have been used.

1. Content Analysis
2. Survey
3. Focus Group Discussions.

In the first method: A time series content analysis was conducted on the AIDS related messages that appear in the print and electronic media in India. Taking a sample of 5 newspapers, the AIDS messages appearing in them were studied during the years 1993 to 1995 and 2000 This process has been described in the following paragraphs. Similarly, a study of audio visual media was conducted through observation method. The details are given in Chapter 6, Part II. This aspect of the study gave the researcher an insight into the involvement of the media with the AIDS issue.

In the second method: A survey was conducted amongst the school going adolescents in Delhi and Ghaziabad. The research design is described in the following pages. This method was utilized to assess the extent of AIDS awareness that is there in the population and the role played by mass media in achieving this awareness.

In the third method: Focus Group Discussions were conducted with the same population to understand the needs of the group and their expectations from the mass media.

Content Analysis

Objectives

1. To identify and analyse the AIDS related content in the prominent Indian national daily English language newspapers.
2. To measure the content quantitatively as well as qualitatively.

Hypotheses

(a) AIDS related reporting in the prominent Indian national daily English language newspapers has increased year after year.
(b) AIDS related news reports focus more on the medical and policy aspect of the news.
(c) Interpretations and human-interest angles have increased.
(d) Sensational stories are very few.
(e) Government messages and advertisements form the bulk of AIDS related content in the newspapers.

Universe

This study considers the AIDS related news content of 5 Indian national daily English language newspapers from November 15–December 15 every year from 1993 to 1995 and from November 15–December 15, 2000.

Sampling Technique

Multi Stage sampling

First Stage

This stage involves sampling of content sources. Out of all national dailies in English, 5 dailies with highest circulation in Delhi are chosen.

Second Stage

This stage involves selecting the time frame of the study. It was found during the pilot study of the newspapers that maximum coverage to AIDS related news was during the months of November and December. Even if the content of the whole year would be considered for analysis, maximum coverage would be found during the said month because all through the year, the news items related to AIDS were few and far between. The researcher conducted a pilot study of the sample papers in 1993, and reached this conclusion. Keeping this in mind, November 15–December 15 was taken as the time period most suited for the study of news regarding AIDS.

A period of three years was considered appropriate to recognize the general approach of the Indian Press towards the issue of AIDS followed by a time series conducted in the year 2000.

Third Stage

Every item which was in anyway related to AIDS, found anywhere in the newspaper, was tabulated.

Unit of Analysis

The unit of analysis in this study is a single assertion about one subject, AIDS. Entire articles or stories regarding AIDS are measured and tabulated in sq.cms.

Categories of Analysis

Categorization was the most difficult part of this analysis. In order to keep the categories mutually exclusive, exhaustive and reliable, the category system was revised three times. With the help of two other coders the final category system was evolved. Since most reports contain many types of news materials, ultimately it was decided to include sub-categories, under the category News Reports. This helped to arrive at a better degree of exclusivity.

The following newspapers were chosen for the content analysis

For the purpose, 5 prominent daily newspapers were selected. The selection was based on their approach and readership in the capital of the country. All figures quoted below are from INS-1993 (Since the sampling required news reports beginning from the year 1993). The selected sample is:

1. *The Times of India*: A prominent daily with nationwide readership. *Times of India* is published from Mumbai, Bangalore, New Delhi, Ahmedabad, Patna and Lucknow. With the introduction of FM radio, *Times of India* has moved on to radio.
2. *The Indian Express*: This important daily with nationwide readership is one of the most popular dailies in the south. Started the trend of local newspapers and foremost in interpretative journalism.
3. *The Hindustan Times*: Largest circulating daily in the Delhi metropolis.
4. *The Statesman*: A prominent newspaper in the eastern part of the country. It is published simultaneously from Calcutta and New Delhi.
5. *The Hindu*: A prominent daily in the south of India. It has a unique page design, which is a special feature of this newspaper. It is known for its serious and literary content.

Time Frame

The AIDS related news reports were analyzed during the period of

15th November 1993–15th December 1993
15th November 1993–15th December 1994
15th November 1995–15th December 1995
and
15th November 2000–15th December 2000

As expected, most AIDS related news items started to appear around 27th November and continued up to 6th December. Although in the year 2000, the period in which the articles appearèd was reduced by 3-4 days.

Categories

Items were divided into 5 broad categories on the basis of their content.

1. *News Report*

Factual reporting with no bias or colour was assigned this category. News reports which gave factual information, data or statement, new policies for HIV testing, government plans for AIDS, medical information, new drugs, opinion from experts working in the field of AIDS, public attitude, programmes taken up by the government and non-government organizations are clubbed together under this broad heading. Sub-categories were created as follows:

(a) *Information*: The first news report. Under this sub-category only the information that was being imparted for the first time was included.
(b) *Policy/Plan*: Any news item that included any mention of a government plan, policy decision taken by a government body or official, any new law or statement made by the government authorities was included in this sub-category.
(c) *Medical*: Any new development in the field of medical research about AIDS, new medicines that have been introduced and if the information appeared as a news report, it was included under this sub-heading.
(d) *Opinion/Attitude*: When the news item reflected opinion of some person, organization or a body of people the news item found its way under this sub-category.
(e) *Activity/Programme*: News items related to any programmes, seminars, rallies, workshops, conferences or any other activity conducted by orgaisations other than the government bodies, were included in this sub category.
(f) *Sensational*: Any exaggerated, attention seeking story about the disease or the affected was allotted this sub-category.

2. *Interview*

Exclusive interviews with government officials, policy makers, programme implementers or anyone connected with the issue of AIDS, even people with AIDS.

3. *Analysis*

In depth analysis of the issue related to the AIDS epidemic, its spread in India, its progress and repercussions.

4. *Advertisements*

Public health messages related to AIDS issued by all authorities.

5. *Human Interest Items/Features*

Sentimental features about people with AIDS and their problems. Articles which carry the items of public concern such as, 'Barber cuts can lead to AIDS' which offer readability although their contents are sometimes dramatized.

Methodology

The data was quantified by means of nominal measurement. The articles were manually quantified thus:

1. *Written Matter*: Total written space occupied by the article.
2. *Photograph*: Photographs have been measured separately without the captions.
3. *Others*: This includes the headlines, by line, captions for photographs and other space left over from the written matter.

The measurement of each article has been carried out in sq.cms.

Time Series study on the content analysis of the five prominent English language dailies in India

In continuation with the content analysis that had been conducted by the researcher for the years 1993, 1994, 1995, a time series study was conducted in the year 2000 to compare the coverage given to AIDS related news reports.

The objectives and the methodology remain unchanged and even the sample newspapers used for the purpose of the study are the same. The time frame of one-month duration starting from November 15 to December 15 was studied.

The categorization remained the same making this study a continuation of the previous one. This method allows for the comparisons to be drawn amongst the previous years coverage and to coverage given to AIDS related news items in the year 2000.

Survey Design

This is the second stage of the study. After a thorough understanding of the mass media's contribution to the cause of spreading awareness about AIDS, the survey was conducted.

The present study strives to assess the level of awareness and knowledge regarding AIDS, exposure to mass media of adolescents in both government and private schools of New Delhi and a satellite town. The target group was chosen after much thought and an exploratory study conducted in Ghaziabad (*Annexure I*) on the same target group. It was a small study but revealed a big problem. AIDS as an issue was not being discussed in smaller towns. The disease was spreading its tentacles into the interiors of the country but the discussions on the issue were taboo in the more orthodox sectors. The results of the exploratory study helped the researcher in finalizing the target group. A workable hypotheses was developed with the initial exploratory study. Null hypotheses were tested with the help of SPSS package.

Hypotheses

The hypotheses for this study has stemmed from the body of theory which affords, by logical deduction, the prediction that if the present conditions prevail, adolescents living in various regions of the country have different expectations from the media and also have various ways of fulfilling these expectations. Theory always represents what is known, logical deductions from this constitute the hypotheses, which must be true if history is true. Having already conducted a study amongst the Ghaziabad school children, an APAC MCRC (AIDS prevention and Control-study by Mass Communication Research Centre) study amongst youth in and out of school at Madras, and a pre-test for the present study amongst Delhi school children, the researcher observed not only a marked difference in the awareness levels but also a difference in the attitude of the youngsters toward discussions about the subject.

Thus the following hypotheses was evolved:

H1: The interaction level with the mass media is significantly greater in a cosmopolitan city (in this case Delhi), as compared to a smaller city (in this case Ghaziabad).

H0: There is no significant difference in the interaction level with the mass media in a cosmopolitan city or smaller city.

H2: It is expected that there will be a positive correlation between socio-economic status of the respondent and his media access and exposure levels.

H0: There will be no significant correlation between the socio-economic status of the respondent and his media access and exposure levels.

H3: The socio-economic status of the respondent will correlate directly with the AIDS awareness levels.

H0: There will be no significant correlation between the socio-economic status of the respondents and his awareness levels.

H4: AIDS awareness levels of the respondents are expected to be significantly greater in a cosmopolitan city as compared to the smaller city.

H0: There will be no significant correlation between the AIDS awareness levels of the respondents and the cosmopolitan city or smaller city.

H5: It is expected that mass media has played a role largely to the AIDS awareness levels of the respondents.

H0: There will be no significant correlation between the role of mass media and the AIDS awareness levels.

H6: It is expected that the respondents would prefer to receive AIDS related information from the mass media.

H0: There will be no significant relationship between the respondent's expectation from the mass media as the source of AIDS related information and its role as the information provider.

H7: There will be a significant difference between the AIDS awareness levels of boys and girls.

H0: There will be no significant difference between the AIDS awareness levels of boys and girls.

H8: There will be significant difference in the AIDS awareness levels and the age of respondents.

H0: There will be no significant difference in the AIDS awareness levels and the age of the respondents.

All procedures, including variables, samples and measurement instruments have been selected and designed in the light of their appropriateness to the hypotheses. In order to produce reliable and valid results the following four aspects have been kept in mind:

1. *Naturalistic Setting*: The study has been conducted under

normally encountered environmental conditions. The subjects were administered the questionnaires in their own classrooms in front of their own teachers. This was important to achieve an honest response to the questions.

2. *Cause and Effect Relationship*: The earliest extraneous variable of location was incorporated in the sample in such a way that it would form a part of the result and not affect the results. Further, whenever the researcher has felt the presence of extraneous variables on the results, it has been mentioned while discussing the findings.
3. *Unobtrusive and Valid Measurements*: The subjects were requested to answer the questions to the best of their knowledge and they were instructed NOT to write their names or the names of their schools on the questionnaires. The location code was added by the researcher separately. This anonymity has helped to get honest answers. In order to assure the validity of the measurement used, an appropriate sample size of 500 respondents was chosen.
4. *Realism*: The study was designed realistically and not idealistically. The researcher has ventured to attempt only as much as was possible. This keeps the study honest and to the point. Thus a multivariate study was designed.

Sample Selection

The first aspect of sample selection was to decide the population. School going adolescents had been chosen as the population to be studied right at the time of the conception of the study. Since comparison between public school and government school had been incorporated in the hypotheses itself, it was important to include these aspects as independent variables. Similarly comparisons between Satellite town and Delhi metropolis were a part of the hypotheses so they too had to be incorporated as independent variables.

Since the study Area and type of sample population had already been decided, a multi stage sampling procedure was used to select the sample for this study.

Before deciding on the suitable sampling technique the following points were considered:

1. *Cost Versus Value*: The sample should produce the greatest

value for the least investment. Since the cost of a very large sample would be too high in relation to the type of quality of information collected, a suitable but small sample was considered the best possible alternative.

2. *Purpose of Study*: This research work would further be used only as an exploratory work for designing measurement instruments or the variable relationships found by this research would act as a first step towards many more researches. Since, the findings of this research would not be used at once for generalization to the population, causal analysis was not conducted.
3. *Amount of Error Allowed*: The researcher was not always able to control the presence of extraneous variables or artifacts in the results. Since no sample is a true representative of the population the researcher feels that the results are as accurate as possible by a single researcher. The primary data collected by this researcher, has been entered into the word processor by the researcher herself at the cost of a lot of time and effort. This has ensured least possible error in data entry.

Selection Procedure for the Study Area and for Sample

The subjects here were selected on the basis of specific characteristics or qualities. The students had to be from the two cities of Delhi and Ghaziabad. This would automatically eliminate adolescents in the rest of the country. The students had to be from government and public schools. This would mean that government and public schools in Delhi and Ghaziabad had to be chosen. A multi-stage sampling procedure was designed.

Multi Stage Sampling

First Stage: Random Selection of Schools

Here the sample had to represent a specific population of public and government schools in the two cities. A list of Delhi Public Schools was drawn and one school was picked randomly. Similarly one branch of Delhi Public School was picked in Ghaziabad. Likewise a list of Kendriya Vidyalays was drawn in Delhi as well as in Ghaziabad and one each was picked up in both the places.

Second Stage: Random Selection

Since the age group of the students had to be between 13 to 17 there was no difficulty in selecting the classes for the study. However, the problem arose as to the selection of the section in each class. Once again Random Sampling method was used. The registers of all the sections of VIII, IX, X and XI classes were placed on the table in a classwise segregation. There was no particular order in keeping the registers of each class. One register was chosen randomly from each class. This gave the sample to be chosen for the purpose of this study. This procedure was followed in all the schools that formed the population.

Sample Size

The primary consideration in determining the sample size is the methodology to be used. Since, here a survey methodology was being used, a large sample size had to be chosen. Initially a sample size of 500 was considered appropriate. On visiting the schools where the survey would finally be conducted the researcher found that each class had nearly five sections each. Since 20 per cent of the population would be adequately representative, the researcher decided to use one section each of 3 classes that formed the operational definition for adolescents in this study. Thus classes VIII, IX and X were used for the study. These constituted mainly of students between the ages 13 to 17.

Thus finally a sample size of 443 questionnaires was drawn.

Survey

This study is based on a correlational descriptive survey. This describes the situation as it is and does not attempt to explain why certain situation exists. This type of survey is best suited for collecting information on audiences and readership also for the purpose of gauging the knowledge levels of a particular target groups. Since the hypotheses did not venture into finding out causal relationships, this type of survey was best suited for this research work. Being correlational in nature its purpose extends beyond merely describing the data. It tries to establish whether or not statistically significant relationship or correlation exists between variables. This goes on to determine whether the relationship between the variables is strong enough to conclude that it did not happen by chance.

Research Tool

A close-ended questionnaire was chosen as the tool for this survey. The respondents were asked to select an answer from a list provided by the researcher. This helped in the final analysis as the responses could be easily quantified.

Pilot Study

A pilot study was conducted amongst 50 school going adolescents in order to test the tool. The questionnaire was improved as per the result of the pilot study. The main concern here was to check whether the terminology used by the researcher was also the one used by young boys and girls. To avoid confusion a focus group of 7 students was used to discuss the terminology. They helped the researcher in the language and proper phrasing of the questions so that they would be understood by the respondents.

As per the result of the pilot study, some questions had to be deleted, some had to be changed, some had to be rewritten to suit the language of the respondents.

Length of the Questionnaire

Although the researcher was interested in keeping the questionnaire short because the attention span of this target group is very short, it was not possible because all questions that covered the topic under investigation had to be asked. Since the survey was conducted in a very formal setting, and an environment in which the respondent is accustomed to writing hour-long tests, it was not a problem to get the respondents to completely answer all the questions. Since the researcher had taken one period out of the timetable, the students loved the distraction from regular study and were very interested in answering the questions. Thus the size of the questionnaire did not prove to be a hurdle in getting adequate response.

Questionnaire Design

Introduction

The very first page of the questionnaire held a letter from the researcher to the respondent. Since the respondents were students, they immediately identified with the researcher as one of them. Special pains had been taken by the researcher to sign all the questionnaires so that the respondent feels important and significant. The introduction had to be short, realistically worded and non-threatening. The legitimacy of the survey and the secrecy that is going to be maintained helped the respondents to trust the researcher and answer all the questions unhesitatingly.

Instructions

The respondents were orally instructed by the researcher to fill only the code numbers in the corresponding boxes. One question was used as an example to illustrate the point. The students were quick to understand the procedure and followed the instructions very carefully.

The instructions were also given together with the questions wherever necessary making the questionnaire self-explanatory.

Order of Questions

The questionnaire was clearly divided into four different sections.

The Demographic Profile

Under this sections questions about the respondents were asked. Their age, the class in which they studied, their family income, the profession and the educational level of their parents and so on. These questions lead to a clear picture of the type of respondent.

The Media Seeking Habits

Under this sections questions were asked about the availability of certain media with the respondent and the media he/she reaches out to for entertainment and general awareness. This section had questions on newspapers, radio, television, cinema, magazines and so on.

Knowledge of AIDS

This section was only to find out the respondent's knowledge about AIDS. The questions began with general health related topics to more specific AIDS related issues.

Sex Education

Under this section an attempt was made to find out the source of information of the respondents. Questions were also asked about the medium through which they would like to get their information regarding AIDS and HIV.

Nominal and ordinal measurement technique has been used for coding. This has helped the research to be mutually exclusive and exhaustive. Each category has been assigned an alphabet code, when one set of alphabets was exhausted, double sets were used.

Example: A, B, AA, BA, CA, DA and so on.

A total of 62 questions were asked with 177 columns to be filled. The respondents took one-hour time to complete the questionnaire.

On final scrutiny, only 4 questionnaires were found to be filled incorrectly and had to be disqualified. Only an enthusiastic and interested respondent could have helped the researcher to collect such a vast amount of data and a final number of 439 questionnaires. Descriptive and Inferential analyses were conducted with the data acquired.

Descriptive Analysis

The descriptive analysis was based on the simple method of frequencies and percentages. In order to find the correlations between variables, in order to prove the hypotheses, further analysis was conducted.

Inferential Analysis

Hypothesis is defined as 'a core concept within the statistical methodology. A proposition that is advanced for testing or appraising a generalization regarding the real social world'.

In a general form

- The null hypotheses (H0) states that there is no structured or systematic difference between two groups in our experiment.
- The alternate hypothesis (H 1) states that there is a structured or systematic difference between two groups in our experiment.

Within the hypothesis testing paradigm the goal is to assess the probability of the null hypotheses being correct. The diagram below is helpful in making the decision whether or not to reject the null hypothesis.

p = 1 ______________ p = 0.05 ______________ p = 0

Cannot Reject H0 Can reject H0

Conventionally, when the likelihood of a null hypothesis being correct is less than 5 in 100 (i.e., $P<.05$ or 5%) we can reject it. In social sciences and media studies, the significance level of 0.05 is used. In this study $p = 0.05$ has been used for all tables.

When chi square test is used on a data, the table first shows cross tabulations between two sets of information. SPSS calls the chi square test as Pearson chi square after Karl Pearson who developed the test. In addition to chi square SPSS also provides other statistics.

The likelihood ratio is an alternative to Pearson chi square. In large samples this statistics is roughly equivalent to chi square as is evident in these tables.

Linear by linear is a chi square test for two continuous variables but it has not been used for the purpose of this research.

Chi square can be defined as the difference between observed data and the expected frequencies. Chi square values for large tables and for small tables are different.

One has to compare the chi square value to the size of the table. The calculations for the size of the table is known as Degree of Freedom (df) of the table. It can be computed as follows:

Df = (no. of rows-1) * (no. of columns-1)

SPSS, however, provides the degrees of freedom in its tables.

In order to find whether the chi square value is more or less than the critical value—the researcher has to look down at the column which denotes the significance level in the chi square tables (Refer Annexure V for chi square tables). While looking down this column and arriving at the appropriate degree of freedom the researcher can get the critical value of chi square.

Thus, if the value of chi square is less than the critical value one cannot reject the null hypotheses. If the value of chi square is greater than or equal to the critical value we can reject the null hypothesis.

It can be summarised thus:

Chi square < critical Value — Critical value — Chi square > critical value

Cannot reject H0 — Reject H0

To find out the level of probability of the differences between our observed frequencies and the expected frequencies, one has to consider the fourth column of the chi square test table, i.e. Asymp. Sig., which is short for statistical term Asymptotic Significance. The probability or p value for the given statistics is reported in this column. Since, for the purpose of this research at p = 0.05, we can reject the null hypothesis, with the value given in the Asymp. Sig. In the table we can further confirm our result and infer whether there is a structured and systematic relationship between the two variables.

This statistical methodology has been used to make inferences about the data as well as to support or reject the null hypothesis.

Developing Indicators

In order to draw correlations between variables it was important to combine various aspects and to construct profiles or indicators.

Depending on the nature of the data and the analysis that was needed, three such profiles or indicators were developed. These indicators were found necessary to test the hypotheses as well as to conduct inferential analysis. These were:

1. Socio-Economic Status Indicator
2. Media Profile Indicator
3. AIDS awareness level score

Each of these indicators prepared with the help of SPSS includes a body of data. Construction of each of the indicators is explained below.

Socio-Economic Status Indicator

In order to correlate the demographic profile with other variables, a socio-economic status indicator (SES) was developed. This indicator combined the following variables each one in an ordinal order.

- Education level of father
- Education level of mother
- Family income
- Type of school and location

Since it was found that city of residence and type of school also made a difference in the AIDS awareness levels they were placed in an ordinal order.

The SPSS added these variables and derived a score chart of 0 to 15. This score chart was categorised into 4 groups:

0 to 5	→	group one
6 to 10	→	group two
11 to 13	→	group three
14+	→	group four

Where group IV is the highest group in the socio-economic status and group I is the least.

These four groups form the SES indicator with those scoring highest belonging to the highest socio-economic strata.

The data of the entire population derived was as follows:

Group	*Frequency*
I	07
II	227
III	172
IV	36

The socio-economic status indicator shows that Groups II and III have highest number of respondents. This indicates that majority of the population belongs to the middle classes and not to the lower or upper classes.

This indicator henceforth referred to as (SES) will be used for further correlations as an index of the background information variables.

Media Profile Indicator

In order to correlate the mass media interaction with other variables and indicators, an indicator of mass media profile was also developed. The variables showing mass media access and mass media reach were clubbed together to develop this profile.

Using the SPSS the following four variables

(a) Do you own/subscribe (1) Newspaper
(2) Radio
(3) Television
(4) Magazines

Were clubbed with corresponding variables of media exposure, i.e.

(b) Do you read/listen/watch (1) Newspaper
(2) Radio
(3) Television
(4) Magazines

Four categories of scores were derived from SPSS

0 ⟶ Do not own and do not interact
1 ⟶ Do not own but do interact
2 ⟶ Do own but do not interact
3 ⟶ Own and interact both

All the respondents fall in anyone of these scores. The data derived finally is:

Newspaper	*Magazines*	*Television*	*Radio*	
20	7	2	2	Group 0
60	144	14	51	Group 1
5	23	5	97	Group 2
354	265	418	289	Group 3

When the whole data is clubbed together a final score is arrived at ranging from 3 to 12. The division of this score gives the high, medium and low media profile of the respondent:

Low (1)	3 to 6	there are 28 cases only
Medium (2)	7 to 9	there are 86 cases
High (3)	10+	there are 325 cases

This index clearly shows that this respondent group has a very high media profile. Henceforth this media profile will be used for correlations.

AIDS Awareness Profile

For the purpose of descriptive analysis percentages of the total awareness were considered but for correlations it was important to get the AIDS awareness score in four groups just as others. Since AIDS awareness profile of the respondents could be easily derived in the form of a score out of a total of 36, scores were taken out. The score chart ranged from 0 to 36, i.e. Minimum to maximum score.

Four groups were made out of this score range.

0 to 9 ⟶ group 1
10 to 18 ⟶ group 2
19 to 27 ⟶ group 3
& 28+ ⟶ group 4

The students belonging to group 1 had the least score and those belonging to group 4 had the highest score and so on. This profile has been used in later calculations.

Focus Group Discussions

"Focus Groups are useful when it comes to investigating what the participants think, but they excel at uncovering why they think as they do". Morgan, D.L. in the book *Focus Groups as qualitative research*. As the findings of the survey suggest, most adolescents interact best with their peers when it comes to information about AIDS and sex. They have rated this group very high in their preference for source of information.

Keeping in mind, that Focus Groups can be used alone or combined with other methods of data collection, it was decided to use the triangulation method, making the focus group, the qualitative part in the wider study. The rationale behind focus groups is that in a group people tell more or give a deeper understanding of what they think or feel about a specific topic. Originally, the focus group interview technique, grew out of Lazarsfeld and Merton's efforts to glean an understanding of how radio audiences evaluate radio programmes and the reasons for their judgment (Steward and Shamdasani).

During Second World War, Merton applied his technique to the study of army personnel who had watched training and morale booster films (Merton, Fiske and Kendall). His research findings, gathered during the war and later at Columbia University, laid the ground work for 'Mass Persuasion' which focused on the persuasive impact of mass media. Soon the focus groups, developed and expanded into such fields as marketing, advertising, programme evaluation, communications and public policy.

The information that social scientists have gathered by applying the technique has contributed to our knowledge about how people think, form beliefs, ideas, opinions and judgments. In 1988, Krueger and Patton, gave the following characteristics of focus groups:

1. 7-10 voluntary members who participate in one meeting that lasts 1-$1\frac{1}{2}$ hours under the directions of a moderator. Members may or may not know each other.
2. Groups share a commonality.
3. Group members generate data that are recorded as observed.
4. The data generated are quantitative—that is, they proceed from in depth, spontaneous natural responses. The data are expressed in the respondents own words and in the context of the questions asked.
5. The in-depth discussion is focused in terms of research interests of the sponsor of the study by the interviewer. The moderator steers the conversation, probes selectively, and maintains the focus of the discussion.

Many researchers have used focus groups as one of the methods in their wider research study. Radway (1987) used focus groups and individual interviews together with other data collection methods to study the readership of romantic fiction among women. Jackson and Holbrook (1995) utilized a number of different methods in their research design, including focus groups, and discuss how these methods worked in their study of shopping and identity. Focus Groups provide space for interaction between participants but they also allow the researcher to access sites of 'collective remembering'. Kitzzinger (1994) used preformed groups, to explore how people talked about AIDS within the various overlapping groups in which they normally operate. The advantage of using participants who know each other means that friends or colleagues were able to relate comments made in focus group to events in their everyday, shared lives. Thus, Kitzzinger was able to tap into fragments of interactions which resembled naturally occurring data. Further, using pre-existing groups is appropriate because groups form a social context in which ideas are nurtured and decisions are made. A focus group is more than a group interview or discussion because of the community of interest shared by the group and the use of participants interaction as research data.

Use of Focus Groups for this Research

The purpose of using focus groups in this research was to interpret the previously obtained quantitative results. In the month of February in the year 2000, the process of conducting focus group discussions among the adolescents from the same sample area was begun. Since the groups used by the researcher had already passed out of their respective classes, VIII, IX, X and XI, the students who were presently studying in these classes were interviewed. The purpose of the research was not to follow the same sample through their life stages but to gauge the level of awareness and involvement into the subject of AIDS of the youngsters of today, studying in these classes. This study deals with the 13 to 16 years old adolescents studying in government and public schools of Delhi and Ghaziabad.

Profile of the Sample

Once the results of the survey were analysed, one dimension of the target group was clear. As a general group of young persons, they exhibited certain marked characteristics. They were mostly from the middle class, came from nuclear families where more mothers were homemakers and fathers were in government service. They spoke Hindi at home and owned most of the tools of media, They read newspapers and magazines and watched a lot of TV. They had heard about AIDS but did not know how it could be prevented. They were unaware of the tests used for the detection of HIV. They had discussed AIDS and sex with friends and wanted to know more. They wanted to hear about it from friends or television. This is a broad generalisation of the type of group that had formed the sample of the survey conducted by the researcher. Armed with the knowledge about the target group, the focus group discussions were conducted with the same sample.

Sample Selection for Focus Groups

Preformed groups work best in studies such as this one. Kitzzinger had already demonstrated that focus groups are appropriate for discussing issues like AIDS because they provide safety in numbers and the company of others who share similar misconceptions, doubts, anxieties or experiences. The sampling process used for the survey was also appropriate for this part of the study. Thus 3 focus groups were conducted in each previously chosen school:

1. Government School in Delhi–Class VIII, IX and XI
2. Government School in Delhi–Class VIII, IX, XI
3. Public School in Delhi–Class VIII, IX and XI
4. Public School in Ghaziabad–Class VII, IX and XI

A total of 12 focus groups were conducted with a gap of one week between each school.

Selection of Groups

Multistage sampling procedure was used for the purpose of the selection of groups. Since the FGDs had to be held in the same schools as the survey the sample had to be chosen from the various classes that formed the universe.

First Stage of Sampling: Random Sampling

Attendance registers from each class were selected at random. Since each class has at least 5 to 6 sections, attendance registers were placed on the table in no particular order. All registers had an equal chance of being selected. At random, register from one section from each class was picked up.

Second Stage of Sampling: Systematic Random

Students, who were to participate in the FGDs were selected through systematic random sampling. Every 6th student was selected from the attendance register, not necessarily starting from roll number 1. In this way the researcher tried to ensure that all numbers had a chance of being included in the sample. Since most sections have 45-48 students, nearly 7-8 number of students formed the focus group from each class. The procedure was repeated for each class.

Knodel has formalized the formation of groups by 'break' and 'control' characteristics. Control characteristic are common to all groups, break characteristics differentiate groups from each other.

Control Characteristics for this Research

1. All groups were mixed groups. No selection bias was made between girls and boys.
2. All were preformed groups and the members in each group knew each other well.

Break Characteristics for this Research

1. All groups were from different age brackets.
2. Groups were divided in terms of type of school—government or public.
3. Groups were divided in terms of location, either Delhi or Ghaziabad.

Thus the control and break characteristics provide contrasting views between subgroups and also establish common views.

Preparation of Questionnaire

Using the survey questionnaire as the base, a schedule was prepared for the focus groups. The role of the researcher in the focus groups is like a silent observer. In this case, however, the researcher had to act like a moderator because the target group was young, nervous and inexperienced. Participants look to the researcher for directions especially during the beginning of the discussion. The researcher had a clear agenda in mind and the schedule only helped as a guideline to prevent the discussion from straying into unrelated areas.

Choice of Location

That which is most difficult task for other researchers, was the easiest for this researcher. Being in the school premises, and with the help of the class teacher, the discussions were conducted in empty class rooms, laboratories, staff rooms or any other vacant room. However, all the locations were familiar to the group members and the group could carry on their discussion, undisturbed for nearly 1 hour.

Group Dynamics

The researcher was mentally prepared to find that groups that are externally similar in appearance. may differ largely when the discussion began. Groups also have a tendency to be led by a leader whenever one member chooses to be one. Unlike the theoretical books on focus groups which lead the researchers to believe that all focus groups run smoothly with well modulated conversations and polite members taking turns to speak, the researcher found that all members want to talk at the same time and soon either there is a bedlam or small groups are formed having their own conversations. The groups comprising of 7 or 8 teenagers talking freely about a subject they have never really discussed in the presence of an adult was a revelation to observe. Not only the students have opinions, they unhesitatingly expressed their doubts.

The researcher found that transcribing the focus groups on tape was not possible as nothing could be deciphered at the end of the day. Finally, the researcher decided to follow the questions and evoke responses, while making extensive field notes. This process helped the researcher to prevent the discussion from degenerating into an incomprehensible noise, while making sure that the students don't feel the presence of an authoritative figure, resulting in loss of fruitful interaction.

Format

A structured format was used for the purpose of this research. A pre-planned set of agenda topics were covered as the issue is relatively well understood and the previous study had already been conducted by the researcher.

This study has been conducted in three stages. Each stage, is complete in itself while also contributing to the overall analysis of the research questions. The tools of content analysis, survey and focus group discussions were used one by one and not simultaneously, so that the findings of each could be used in the inquiry. The method proved fruitful as the findings of the content analysis helped in designing the questionnaire and the findings of the survey helped in designing the schedule for the focus group discussions.

5

Media Coverage and the Adolescent

Mass media are generally defined as those channels of communication which are capable of reaching heterogeneous audiences simultaneously with uniform messages. These include radio, television, the press and cinema. Despite the overwhelming evidence of mass media effectiveness in raising awareness, increasing knowledge and changing behaviour, doubts still remain among non-specialists and media critics. These may be due to a failure to realize that there are two distinctive ways of media utilization, the first being the usual media coverage of news events, regular programmes and entertainment material, and the second is the use of mass media in the context of a planned and systematic process for the clear purpose of influencing attitudes and behaviour.

The present study was designed with the idea to find out the treatment given to AIDS related news by the mass media and also the access and reach of mass media amongst the target populations. Since, the study attempts to concentrate on the main components of the communication process, viz., the message as well as the feedback, it was important to analyse the content of the mass media and also conduct a survey with the target population to discover the reach of the medium as well as the message. In order to interact directly with the members of the target group and fill in the gaps left over by the quantitative methods, a focus group discussion was designed. All the three methods have given this study an understanding of the AIDS coverage from the point of view of the sender as well as the receiver.

As we look back at the history of the epidemic, it is obvious that the nature of press coverage of the disease has changed dramatically. The amount of press attention to the epidemic goes on in cycles. With major deaths related to AIDS, fresh statistics on every AIDS day, celebrity involvement in the AIDS issue, the press coverage goes up. On ordinary days, in normal times, the press is quiet about the issue. However, the overall non-tabloid, non-sensational elements of the media's efforts have been rather satisfactory. The fact that AIDS, has received more 'regular' media coverage in some countries than any other health issue in the history of humanity could very well be due to the fact that AIDS is a disease that involves, women, sex and death, thus providing journalists with all the ingredients of a sensational copy (Brown, P., 1992). The journalists may be reporting AIDS in a manner which reflects their own prejudices. Journalists have always emphasised rare or bizarre ways in which HIV can be spread rather than the common modes of transmission. Media coverage of AIDS has been described as having been, slow, erratic, distorted and bizarre (Poitrow, P., Meyer, R.C., Zulu, B.A., 1992). While it may seem that news organisations are doing a public service by communicating important health messages to their audiences, they do so not because of an altruistic desire to better human condition, but to sell more newspaper space or charge higher rates for commercial time (Dann, B.B., 1992). A leader in the news media claims that it is unrealistic to expect that the media will systematically pass on repetitive messages from the medical community or anyone else (Sullivan, S., 1993). However, it would not be fair to condemn the mass media for their market orientation, which is the need of the hour. Mass media has displayed a sense of responsibility as far as the issue of AIDS is concerned. Looking back, it is evident that the style of AIDS related coverage has undergone a lot of change.

Initial Coverage of AIDS News

Since 1981, when the first reports of a rare pattern of 'opportunistic infections associated with immunosuppression in homosexual men' appeared in *American Medical Journals* (Brown *et al.*, 1989) the world has struggled to cope with the disease that has pushed issues of sexuality into the foreground of political, religious and medical debate (Bruss and Greenberg, 1989). Mass media has been involved in the struggle since the very beginning. Mass media deliberates on issues of public interest and plays the role of a watchdog, acts as a forum for discussion, has the ability to influence the salience of events in the public mind— as Walter Lippman described— 'pictures in our heads'. Maxwell McCombs and Donald L. Shaw, offered in 1972 their scientific concept of agenda setting function, that media emphasis on an event influences the audience to also view the event as important. Bernard C. Cohen declared in his book, '*the Press and Foreign Policy*' that 'the press may not be successful much of the time in telling people what to think, but is stunningly successful in telling its readers what to think about (Agee *et al.*, 1985). Communication researchers believe that mass media have effects and are used by many people in ways important to them. A survey by McDermott *et al.* (1987) found that young people reported TV as the major source of their knowledge about AIDS, followed by newspapers and magazines (Pitts and Jackson, 1993).

During the first decade following the outbreak of the epidemic, the media in San Francisco carried more stories about AIDS than media in other urban centres of United States. During the 1970s San Francisco with its liberal lifestyles was a magnet for gay men and women. Homosexual men and women from all over United States travelled to San Francisco when the news spread that the city had tolerance for diverse lifestyles. The city also witnessed the first awareness campaigns about AIDS. The issue found a place in the media agenda of the press in San Francisco much before it did in any other part of the world. The reasons cited for the issue to climb the San Francisco media agenda are:

(a) The highest rate of HIV infection of any North American city.
(b) A strong commitment to the issue by several local journalists.
(c) The network of homosexual persons and medical professionals who organized for self help, such as by forming non profit organisations (Dearing W. James and Rogers M. Everett, 1996).

The importance of citizens organisations and grassroots advocacy—the attentive and active public that worked together to boost an issue are the ingredients that turned media agenda into public agenda.

The media, when it is involved in the coverage of AIDS issue cannot remain emotionally immune to this epidemic. For the press people who have been covering it since the first Kaposi Sarcoma days, have waited outside AIDS wards, have interviewed people with AIDS, have spent time with the carers, AIDS issue just cannot be sensationalised. There have been irresponsible aspects to the press coverage about the issue but the genuine, factual information certainly is far ahead in terms of both quantity and quality.

The earliest press coverage of the disease was when it first surfaced as a gay disease. The initial shock of hearing about a non curable disease was not as much as the shock people felt on hearing about homosexuality. This appeared in the form of judgmental shock in the press. Over the years the nature of press coverage of the disease has changed dramatically. Initially the press coverage could be called crude and insensitive as it emphasised on the sex lives of a certain group and only reflected the public opinion at that time. As the society matured in its attitude the press too grew. By 1983, the press had taken on a responsible role and stressed the real risks and tried to calm down public hysteria over the disease (Garret, 1994).

As the society grew in its attitude, the media too reflected its maturity. In 1982, the American newspapers referred to the disease as 'gay plague' or 'gay epidemic'. The gay community objected to it and its representatives stepped forward and said, "You are cutting the throat of American people if you let the public believe this is a gay disease only." (Quoted by Garrett Laurie, in reference to a specific case of San Francisco Chronicle, at a conference held in Atlanta on February 19-20, 1987). By 1983, any phraseology of this kind was dropped by the American press. By the time the disease reached India, the press and the public here were much more knowledgeable than their American counterparts had been. That is why press here has always treated AIDS as a serious issue that could not be sensationalised.

The major turning point in public attitudes and media coverage of AIDS came when Rock Hudson died in 1985. The death of a national hero, of a man who had a macho image in America, made AIDS a real issue with the Americans. Suddenly AIDS news was on front pages of all newspapers. The public grew aware of the issue and at the same time the confusion about the issue also increased. There was a great pressure for accuracy amongst the press persons. The stress on right terminology, the medical accuracy, the sensitive handling of the story, made it really difficult to report AIDS. Yet, the reporting continued. By 1986, when AIDS travelled to India, the story was already known. Educated Indians had heard about AIDS when Rock Hudson died. The press here did not have to face the confusion which the American press did. However, the social conditions in India made it difficult to talk about taboo topics such as sex and sexually transmitted diseases in the press. That was a hurdle the Indian press had to cross. By 1990, the Indian press could report about AIDS and not worry about the social stigma.

As of now, the mass media's involvement in the issue cannot be denied and one comes across items related to AIDS on all the media. However, issues are played up or played down by the media occasionally. Topics related to the disease appear in the newspapers or television towards the AIDS day and gradually other issues take precedence over the AIDS news. It has been a subject of study of many researchers that as time goes by, attention to particular social problem will wane, even if the objective conditions related to that problem have not changed. Some argue that public boredom leads to waning attention, the issue simply dies away (Downs Anthony, 1972). Hilggartner and Bosk (1988) state, 'The collective definition of the social problems occurs not in some vague location such as society or public opinion but in particular public arenas in which social problems are framed and grow.' They state that news media act as public arena. The press according to them has the capacity to carry an issue on its shoulders and make them social agenda. The development of AIDS as a social problem was tested as an example of this theory set out by Hilgartner and Bosk, by Hertog, Finnegan and Kahn (1994). However, they did not find very strong displacement reactions. The effect of public arenas model is far less dramatic than what was proposed. Similarly the knowledge gap hypothesis, which states that individuals with higher levels of education are able to process and understand information in the news media better than those with less education, was tested by Wanta Wayne and Elliot William R. (1995) on the subject of AIDS. The hypothesis was not supported. All individuals moved from fairly low knowledge equally to higher knowledge levels, but the knowledge gap narrowed as a proportion of the difference between high and low education groups.

AIDS and the Print Media: An Analysis of AIDS Coverage by the Press in India

This content analysis was conducted to review the role played by the Indian print media in disseminating information about AIDS. Most media studies of this nature have focused on the western media with a few exceptions of studies in the developing countries. Pitts and Jackson (1989) described an initial survey of newspaper coverage of AIDS in Zimbabwe, Ogunyakin and Jinadu (1990) looked at the coverage in Nigeria, and Adeodato Filho and Longo (1990) reported a survey in Brazil (Pitts and Jackson,1993). The AIDS epidemic has caught up with the Asian continent. Even as the infection rates have peaked in other parts of the world, it is still exploding in Asia, where the virus is spread predominantly through sexual intercourse.

In May 1995, 2,507,908 samples were screened in India by the National AIDS Control Organisation, and 18,291 were confirmed by Western Blot, total number of AIDS cases was found to be 1139 (Sreedhar,1995). By the turn of the century, more people are getting infected each year in Asia than in the rest of the world combined

(IHO,1995). From 1981 to 1999, 33.6 million cases of AIDS have been diagnosed. The developed countries have reached a plateau and 95 per cent of new cases are being reported in the developing countries (N.M. Sharma, 2001). According to Dr. I.S. Gilada, of the Indian Health Organisation, by the year 2010 AD, India will have at least 30 million HIV infections, killing 10,000 of them everyday— "At present, AIDS cases are under diagnosed, under reported, and ill treated while fear and ignorance about AIDS compound the difficulty in controlling its spread" (News Report, TOI, 1995).

India is on the threshold of a dual epidemic of AIDS and Tuberculosis with an alarming increase in the TB cases. Within nine years of the first AIDS case being reported in Bombay, in 1986 India had the second highest incidence of HIV +ve cases in South East Asia after Thailand according to Dr. N.K. Shah, India's representative in the WHO (News Report, *Statesman*, 1995).

In such a scenario one would expect the country's media to focus on the issue with regularity and perform its function of agenda setting as well as provide forum for discussions.

Findings

Study of the AIDS news published during the month of November-December, reveals initially a spurt of concern for the subject which gradually changed into a more meaningful understanding. As, is evident from the figures, AIDS news enjoyed maximum coverage in the year 1994 as compared to the years 1993 and 1995 and after a gap of five years, there was not much difference in the amount of reporting although the situation of HIV in the country was turning grim by the day.

The year, 1993 saw a total of 36 news items measuring 5658.75 sq. cms., in the year 1994 the number more than doubled itself (85 news items) and the total space occupied by AIDS related material was 18461.6 sq. cms. (Refer Fig. 5.1). However, in the year 1995, the number fell to 41 and the space covered by the AIDS related material was 14282.55 sq. cms. In the year 2000, the number of AIDS related articles was 50 with 16871.96 sq. cms coverage.

Although there is an overall increase in AIDS reporting the year 1994 forms a peak where the number of news items as well as the space covered by them is concerned. This leads to disapprove the first hypothesis that AIDS related coverage was on the rise. This only shows that there is no steady increase in the AIDS related coverage. The public

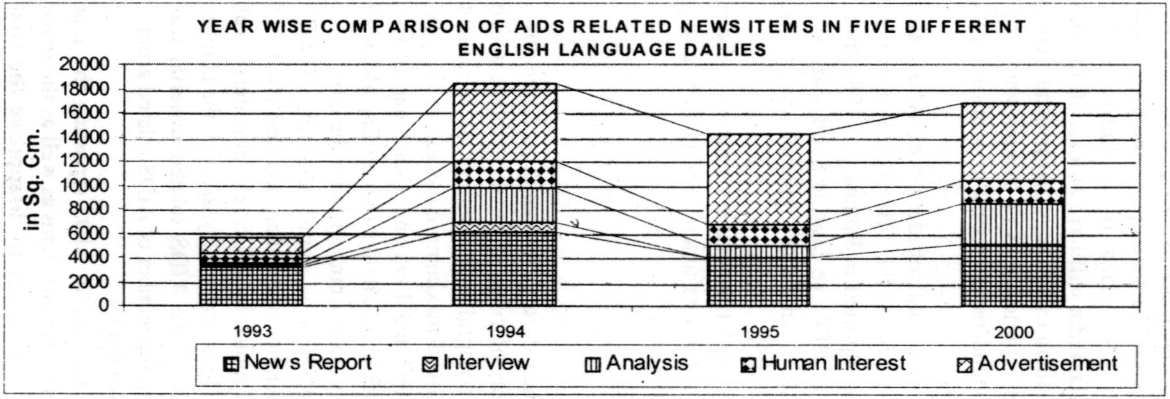

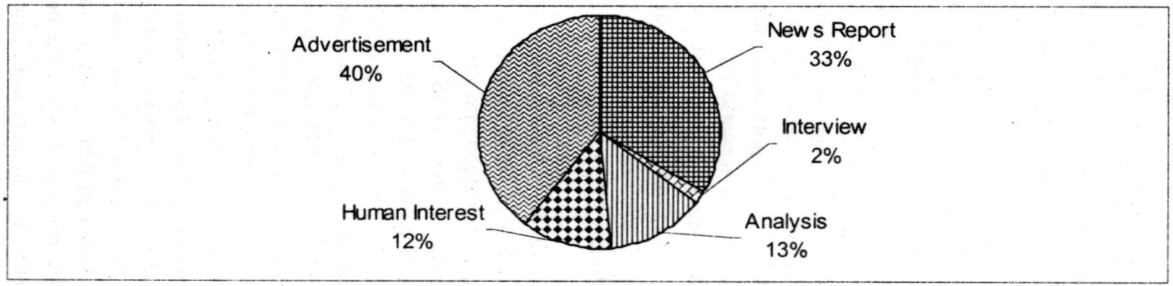

Fig. 5.1 : Content Analysis of Print Media

interest and the issues foremost on the public agenda make headlines. Hence the first hypothesis (a) stands rejected. The news regarding AIDS does not increase year after year although there is an overall increase in the news coverage.

This increase in AIDS reporting can be attributed to growing awareness and serious concern about the subject. The media has acquired a more open stance in discussing sensitive issues such as sex, sexuality, sexually transmitted diseases and AIDS. However, the press is not consistent in its coverage. The year 1994, got special attention as AIDS as an issue was gaining importance in the public mind. The press as it is prone was only a reflection of the public concern. By the end of 1994, the initial interest of the public in the subject waned, as AIDS control efforts were getting concentrated towards the high risk groups and this reflected in the media as well. It was during this time high risk groups were being identified and extensive interventions were being planned for them, leaving the general public complacent about the issue. With passing time AIDS as an issue had to compete with so many other important events for coverage in our dailies. This is evident in our finding about the extent of coverage given to the issue in 2000. Despite the mounting concern for the issue displayed by the articles, the coverage in terms of space occupied still could not beat the then newfound issue in the year 1994.

Maximum amount of coverage has been given to news reports. This category leads others by a wide margin in all the years, both in terms of numbers as well as the space covered by it. While there were 24 news items in 1993, there were 57 in 1994 and only 26 in 1995, and a total of 3168 sq.cms. was occupied in 1993, which increased to 6143.8 sq. cms. in 1994 and fell again to 4077.45 sq. cms. in 1995. Advertisements followed next with 8 advertisements in 1993 and 4 advertisements in 1994 and 1995 each. However, advertisements do cover a lot of space as they are either full page advertisements on World AIDS Day or half page, thereby covering 6489 sq.cms. in the first year and 1278 sq.cms. in the next year and the third year led them both with maximum space covered by advertisements 7516 sq. cms. that is also the maximum space covered by any single category in any year. It is interesting to note that no advertisements or public health message related to AIDS appears at other times of the year (Refer Figs. 5.2, 5.3, 5.4). Advertisements do form the largest single category in both 1994 and 1995. This shows that although public or the press was not paying enough attention to the epidemic the government on appropriated days continued to give full

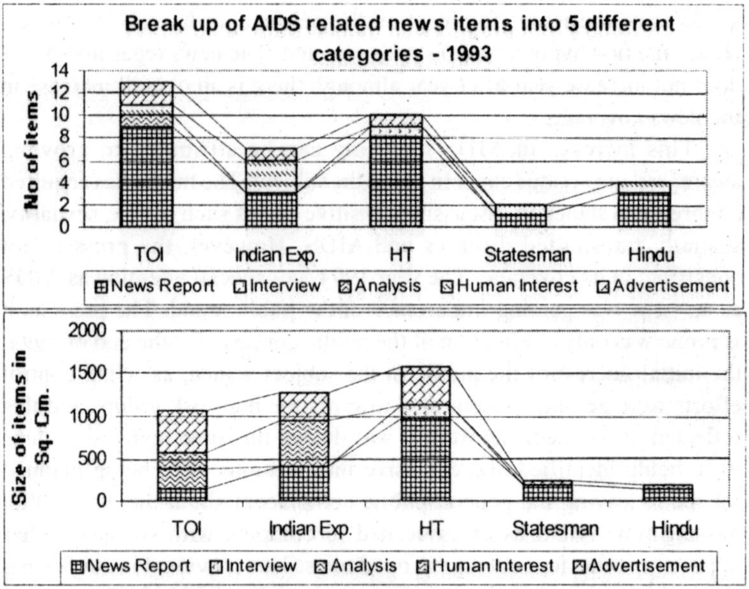

Fig. 5.2: Content Analysis of Print Media (1993)

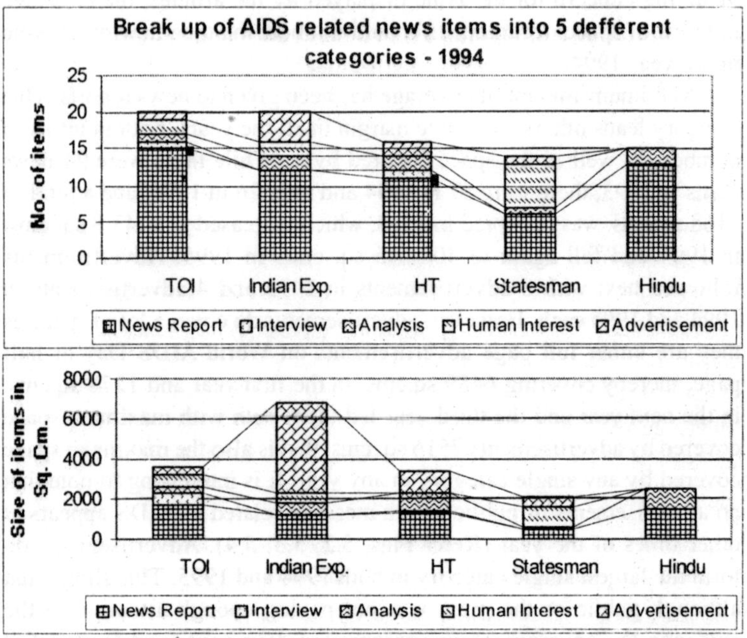

Fig. 5.3: Content Analysis of Print Media (1994)

page messages in major national dailies. Messages by the President, Prime Minister, Health Minister and other dignitaries filled the pages. The same argument continues, now five year hence, advertisements which are usually full page insertions do form the largest single category. However, since the past years there appearance has been only once an year and that is inadequate.

Hence the last hypothesis (e) has been proved. Advertisement cover the maximum space as far as AIDS coverage is concerned.

Categories such as Interviews and Human interest stories appear during some prominent conferences, or rallies. Although AIDS is an all time issue, it receives coverage only for about 15 days in the whole year. Whenever, a conference is organised in the capital, which is generally to mark the AIDS Day, it receives coverage in the national newspapers. A number of health officials and experts who are in the city to attend the conferences are interviewed and no follow up stories are carried out once the event is over.

News analysis of AIDS stories was found to have increased since 1993. Maximum analysis was carried out in 1994 with 8 articles covering 2905.85 sq. cms. which was quite a leap from just one analytical report in 1993 covering only 225 sq. cms. space. The year 1995 however showed an average coverage with 5 articles covering 936.45 sq. cms. However the category of news reports is the dominant category and although interpretations have increased they have not out done the basic factual news reporting (Refer Fig 5.6). Analysis formed the second largest category in the year 2000, with 10 articles covering a total space of 3299.2 sq. cms. (Refer Fig. 5.5).

Articles outlining the enormity of the task and the inaction on the part of the government (December 4th, 2000, *The Times of India*) have stressed on the need to accept the problem and find a solution. AIDS is all set to beat TB as the leading cause of premature death among Indian adults. Faced with these nightmarish facts, the politicians and officials in charge of health instinctively resort to some form of denial. On the other hand there is a huge chasm between the realities of the general public's health behaviour and the nationalistic myth that all Indians are monogamous. The articles appearing mainly in *The Statesman* and *The Indian Express* are to the point and hard hitting. In one article (AIDS project funds lying unused in Orissa, 4th December, 2000, *The Statesman*) the State AIDS control programme has been criticised for not having used Rs. 1.10 crore out of the grant that it had received for the AIDS prevention programmes.

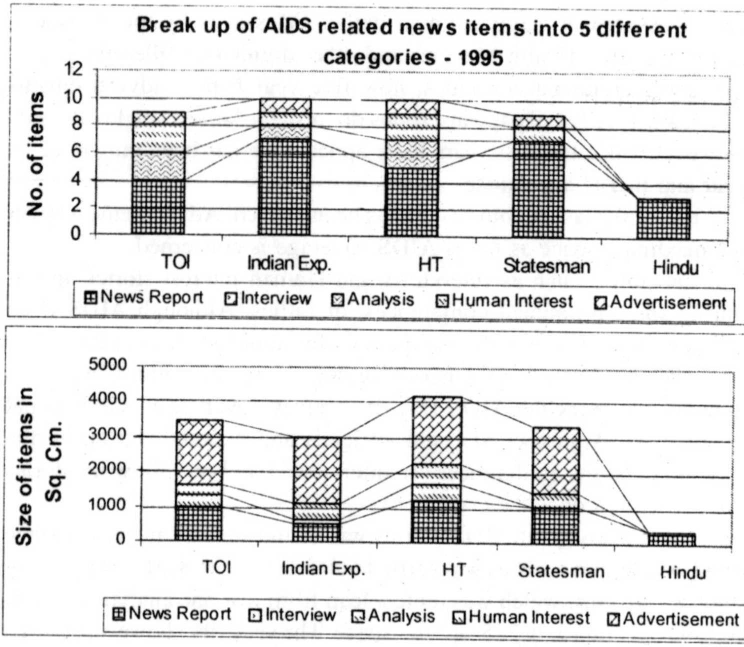

Fig. 5.4: Content Analysis of Print Media (1995)

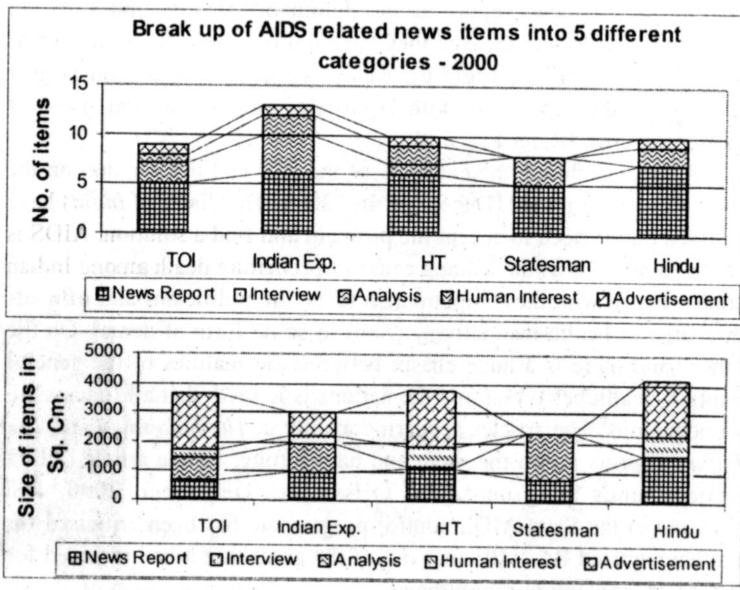

Fig. 5.5: Content Analysis of Print Media (2000)

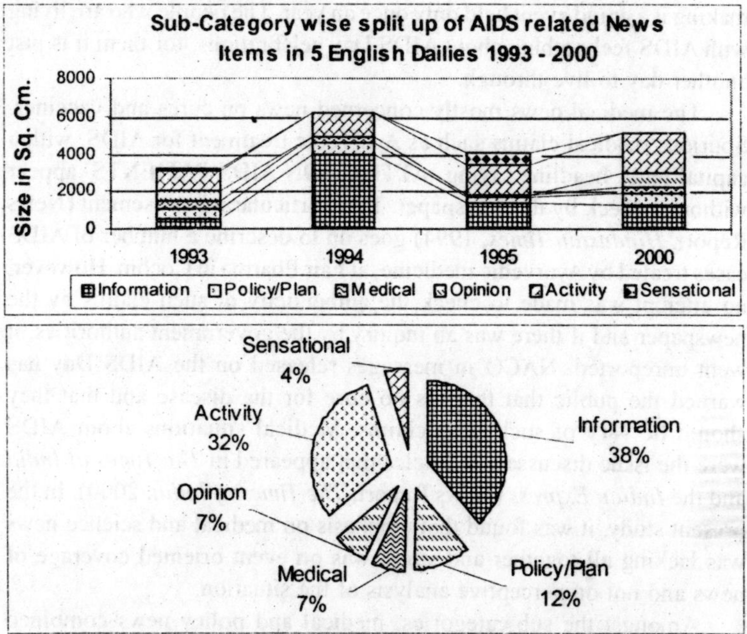

Fig. 5.6: Content Analysis of Print Media (1993-2000)

Hence the hypothesis (c) which says that interpretations and human interest stories have increased has been proved.

Sensational news was given very low priority with only one item appearing in 1993 covering a space of 90 sq. cms., no sensational story was found in 1994, and only 1 in 1995. By the year 2000, one finds the reporting more mature, with sensitive handling of the subject and no sensationalism of this serious issue.

Hence hypotheses (d) which says that sensational stories are few has been proved.

Indian public seems to show no interest as not a single letter was published in any of the newspapers in the three years. This lack of participation could be a result of low awareness levels or perhaps the seriousness of the issue has not sunk in the public psyche. It is possible that the general public is still under the 'denial stage' as they believe that AIDS cannot happen to them. Lack of initiative from the public was evident even after the time gap as no one bothered to give any feedback to the newspapers. However, public has been showing concern by way of participating in rallies and other functions organised on the AIDS Day. The activities related to the event have increased manifold making it a grand event held only once an year. The people who are living with AIDS feel nothing about AIDS Day celebrations, for them it is just another day to live through.

The medical news mostly concerned news on cures and vaccines. Spurious medical claims such as Ayurvedic treatment for AIDS, with a capital letter headline saying 'ATTENTION AIDS PATIENTS' appear without a check by the newspaper. This particular advertisement (News Report, *Hindustan Times*, 1994) goes on to describe a number of AIDS cases treated by Ayurvedic medicine, at Fair Pharma in Cochin. However, no attempt was made to check the authenticity of such claims by the newspaper and if there was an inquiry by the government authorities, it went unreported. NACO in messages released on the AIDS Day has warned the public that there is no cure for the disease and that they should be vary of such false claims. Medical situations about AIDS were the issue discussed in articles that appeared in *The Times of India* and the *Indian Express* (News Report, *The Times of India*, 2000). In the present study, it was found that emphasis on medical and science news was lacking all together and stress was on event oriented coverage of news and not on perceptive analysis of the situation.

Amongst the sub-categories, medical and policy news combined could not beat the information category. In 1993 the information category had total of 4 articles covering 499.5 sq. cms., whereas medical news had 3 articles covering a space of 450 sq. cms. and policy news had 4 articles with 571.5 sq. cms. covered. However, in the next two years the information category covered 3964.05 sq. cms. (39 items) in 1994 and 1402.6 sq. cms. (14) items in 1995. The medical news had only 3 and 2 articles only in 1994 and 1995 with space of 288.045 sq. cms. and 162.9 sq. cms. respectively. The policy news was also 6 and 2 articles only covering 628.2 sq. cms. and 298.8 sq. cms. in the next two years.

Over the years AIDS Day celebrations have become popular with not only the government but also NGOs and Voluntary organisations coming forward to celebrate the day. All this has lead to increase in the reporting about the activities held on the AIDS Day making this the largest covered category after advertisement with 13 articles covering 2135.11 sq. cms. (Refer Fig. 5.10).

Therefore, one can say that save the first year of the study, the next two years saw more information based articles and less of medical or policy news items. In fact the other category which seems to attract maximum attention seems to be the sub-category of 'activity'. More news items related to various activities held in the capital were found when compared to medical or policy news (Refer Fig. 5.7, 5.8, 5.9, 5.10). Earlier the scientific community was suspicious and reticent to trust the most responsible science reporters with their secrets. They felt that the scientific abstracts could not be effectively translated into layman's language and that the journalists have a way of sensationalising every event. The responsible science reporters have worked very hard the world over to bring science news to the common man. Thus, a mutual growth of confidence benefited both the scientists and the journalists. However, news related to science just cannot be written off the cuff and requires considerable research (Hohenberg, John, 1973). Studies have demonstrated that Science and Medical news are often inaccurate (Nelkin, 1987; Singer, 1990). Certain tendencies of journalistic style—especially the emphasis on conflict, controversy and sensationalism—present hurdles to overcome in disseminating medical and science information from experts to the populance (Klaidman, 1990, Winsten, 1985). However, other researchers have found that errors in reporting exist, but they do not act cumulatively, so although each report may exhibit errors of omission or commission, the population of messages conveys a fairly accurate picture of the authoritative medical consensus (Hertog and Fan, 1995). The Indian media, with its market orientation covers the HIV related news in a very casual manner. UNDP Regional and the Centre for Media Advocacy and Research held a National Consultation on HIV/AIDS in New Delhi in the third week of June 2001. This was a forum of editors and journalists to discuss the issues that revolve around the disease. The concerns of the affected too were discussed, as was the need for reviewing the news gathering and reporting process to enable informed, sensitive reporting on the subject. Dr. Nirmala Lakshman, Joint Editor of *The Hindu*, in her inaugural address set the tone of the deliberations by saying, 'our preoccupation with a different kind of journalism deters us from bringing these issues to centrestage' (News Report, *The Hindu*, June 2001). Obviously, the market orientation is being felt within the journalistic community. In the future perhaps the scenario would change but presently, the hypotheses (b) which says that news reports focus more on policy and medical aspects of news has not been proved.

Pediatric AIDS does not receive much coverage as child mortality due to AIDS is not a big issue in India as yet. The epidemic has yet to reach a stage when people can see other people dying of it. As it is, more children die of malnourishment in the country. As far as pediatric health is concerned, more emphasis is on vaccination programmes and

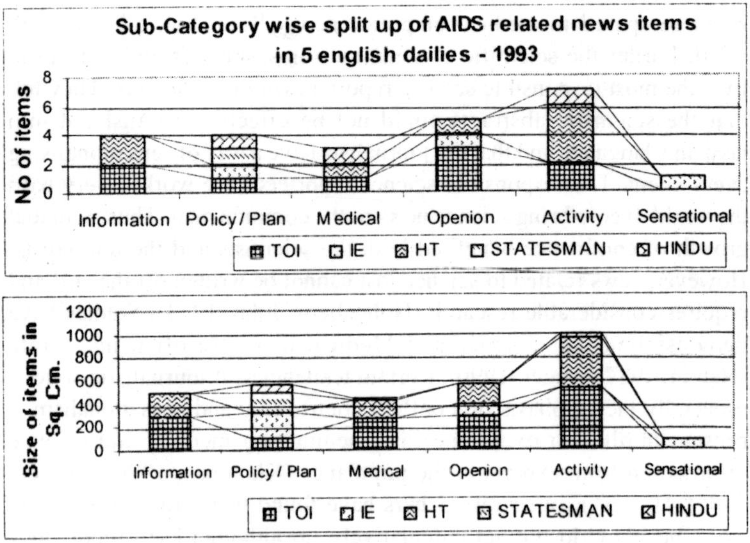

Fig. 5.7: Content Analysis of Print Media (1993)

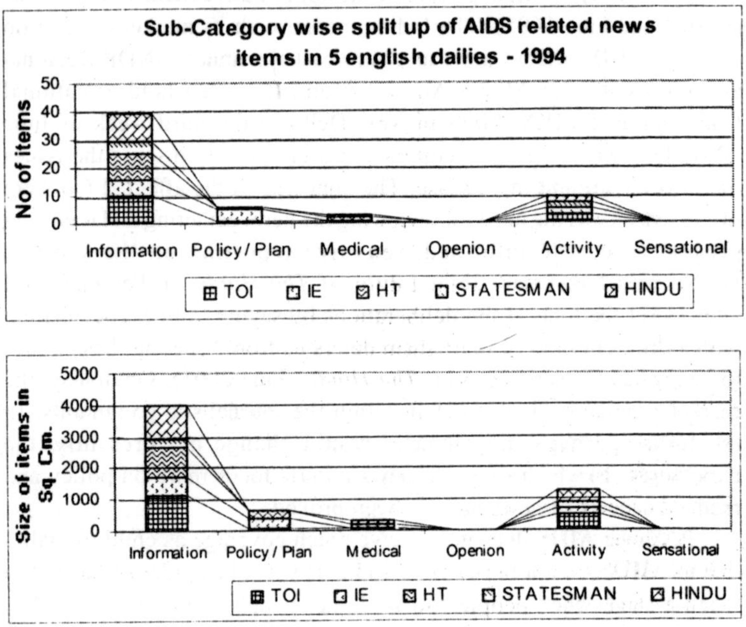

Fig. 5.8: Content Analysis of Print Media (1994)

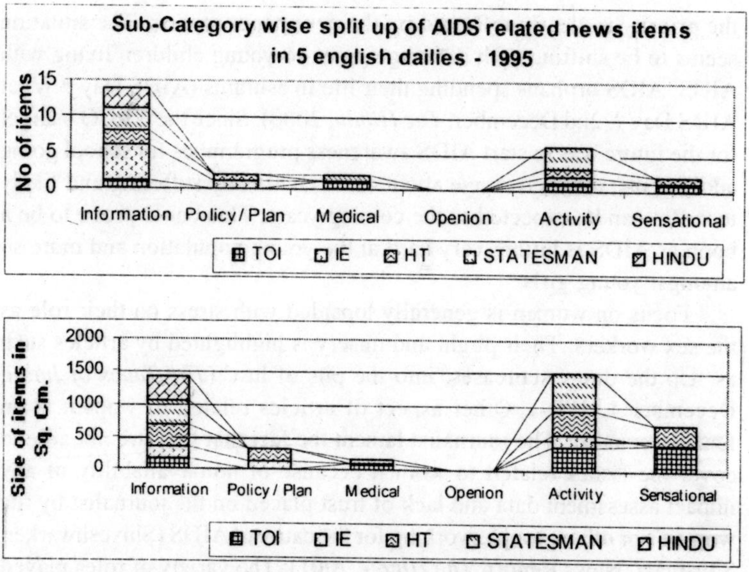

Fig. 5.9: Content Analysis of Print-Media (1995)

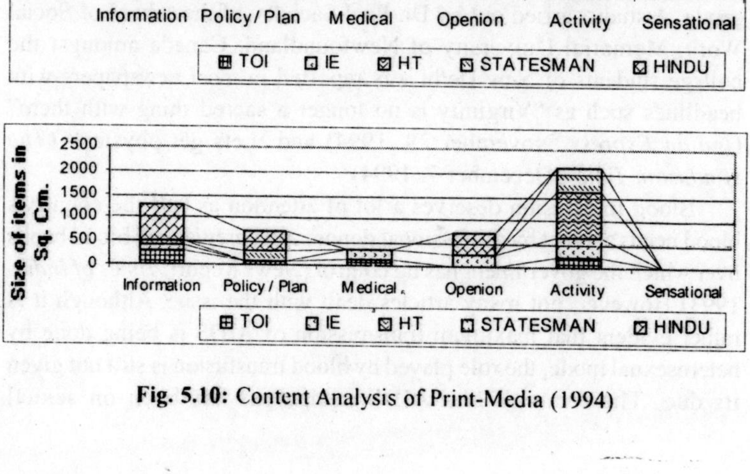

Fig. 5.10: Content Analysis of Print-Media (1994)

the priority is clearly reflected by the newspaper reports. The situation seems to be shifting with coverage given to young children living with AIDS, AIDS orphans spending their life in ashrams (AIDS Day ? What AIDS Day ?. 2nd December, *The Hindu*, 2000). Since the NACO's target for the future was to start AIDS awareness programmes for school going adolescents, more coverage about children already suffering and likely to suffer can be expected in the coming years. This could prove to be a boon as AIDS is hitting very hard at the young population and more so amongst young girls.

Focus on women is generally lopsided with stress on their role as the sex workers. Their plight and misery is highlighted by articles such as 'Up the dingy staircases, into the pits of lust' (*The Times of India*, December 1, 1994). Other aspect of articles related to women is on female sexuality. The journalist lament the fact that they are not able to cover the issues related to women because of non-availability of any impact assessment data and lack of trust placed on the journalist by the women's or other groups, working for the cause of AIDS (Shiveshwarker, Shyamala, News Report, *The Hindu*, 2001). The variety of roles played by women as caretakers, sufferers and victims are not stressed. AIDS is generally treated as an issue for anonymous people with whom the general public is unable to identify. The focus on the commercial sex worker seems to have shifted in favour of the social worker. More and more women are coming forward to observe the AIDS Day and these women being high profile socialites manage to get the flashbulbs and the news print is splashed with their photographs the next day.

News reports on adolescents and youth have found their way into the newspapers as major studies have been carried out with this target group. A study carried out by Dr. Paul Sachdev of the school of Social Work, Memorial University of Newfoundland, Canada amongst the college students of New Delhi was reported in most newspapers with headlines such as "Virginity is no longer a sacred thing with them" (*Indian Express*, November 29, 1994) and 'Lets get physical' (*The Hindustan Times*, December 7, 1994).

Blood transfusion deserves a lot of attention as half the country's blood needs are met by professional donors and unregistered blood banks over which the government has no control (News Report, *Times of India*, 1993) However, not many articles dealt with the issue. Although it is rather evident that maximum transmission of AIDS is being done by heterosexual mode, the role played by blood transfusion is still not given its due. The focus of anti-AIDS campaigns has been on sexual relationships, there is comparatively little social advertising on precautions regarding blood transfusion and other such issues. Reports were published regarding the controversy about NACO guidelines, which assures anonymity to the blood donors. The donors are not informed about their HIV status which is proving to be a very harmful practice. The NACO faced a lot of flak regarding this policy which was born more out of sympathy than out of common sense (News Report, *The Indian Express*, 2000).

Issues of counselling and care are not tackled at all and the general emphasis is only on information. Information on the increasing number of AIDS cases, on death of an AIDS activist abroad, on government policies, grants and on the reports issued by National AIDS Control Organisation on the eve of World AIDS Day form the gist of newspaper reporting on AIDS.

Headlines

A study of the headlines reveals a series of terms like, 'Warning', 'Horror', 'War against AIDS', 'Alarming spread', 'AIDS threat', 'Taboos hinder AIDS education', 'AIDS soars', 'AIDS victims'. The terminology shows a pessimistic attitude and an effort is needed towards the use of more non threatening language.

The term 'AIDS victims' is used to describe people with AIDS and in interviews with them their suffering and the ostracism by the public is highlighted. One news item titled 'Bombay hospital worker tests HIV positive' (*The Indian Express*, November 20, 1994) reports the HIV +ve status of a mortician in a Bombay hospital. The lead of the news reports says 'Cynics who believed that the medical fraternity's fears of a possible transmission of the Human Immunodeficiency virus through health care were unnecessarily alarmist, may now have to concede that those concerns were not entirely misplaced. It has already happened.' The news report described that the mortician has acquired HIV, during a post mortem on the body of a person who was infected with HIV. The colleagues of the mortician have vouched for his 'clean moral history'. The concerned hospital had stopped undertaking any more post mortems of such nature.

This report can have very serious repercussions on the medical assistance being given to people with AIDS. There was no follow up of the report in any of the newspapers and the matter was just dropped. It would have been more appropriate to investigate into the issue and clarify the matter.

This report also unwittingly raises the issue of morality. It reflects that the society still believes that AIDS is a disease of the 'immoral'. This sentiment is emphasised by the press too.

Other headlines such as 'Breastfeeding may guard against HIV' may mislead the public into believing that breast feeding may act as a barrier against the virus, which is not true. In the developing countries breastfeeding is encouraged since bottle milk is a luxury and babies could die more out of malnutrition than because of HIV which has only 30 per cent chances of passing through breast milk. Other than this, most headlines were comparatively non threatening and positive.

Advertisements

All the public health messages which appear during this period mark the World AIDS Day. Other times of the year hardly any advertisements related to AIDS make an appearance. These messages describe the modes of transmission of AIDS, compare AIDS with other sexually transmitted diseases, stress on the use of condoms and also try to make AIDS a topic of everyday conversation with captions like, 'Is your family ready to talk about AIDS ?' If these messages were to appear more frequently, it would help a lot in making AIDS a more talked about issue. An insertion once a year, however, well worded it may be hardly serves the purpose. The theme in the year 2000 being 'Men can make a difference' advertisements appeared emphasising the theme. NACO advertisements spoke in great detail about its vision, plans objectives for the second phase of the programme (1999–2004).

Other advertisements were announcements by Television channels about their forthcoming programmes about AIDS, as they also mark the AIDS week with a series of films on the subject.

Newspaper-wise Coverage

The maximum number of articles appeared in *The Times of India* followed by *The Hindu* and *The Hindustan Times*. The articles were mostly news reports and news analysis in the form of editorials. *The Hindu* published more analysis and discussions. *The Times of India* published the only article related to the economic aspect of AIDS. Maximum number of public health messages appeared in the *Indian Express*, some of them covered the entire page of the newspaper. Maximum number of human interest stories appeared in the *Statesman*.

(Refer Figs. 5.6, 5.7 and 5.8) During the period Novenber-December, 2000 the maximum number of articles appeared in *The Hindu*. This newspaper has given serious thought to the issue and a number of thought provoking articles on various aspects of the disease have appeared. News value of this issue was recognised by *The Statesman* as it had maximum number of photographs along with its stories (Refer Fig. 5.12).

In the final analysis, the *Times of India*, was found to be the only newspaper which covered a range of subjects on AIDS. It has shown a consistent concern for the issue as it has maintained an interest in the subject during all the three years.

In the year 2000, *The Hindu* has exhibited concern for the issue. *The Times of India* continues as before. However, it was found that although the quantity of the articles may not have increased in these years, the quality has certainly improved. The newspapers depict better understanding of the problem, they are now in a position to criticise the government laxity when they see it. They are able to act as watch dogs which they could not do five years back as they were still coming to grips with the subject and merely following government policies.

The coverage given to AIDS related news stories shows that the grimness of the situation is not apparent in our print medium. In the last five years, the number of people infected with HIV has increased manifold but the coverage given to AIDS related news matter has not increased proportionately.

The year 2000, saw a total of 36 news items related to AIDS (This does not include the messages inserted by the various government agencies which have been included in the category 'advertisement'). The total space covered by AIDS related news was 10477.45 sq. cms. (Refer Fig. 5.9) which was more than all the previous years. Maximum space was covered by advertisements as all the previous years and news reports lead the other articles because most of the news reporting regarding the issue is event reporting (Refer Fig. 5.5).

Analysis of Audio Visual Media

Newspapers have been covering the issue of AIDS since the time, AIDS was first detected in India. However, in a country like India, where a large section of the population lives below poverty line and the literacy levels are rather low, newspaper is certainly not the medium for the teaming masses. Besides, the press coverage is not the only mass communication method by which the issue of AIDS can be tackled.

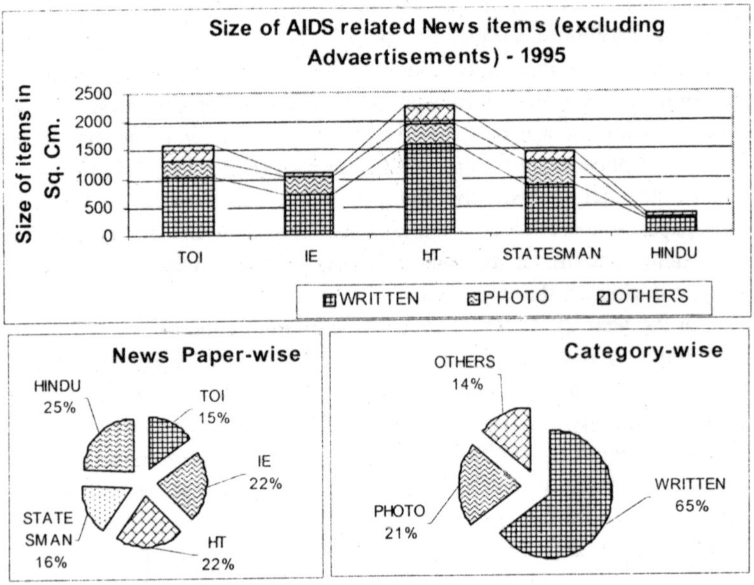

Fig. 5.11: Content Analysis of Print Media (1995)

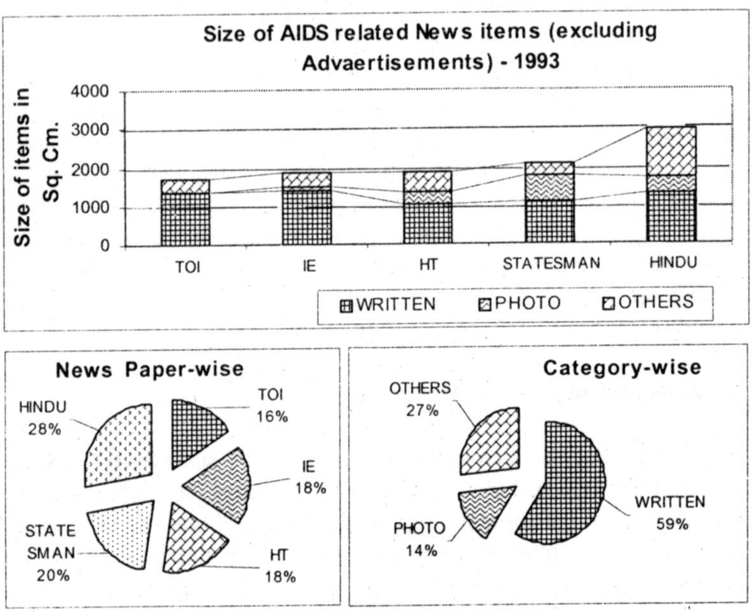

Fig. 5.12: Content Analysis of Print Media (1993)

Communicating about AIDS/HIV/STD is extremely difficult as it requires detailed discussions on sex and sexual practices, a topic many people would rather avoid. To achieve this, consistent and clear messages from all channels—mass media, traditional and interpersonal media, need to work together.

The media impact on public beliefs is one of the most enduring concerns of mass communication research. In a study of impact of news magazine coverage of AIDS from 1987 through 1991 on public beliefs concerning the likelihood of HIV transmission via toilets, sneezing and insects, a significant relationship was found—news content formed public opinion (Hertog, K., James, Fan, P., David, 1995). Noelle Neumann (1973) had argued that media effects are gradual and cumulative. Neumann wrote: "Communication flow conjures up the notion of a steady stream of information, ideas and images that over a long period of time, influence public thinking as the flow of a river etches clearly discernible patterns in the rock of the river bed."

AIDS represents a unique test case for the impact of media coverage on public beliefs because before 1981 the disease was unknown and whatever the public knows about the disease is from the reports that they have read or the messages that they have seen on television. The public opinion that has been created over two decades of AIDS has been the result of the media messages that they have imbibed. It is easy in this case for media to have an impact because the whole concept is absolutely new. Media does not have to negate certain old beliefs or fight any religious notions about the subject. Since the phenomenon is a new one, it helps the media to create opinion when there is none. However, there is a flip side to the issue. Since the AIDS awareness strategies are all new and designed only as the epidemic hit, there is no precedent to fall back on. The media has no previous researches to help it design its messages. The researches are being conducted side by side while messages are being designed. This may lead to mistakes or even blunders.

Earlier Campaigns

Although mass media in isolation have little effect on health related behaviour change, but it has been seen that people do learn from mass media. Not only do they learn factual information but also learn how much importance is to be attached to an issue or topic by the emphasis placed on it by the mass media.

In 1921 when a campaign was designed to control the spread of STD, a massive research was conducted by psychologists Lashley and Watson. After interviews and questionnaires covering 4800 people they concluded that hard facts presented in a serious, straightforward scientific manner was the best method to give information regarding STDs. Facing a similar problem with AIDS in 1986, the earliest campaigns reflect the general feeling about the epidemic. Just as the mass media called it a gay disease, the electronic media campaigns stressed on the 'Fear Appeal'. The Grim Reaper campaign of Australia created such a scare amongst the public that people actually thronged the hospitals for tests. Later it was suggested that such campaigns create fear in the minds of the general public instead of warning the high risk groups (The concept of high risk group was prevalent at that time). The next lot of campaigns and films showed the protagonist as a sex worker or a homosexual and even truck drivers (Piotrow, P., Mcyer, R.C., Zulu, B.A., 1992). Although the issues tackled were informative, the identification of high risk persons led to the denial syndrome amongst the general public. Ultimately learning from past mistakes it was realised that: (1) Fear campaigns are not effective and cannot be sustained, (2) Stigmatizing one group leads to the denial or blame attitude in the general public, (3) Moral messages turn away the very people you want to reach, (4) The messages should be consistent and accurate, positive, objective and action oriented.

As the press coverage shifted from confinement of the epidemic within the so called high risk groups to an image of susceptibility, public opinion followed. The electronic media too addressed the issues to the general public. Even when AIDS is a theme in television material, it is often not addressed in the most responsible way, because television is a business and customers must not be offended. For example, it was found in a study conducted by Palmer P. and associates, that of the AIDS cases portrayed on television, 37 per cent were caused by blood transfusion, while the actual figure does not exceed 3 per cent (Palmer, P. *et al.*, 1988). Planned entertainment material has achieved impressive results. In the Philippines, a popular music video, intended to encourage young people to postpone sex and avoid unwanted pregnancy, resulted in enhancing young people's communication with their parents. It also motivated over 150,000 Fillipino youth to call a sexual responsibility hotline, as promoted in the television video featuring musical stars, and 25 per cent of young people sought contraception information as a result of the song (Turner, R., 1992). As many as 240,000 women in Turkey are estimated to have adopted modern family planning methods as a result of television dramas and humorous spots (Church, C.A., Coller, J., 1989). In Mexico, which has been a pioneer in the deliberate use of soap operas for educational purposes, soap operas were the primary cause of a 63 per cent increase in the adult literacy centres in one year, and a rise of 560,000 in those adopting family planning methods (Brown, W.J., Singhal, A., Rogers, E.M., 1989). A Ugandan film *Its not easy*, was so effective that those who had seen it were more than twice as likely to have used condoms in the two months prior to the interview, as were those who had not seen the film (Piotrow, P., Meyer, R.C., Zulu, B.A., 1992). Most electronic media messages are based on the approach that entertainment not only mirrors social reality but also helps to shape it by depicting what constitutes popular opinion, by influencing people's perception of the roles and behaviours that are appropriate to the members of a culture, and by modelling specific behaviour. The strength of this approach is that short messages, embedded with dialogue, are casually presented by characters who serve as role models within a dramatic context, thereby facilitating social learning (Sherr, L., 1988).

Media and entertainment can be compared to nuclear power: they are neither good or bad in themselves; it all depends on how they are used and for what purpose. The following section reviews the efforts made by the electronic media in the country to increase AIDS awareness and make it a regular topic of conversation.

Television

The earliest television messages appeared in the early 90s, when a socially conscious actress Shabana Azmi was chosen to deliver the message. These public service messages were designed by the National AIDS Control Organisation. The message showed Shabana Azmi walking into an AIDS ward and hugging a little child with AIDS. The spot clearly explained the modes of spread of the disease and also the ways in which it does not spread. The underlying theme of the spot clears many issues: (1) The initial inhibitions of the press reporters are shown to be shed towards the end of the spot signifying a positive step towards attitude change. (2) It tackles the issue of pediatric AIDS. (3) By showing a child with AIDS it also clears the misconception about high risk groups. However, since the spot shows a change in behaviour of press persons, it stops short of addressing the general public. The press has the image of being more socially aware and also risk taking group. The common man cannot identify easily with press persons. On the other hand, using a film star with a reputation of being a social worker adds to the salability of the spot.

On the similar lines of celebrity recommendations there are spots with Shah Rukh Khan, Aparna Sen, Kabir Bedi, Sarika, Jaspal Bhatti and many more. The Aparna Sen spot is produced by *Chitrabani*, Kolkata but is used by National AIDS Control Organisation for telecast all over India. Here again Aparna Sen sends across the message of indiscrimination against the HIV infected groups. The Kabir Bedi spot is a bit controversial because he uses the terms such as '*Chakkar*', obviously referring to multi partner sex. Use of such colloquial language gives the spot a frivolous image. He also says, 'Death is the only cure'. Although technically correct, the undertone of threat that is present in the message make it sound like a warning sign. The fatal nature of AIDS can be put across with terms such as, 'incurable' or 'fatal' which certainly sound less sordid than 'Death'. The punch line of the spot is once again, 'Condom or Death'. The threat, fear, blame messages make the low risk population such as middle aged and old people unnecessarily worried. If fear messages had worked then no packet of cigarettes would ever have been sold.

Another message which effectively stresses the use of condoms is one in which male and female hands keep passing the packet of condoms to each other while the woman is trying to convince the man to use a condom in the voice-over. It is a one minute spot and the voice-over explains the modes of spread, fatal nature of AIDS and the significance of the use of condoms. In another spot Manohar Singh, noted theatre personality, acting as a shopkeeper explains to teen aged boys to overcome their shyness in case they want to buy condoms. Two minutes of shyness can lead to a lifetime of regret.

The role of parents, teachers, seniors, uncles and aunts etc. in giving information about sex and AIDS to their children or wards is depicted in another one minute spot. An uncle passes on a packet of condoms to a fun loving nephew, while explaining to him the seriousness of AIDS. The spot attacks the inhibitions that are present in our society. The parents are generally wary of giving information about sex, sexuality or STDs to their children so a friendly uncle has been chosen to do the needful. The attitude of elders in not recognising the sexuality of their children can result in disastrous consequences. In another spot two friends are shown discussing their sex life in the context of AIDS.

Issues on AIDS are being discussed on popular TV shows such as Donahue, Oprah Winfrey show and also various Indian talk shows such as Shakti. Star TV celebrates AIDS week every year with 'Think Again series' of films on people with AIDS. Many documentaries are being made and telecast on different channels.

Recent Messages

Lately, film star Madhuri Dixit has appeared on endorsements messages about the inherent strength of women in not only protecting themselves from unsafe sexual practices but also taking on the responsibility of educating their teenage children about safe sex. The messages urge the women to be unabashed while talking about AIDS as they have been depicted as the stronger sex. Although the messages help boost the morale of women, they certainly undermine the role that can be played by men as sexual partners, husbands and fathers. Men are depicted as careless and frivolous in their attitude. The fact is that men do take on the dominant role whether in sexual matters or in domestic matters. They act as decision makers in most of the homes. While it is creditable to help women to emerge as decision makers men should also be shown as responsible lovers and sensible fathers.

The latest spots sponsored by Cipla for social causes, shows endorsements by people with AIDS. For the first time in Indian television the persons with AIDS are shown as healthy human beings who lead normal lives and also urge others with the same predicament to lead regular lives. The TV spot seems to have come of age. From that little ill looking girl who was hugged by Shabana the portrayal of the people with AIDS has improved dramatically. He is no longer a person shunned by the society. He looks normal, is optimistic about his future, understands the implications of being infected with HIV and is ready to fight the disease and not let the disease overcome him. The effects of this spot have yet to be seen but credit goes to Cipla for taking the lead.

As is evident from the above review that more research is needed before Television starts to telecast AIDS related messages in a big way. Most of these messages appear only in November and December. AIDS is not a seasonal disease. The emphasis on public service advertising should be made all the year round.

Radio

The last two decades have witnessed a phenomenal growth in the field of media technologies. From, television to computers to the internet, many new and faster means of communication have emerged. Despite the veritable flood of new media on the scene, radio has maintained its identity, and a steady upward climb. It can boast of 100 per cent reach in India, with the FM channel reaching the young population of major metros. It caters to the youth and its programming is based on their likes and dislikes.

The National AIDS Control Organisation has produced a number of audio spots designed by the DAVP for broadcast during popular film song programmes like Jaimala and Chhayageet. NACO has one-hour programme during the lunch hour from 1-2 p.m. To disseminate the information of AIDS on FM channel. The NACO Filmi Parade, is designed to provide information on preventive aspects of AIDS. This was done by tying up with FM Times network, of *The Times of India* group (Bamezai, G, Shukla, A., 1998). This programme is padded with the facility of individual information through NACO hotline. Prior to this NACO had also broadcast a programme Balance Baraber, which ran for almost an year in 1994-95. The presenter, as a friend, acted as adviser and counsellor to people who called in with queries. Average number of calls per week were 100-150 and boys and girls participated equally in the programme. The programme was sponsored by Population Service International. Another programme, on similar lines, called *Kam Ki Baat*, was launched with the help of another NGO, Marie Stopes. It ran from July, 1995 to May, 1996. The format was similar to Balance Baraber, and average age of the callers was 20. Both the programmes made liberal use of film songs to attract young audiences.

Besides the NACO, State AIDS Cells operate at state level, with their own managerial bodies under the state administration. Among the various State AIDS Cells, the Government of Maharashtra has been the most active in the production of audio and video materials for AIDS prevention and control.

The radio spots are mostly of one minute duration and provide all the information about the spread, the precaution and also the seriousness of the disease. Many of them have voice-overs in the voices similar to popular film stars in order to attract the general public. Celebrity endorsements may work in cases where elders such as parents, teachers do not discuss the issue openly, and young people like to follow in the footsteps of their favourite film star. The background music of these spots resembles film songs and the endorsements are in dialogue form. Chitrabani in Calcutta has also produced some spots in various formats such as quiz shows, studio format etc.

Most of the radio jingles use the word 'Suraksha' every time they have to refer to the condom. This may lead to misconceptions in the mind of the public. It also reflects that the DAVP or the government in itself was wary of using direct straightforward language while talking about AIDS. Such messages contradicted the Talking about AIDS programme launched by the government. Later messages have used the word condoms and have stressed that 'lubricated condoms' are the road to safety for everyone. In another jingle, streetplay format is used where a *Madari* and a *Jamura* discuss AIDS and stress on shedding inhibitions while buying condoms. The jingle makes it clear that if you are shy of buying a condom you will die of AIDS. While trying to be too straight-forward, such jingles may end up making the people confused about the issue. Most of the radio jingles target the youth. In one such jingle two young men are arguing about whose turn it was to buy a condom. They seem to be passing the responsibility to one another. This reflects the desire for sexual experience but a hesitancy in buying a condom. Most of these jingles have been designed by Lintas, Bombay under the guidance of Dr. Subhash B. Salunke.

DAVP too has produced a few jingles for radio. These have similar formats as the above and are of 30 seconds duration each. These messages stress on the spread of AIDS through heterosexual relations. They use punch lines such as '*AIDS se bachne ka adhar, pati patni ka sachcha pyar*'. The false morality exhibited by the common Indian has been tackled in these jingles. One of the jingles also discusses the homosexual partners. The voice-over of two men discussing safe sex methods is used and the lines of popular film song '*gore gore o banke chhore, kabhi meri gali aaya karo*' play in the background. Some of the jingles do turn didactic. Value laden messages which advise abstinence from sex are also used as the punch line of most of these jingles is '*Sanyam ya Suraksha*'.

However, despite the shortcomings, these jingles are the earliest attempt being made to reach the large population of people that relies on radio as a medium of information either because of illiteracy or because of its easy availability. Besides radio is a medium which can be turned on in public places such as the tea and *paan* stalls and may acquire many casual listeners. Public discussion may follow the broadcast of such jingles.

Hotlines have been started by the efforts of UGC-UNIFPA's Adult and Continuing Education and Extension Department. The response to this hot line has been tremendous. Initially started for the students, it now gets calls from housewives, businessmen, young married couples and people on the verge of getting married. The calls reflect an ignorance about the subject merged with fear. The calls made by a diverse section of the society also reflect the readiness in the society to discuss such matters, but a desire for anonymity while doing so (Savvy, 1995).

In order to reach different sections of the population messages are also inserted in audio cassettes. The Department of Youth and Sports (Ministry of HRD) has even released a special cassette of Punjabi songs related to AIDS for truck drivers. There are messages on bus stops, backs of city buses, bill boards, cinema hall slides, in front of major hospitals. National AIDS Control Organisation, premier body for AIDS control and research, has designed most of the messages in this medium. The emphasis of its campaign is on large scale awareness for behaviour change, as well as targeted intervention for high risk group such as sex workers, truck drivers, drug users and infected blood donors. The State AIDS cells of NACO too keep organisng seminars and entertainment programmes aimed at different sections of society, whereby they spread the message of AIDS awareness. For, instance, the Tamil Nadu State AIDS cell organised a cultural show with popular singers 'Colonial Cousins' singing the message of AIDS.

BBC has also realised the potential of radio in influencing behaviour and using it to combat AIDS in the Asian subcontinent. BBC undertook a campaign in 1995-96, for spreading information about AIDS to Pakistan, India, Bangladesh, Iran, Nepal, Sri Lanka and Maldives. In association with the BBC Radio, International Planned Parenthood (South Asia Region), and the Family Planning Association of India launched a joint project in broadcasting a series of sexual and reproductive health education broadcasts with a particular focus on young women and men (Bamezai, G., Shukla, A., 1998).

The Asia Pacific Network, an organization that brings together People with AIDS, has set up an electronic mail service called APN-Plus Share. APN is a network of people living with AIDS. APN Share strives to provide support to AIDS patients and their families and friends by helping them to communicate with others infected with HIV. APN has members in 13 countries in the region. With AIDS crossing all national frontiers, the people living with AIDS can share experiences with people from different countries and this will give them a feeling of solidarity and also a feeling that they are not alone in their struggle.

Discussion

Indian society is multi-ethnic, muti-cultural and multi-linguistic. Folk culture is the most acceptable medium through which a social or educational message could be driven home. In rural India people learn their behaviour pattern from the folk media. In the folk medium which is based on entertainment, the influences of social message on behaviour is for a short while, but where the message is integrated into the medium with creativity and care, it can bring about radical and lasting changes in the basic attitude of the audience.

This study provides an analysis of AIDS related news material which appears in the 5 prominent newspapers of the country. Further it provides an analysis of audio visual messages that have been presented to the audiences since the last decade. The analysis is both qualitative as well as quantitative. It was found that the society as well as the media has yet to accept that AIDS is an issue of each person's concern. Moralistic stands, denial, prejudice, lack of research and follow up has been seen in the news reports. Some of the reports do reel out baffling statistics of people who have been infected by HIV, but on the whole AIDS is still a disease which happens to other people.

In a country like India, press can play a crucial role in spreading awareness about AIDS, but we find that the newspapers publish advertisements by healers who claim to have found a cure for AIDS. As a nation, which still believes a lot in alternative forms of medicine, such advertisements can misguide the public. There should be system to check these spurious claims.

The year 2000, had always been cited as a landmark year by the experts on AIDS. All predictions were targeted at year 2000. Whenever the seriousness of the AIDS scenario had to be depicted, the year 2000 situation would form the basis of the message. By the time one arrived at the year 2000, AIDS was not an issue on the top priority list. The figures which are repeated year after year on World AIDS Day were repeated once again and they certainly painted a grim picture.. Yet, in the year 2000, while there was the regular run of the mill news reports of gala get togethers on AIDS Day by glamorous socialites there was more sensitivity in the writing style when human interest and analytical articles were concerned.

All the predictions for the year 2000 came true. India had 3.7 million HIV positive people, the highest in the world. 80 per cent of these cases were from 18–40 years age group (*The Statesman*, December 4, 2000). While countries like Holland, Thailand, Uganda and Australia managed to control the epidemic, India with its special brand of moral hypocrisy did not invest sufficiently into the prevention programmes. However, despite the growing seriousness of the situation, it does not get reflected in the columns of our newspapers, who awaken to the issue of AIDS only when the AIDS Day approaches.

The news items about AIDS begin to appear towards 27th of November and taper off by the 3rd of December. As compared to previous years, the high coverage period of AIDS related news items has reduced by 4 to 5 days. The World AIDS Day seems to have turned into a kind of circus when the government and private machinery goes on top gear organising rallies, get togethers, parties where the top film stars and sundry other stars are invited to pin red ribbons on each other, sing a few songs, mouth AIDS awareness slogans, get photographed, and disappear till the next AIDS Day comes around. Besides, various other days that are celebrated in the same week and the next one jostle for space in the newspapers. On 30th November, just one day prior to the AIDS Day, *The Hindu* carried a 4 column advertisement for World Disabled Day which falls on 2nd December. The Pulse Polio drive which was on full swing during this period acquires full page insertions on 9th, 10th and 11th of December. The Human Rights Day is given insertions on 10th and 11th of December. The AIDS Day seems to be no longer a novelty.

In the year 2000, the AIDS related news had to vie for space with so many other market friendly news stories. The months of November and December had stories about cricket scams, release of film star Rajkumar by Veerappan, and to top it all the Miss World. On 30th of November *The Times of India* carried various insertions given by commercial organisations to wish good luck to Priyanka Chopra for the Miss World contest. With the changing concept of news, the crowning of Priyanka Chopra as the new Miss World on 1st of December, made AIDS news take a back seat. The newspapers rejoiced with Priyanka and the rest of the nation, while keeping their advertisers happy, covering every aspect of the event, with stories of all types and styles. News reports, close up photographs, human interest stories, interviews with people who helped her and so on. Sadly for those who are concerned with AIDS as an issue, this mega event happened on the 1st of December, i.e. the World AIDS Day. Most of the newspapers carried AIDS related news stories on the 2nd of December. Obviously these were just regular reports of the various activities that were held to mark the World AIDS Day.

The reportage given to the issue of AIDS would be more effective if the media can participate in the awareness programme not as an outsider but as a partner. Some of the means by which the mass media can gain the trust of the public and the organisations working in the field are: (a) providing more detailed and comprehensive coverage to the issue, (b) making AIDS an everyday issue by encouraging the readers to participate in the discussion through the letters column, (c) Using more acceptable terminology, so as not to generate fear, (d) Providing appropriate follow up of sensational news reports, which might inadvertently affect the issue adversely.

If the media takes up the issue more constructively, then the government will also be more serious about the matter. The government grants could be used more effectively if the press kept a watch on the ongoing programmes. While topics of concern for the government and the press are many in this country, a better media coverage could put AIDS too on the agenda and help the people to understand AIDS and deal with it more effectively.

Since the NACO has decided to take up traditional media such as folk arts and street theatre it is for all to wait and see how far does the effort reach the people. Even in the presence of other media, newspapers, cannot underestimate their reach and potential as far as the reading public is concerned. A concentrated effort is needed to take the message far and wide. AIDS is not an issue of just a certain set of people. It should be made an issue of all people where everyone should participate in overcoming it. Newspapers have an enormous task of making this issue an important public agenda in the coming years.

A multi media approach is relevant in this context to cover a wider category of audience with a diverse orientation and mind sets. A large section of the people are starved for education by the normal processes, information and knowledge on social and health issues could be disseminated through folk media (Multi media workshop on AIDS, Educational material).

The impact of media coverage of any subject depends on the interaction of several factors, including the previous knowledge of the readers or the audiences, the content of the message, the credibility or otherwise of the journalist, the reaction of the people with whom the reader or viewer goes on to discuss what they believe they have read, seen or heard. The aims of the mass media should be to set the agenda for the development of public policy and influence the actions of those who have the power in our society. In approaching the role of mass media in relation to AIDS, the media need an idea, of where the public interest lies, of how the public policy should evolve. Such an idea must clearly be founded on the best available medical knowledge and on social research. Unfortunately this knowledge accumulates over time and interventions have to be planned side by side.

Finally, there is the issue of what is left unsaid in the media and why it matters ? Worldwide HIV is predominantly a heterosexually transmitted infection. There is no reason to believe that in the long term it will be confined to the groups currently identified with it. One of the biggest problems of the observation with the particular mode of transmission is that it distracts the public from the central issue, which is change in social attitude towards AIDS through awareness and widespread diffusion of the correct information and knowledge. The limitation of the news media as a mode of education and communication is very sharply exposed; what is new is news, but the background to it does not have anything like the same news values. If mass media was an excellent source of public education, no one in India would smoke cigarettes. Nobody would take drugs, nobody would eat cholesterol rich food, no child would be inflicted by polio, all men and women would understand the necessity of birth control, no one in the country would have more than two children. If all it took was to hear that something was dangerous and behaviour would change. It is not so. Press is good at raising fear or concern, but it takes more than just fear or concern to move people to make rational, pragmatic action. AIDS awareness must involve every element of society that influences what people believe in, media can only fill in the details of public information. The first step then is to begin by filling those details of public knowledge about AIDS.

Survey: Findings

The main aim behind this survey was to find out the mass media access and reach status and the AIDS awareness level of adolescents from two different settings.

The analysis of data has been structured according to these variables. The findings are divided into 5 different sections for clear and thorough discussion. The sections are:

1. Demographic Profile
2. Mass Media Profile
3. AIDS Awareness profile
4. Knowledge about AIDS
5. Sex Education

In order to have a complete overview of the data each section was first studied independently and later co-relations were found between the different sets of variables.

Demographic Profile

The respondents came from four different schools and from two different cities. Both girls and boys were administered the questionnaires. The total population of students was 443.04 questionnaires were disqualified at the time of analysis. A total of 439 questionnaires were analysed. Boys were more in number as compared to the girls but since all the schools visited offered co-education, the difference is not intentional (Boys 243, Girls 196). It is interesting to note that although boys outnumber the girls in the overall population but in the public school population the girls are more in number. The girls lose out on strength in the government schools (Refer Fig. 5.14).

Classes VIII, IX, X and XI and chosen for the study because the age group of the students in these classes was the appropriate target group suitable for this study. The ages of the students ranged from 13 to 17 years. However the biggest group was the 13 and 14 years old. This is an apt age for starting sex education in schools (Refer Fig. 5.15). This division is also not intentional.

Most of the students were Hindi speaking, which was rather obvious. Most of them had educated parents. The most common qualification for fathers was found to be a professional degree (33.3%) and the mothers in most cases were graduates (33.4%). The majority of students were from nuclear families (79.2%) with average income of the majority being Rs. 5001 to Rs.10,000 (37.4%) (Refer Figs. 5.16, 5.17, 5.18). More number of fathers were in government service as compared to any other category (65.4%). The reason could be that two schools out of four were government schools. Most of the mothers were housewives (81.3%) and some of them were school teachers (Refer Figs. 5.19, 5.20).

Although an effort was made to keep the population of the Delhi metropolis and the satellite town of Ghaziabad, as same but it was practically not possible. The researcher chose a class of students for administering the questionnaire by the process of random sampling. One section in each class was chosen. The metropolis had **213** students and the satellite town had **226**. Correlations of media profile and locations have been detailed under the section 'Correlational findings'.

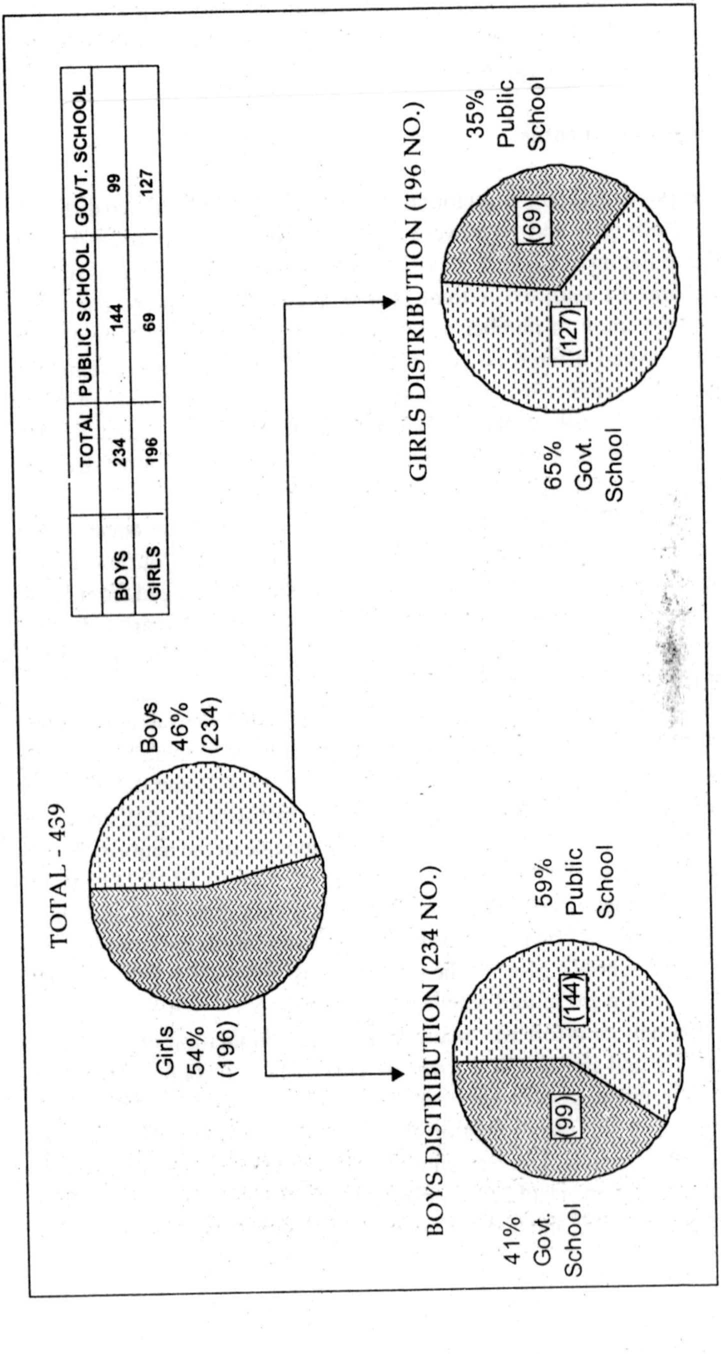

	TOTAL	PUBLIC SCHOOL	GOVT. SCHOOL
BOYS	234	144	99
GIRLS	196	69	127

Fig. 5.14: Profile as per Sex and School

AGE DISTRIBUTION	13Yr	14Yr	15Yr	16Yr	17Yr
BOYS	50	88	36	54	12
GIRLS	77	48	26	38	7
TOTAL	127	139	62	92	19

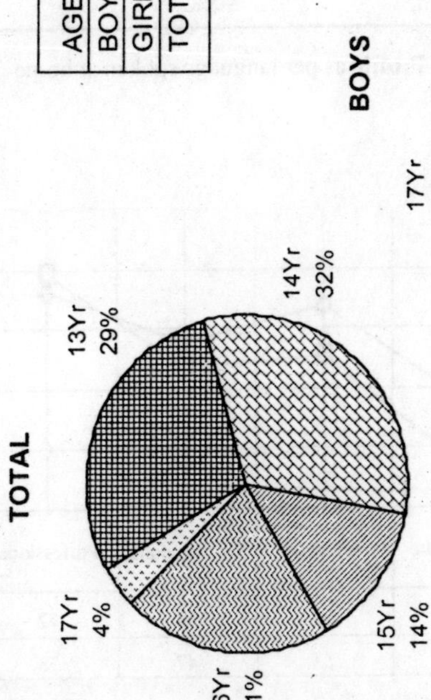

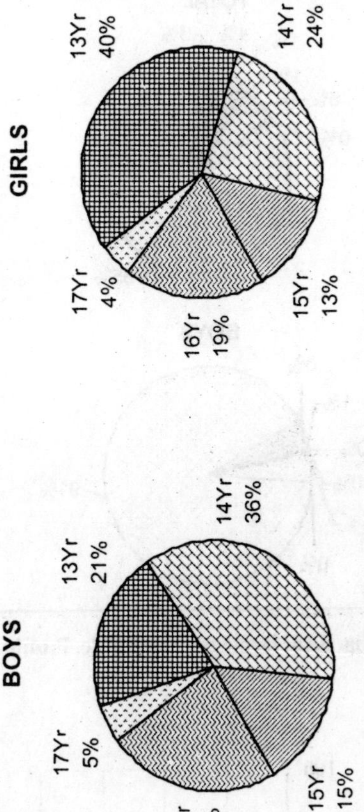

Fig. 5.15: Demographic Profile: Profile as per Age and Sex

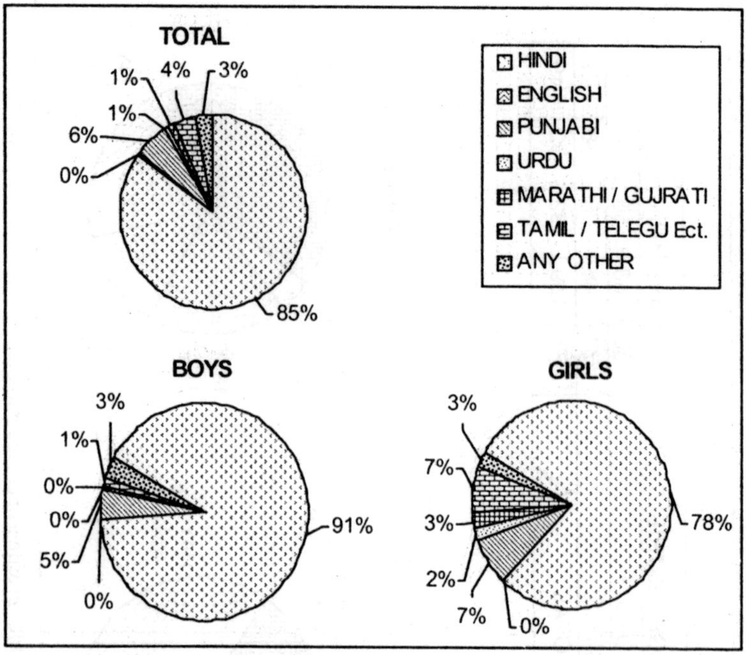

Fig. 5.16: Demographic Profile: Profile as per language spoken at home

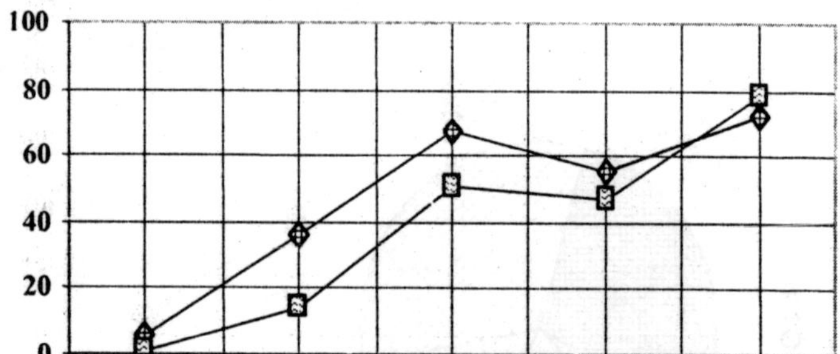

	Middle School Passed	Matriculate	Graduate	Post Graduate	Professional
BOYS	6	36	67	56	72
GIRLS	1	14	51	47	78

Fig. 5.17: Demographic Profile: Profile as per Education level of father

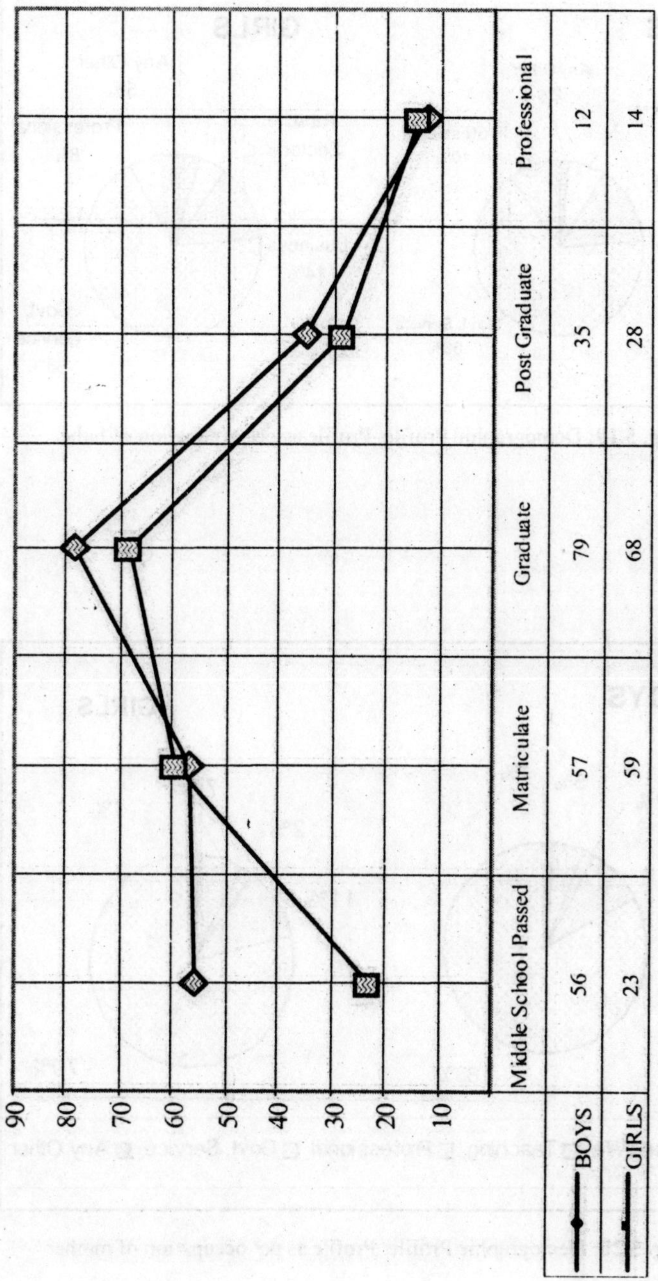

Fig. 5.18: Demographic Profile: Profile as per educational level of mother

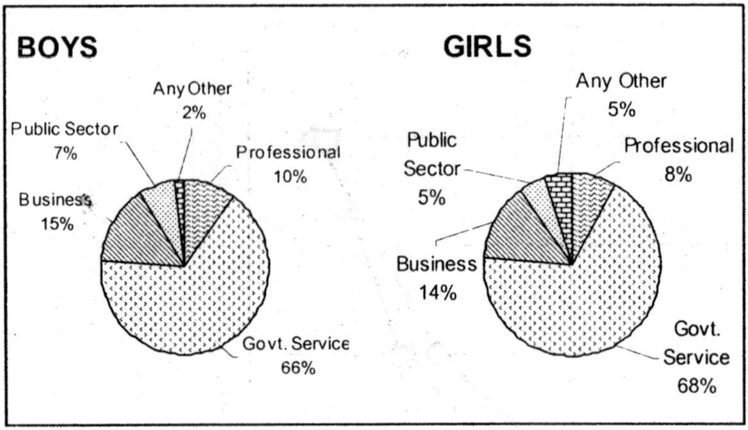

Fig. 5.19: Demographic Profile: Profile as per occupation of father

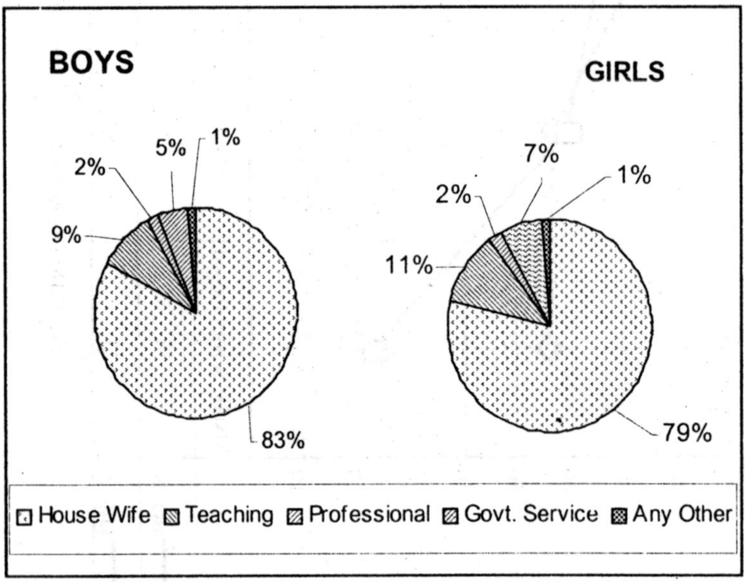

Fig. 5.20: Demographic Profile: Profile as per occupation of mother

Media Profile

The media access study was interesting as the data showed that more students own Television sets (97.2%) than those that subscribe to any newspaper (82.9%). Radio ownership varied as 98.2 per cent of the metropolitan public school students owned a radio, only 79 per cent of the satellite town public school owned radios. Even amongst the government schools, 90.2 per cent students in the metropolis owned radios whereas 88.8 per cent of the students from satellite town owned radio sets (Refer Fig. 5.21).

	% Distribution of population, categorywise, based on Media Access as per location and type of school							
	Govt. School				*Public School*			
	Metropolis		*Sattelite*		*Metropolis*		*Sattelite*	
	No.	*%*	*No.*	*%*	*No.*	*%*	*No.*	*%*
No. of respondents	102	–	116	–	111	–	110	–
Newspaper Subscription	86	84.3	81	69.8	105	94.6	92	83.6
Magazine Subscription	70	68.6	63	54.3	93	83.8	69	62.7
TV Ownership	101	99	116	100	110	99.1	102	92.7
Radio Ownership	92	90.2	103	88.8	109	98.2	87	79.1
VCR / VCP Ownership	34	33.3	19	16.4	71	63.9	34	30.9
Audio player Ownership	66	64.7	67	57.8	103	92.8	79	71.8

Fig. 5.21

The media exposure findings reveal that maximum number of students are exposed to the television and only half the number read their newspaper daily (98.8% watch television and only 40% read the paper everyday). Even when studied independently it was found that amongst the government schools, 99 per cent students in the metropolis and 98.3 per cent students in the satellite town watched television regularly whereas 43 per cent in the metropolis and 38 per cent of the government school in the satellite town read daily newspapers. From amongst the public school students 48 per cent in the metropolis and 46 per cent in the satellite town read the newspaper everyday (Refer Fig. 5.22).

	% Distribution of population, categorywise, based on Media Exposure as per location and type of school							
	Govt. School				*Public School*			
	Metropolis		*Sattelite*		*Metropolis*		*Sattelite*	
	No.	*%*	*No.*	*%*	*No.*	*%*	*No.*	*%*
No. of respondents	102	–	116	–	111	–	110	–
Listen to radio	64	62.7	83	71.6	83	74.8	75	68.2
Watch TV	101	99	114	98.3	109	98.2	110	100
Read daily newspaper	44	43.1	38	32.8	48	43.2	46	41.8
Read Magazines	82	80.4	95	81.9	97	87.4	78	70.9
Watch Films	98	96.1	116	100	109	98.2	107	97.3

Fig. 5.22

Cinema viewing seems to be very popular as 97 per cent of the students from the metropolis watched films and 98.6 per cent students from the satellite towns also watched films. Radio listenership lagged behind television and films although it was still far ahead of the newspaper readership. Amongst the government schools, 62.7 per cent students in the metropolis and 71.6 per cent students in the satellite town listened to the radio and amongst the public school students, 74.8 per cent in the metropolis and 68.2 per cent of the public school students in the satellite town listened to the radio. The findings, if studied all together reveal that media habits of most youngsters regardless of the school they studied or the location where they resided are nearly the same. Television and cinema win hands down as the most popular media, with radio having an average listenership following them. Newspaper reading loses out making it seems that the target group has yet to develop a habit of reading the daily newspaper and rely more on electronic media for their entertainment and general awareness. However, since this survey was conducted, the print media has begun in a big way to woo the young readers with their own supplements and perhaps this will increase the readership amongst the school going youngsters of today.

Since the electronic media was found to be the most popular, further analysis was conducted to find the most popular time of the day when the teenagers switched on their radio sets. First of all a strange finding is that girls in the metropolis and boys in the satellite town are more radio friendly. Evening time is most popular (43.7%) followed by morning time (38%). The reason could be that most houses have the radio on before everyone leaves home for the day and evenings could be spent with the radio as other chores go on. The afternoons are spent in school and in commuting from school while the nights are reserved by the television. The most popular programme that was tuned in by the radio listeners were the Hindi music programmes followed at a distance by the news and English music (Refer Figs. 5.23 and 5.24). Whatever the popularity of radio may be, it pales in the light of the power wielded by the medium of television.

	% Distribution of population, categorywise, based on Time of Radio Listening as per sex and location							
	Metropolis				*Sattelite*			
	Boys		*Girls*		*Boys*		*Girls*	
	No.	*%*	*No.*	*%*	*No.*	*%*	*No.*	*%*
No. of respondents	144	–	69	–	99	–	127	–
Morning	36	25	29	42	63	63.6	39	30.7
Afternoon	19	13.2	23	33.3	47	47.5	22	17.3
Evening	47	32.6	47	68.1	55	55.6	43	33.8
Night	36	25	30	43.5	55	55.6	27	21.3

Fig. 5.23

	% Distribution of population, categorywise, based on Most Prefered Programe on Radio as per location			
	Metropolis		*Sattelite*	
	No.	*%*	*No.*	*%*
No of respondents	213	–	226	–
Hindi Music	84	39.4	102	45.1
Film	15	7	8	3.5
Drama	3	1.4	8	3.5
News	15	7	24	10.6
English Music	20	9.4	9	3.9
Youth Programme	8	3.8	1	0.4
Any Other	3	1.4	4	1.8

Fig. 5.24

The girls in the metropolis and the boys in the satellite town had a 100 per cent television viewership at night time and 67.4 per cent of the boys in the metropolis watched night time television and 59 per cent satellite town girls watched night time television. These are also the maximum scores in each category making night time television the most popular. An interesting similarity in media reach behaviour is being displayed by the satellite town boys and the metropolitan girls. Both the categories seem to be more radio friendly and television friendly too. The least media friendly group of the lot seems to be the girls from the satellite town. The reason could be that since many students in the satellite town of Ghaziabad came from nearby areas such as Dadri and Hapur for their schooling, these being backward areas, the girls had to return home to help in the household whereas the boys were comparatively free (Refer Fig. 5.25).

	% Distribution of population, categorywise, based on Time of TV Viewing as per sex and location							
	Metropolis				*Sattelite*			
	Boys		*Girls*		*Boys*		*Girls*	
	No.	*%*	*No.*	*%*	*No.*	*%*	*No.*	*%*
No. of respondents	144	–	69	–	99	–	127	–
Morning	27	18.8	23	33.3	65	65.7	29	22.8
Afternoon	69	47.9	60	86.9	71	71.7	40	31.5
Evening	72	50	46	66.7	97	97.9	62	48.8
Night	97	67.4	69	100	99	100	75	59.1

Fig. 5.25

As regards the most popular programme on television, the category of songs wins hands down with 30.5 per cent students in the metropolis and 42.5 per cent in the satellite watching them. This category was followed by the television serials and feature films (Refer Fig. 5.26).

Since cinema was found to be a rather popular medium, an analysis was made to see the most popular location of cinema viewing. Maximum number of students watched films on television (38.2%) followed closely by cinema halls (36.6%).

The per cent of film viewing on television is maximum amongst the satellite town boys and girls and this ratio seems to have affected the overall percentage because in the other categories cinema halls are found to be more popular. In the metropolis, 43.8 per cent boys and 43.5 per cent girls watched films in cinema halls. In the satellite town 29.3 per cent boys and 30.7 per cent girls watched films in the cinema halls. On television 29.2 per cent metropolitan boys and 17.4 per cent of the metropolitan girls watched films whereas 52.5 per cent satellite town boys and 48.8 per cent satellite town girls watched films on television. The reason of better cinema hall attendance in the metropolis could be the better condition of cinema halls whereas cinema halls in the satellite towns may not be in such a good condition to be able to attract audiences. However, film viewing on video CD was very limited (Refer Fig. 5.27).

	% Distribution of population, categorywise, based on Most Prefered Programme on TV as per location			
	Metropolis		*Sattelite*	
	No.	*%*	*No.*	*%*
No of respondents	213	--	226	--
Songs	65	30.5	96	42.5
Serials	54	25.4	50	22.1
Feature Films	33	15.5	48	21.2
Film based programmes	10	4.7	6	2.7
Talk shows	16	7.5	9	3.9
Interviews	19	8.9	17	7.5
Others	5	2.3	3	1.3

Fig. 5.26

	% Distribution of population, categorywise, based on Place of Cinema viewing as per sex and location							
	Metropolis				*Sattelite*			
	Boys		*Girls*		*Boys*		*Girls*	
	No.	*%*	*No.*	*%*	*No.*	*%*	*No.*	*%*
No. of respondents	144	--	69	--	99	--	127	--
Cinema Hall	63	43.8	30	43.5	29	29.3	39	30.7
Video	39	27.1	21	30.4	17	17.2	24	18.9
Television	42	29.2	!2	17.4	52	52.5	62	48.8

Fig. 5.27

AIDS Awareness Profile

The AIDS awareness profile was found by correlating the demographic and the media profiles with the overall AIDS awareness level of the target group.

Mean AIDS Awareness

In order to reach an average about knowledge of AIDS, correct responses of all the AIDS information related questions were consolidated. Each questionnaire had a certain number of correct responses out of 36 all correct responses.

The correct answers of each questionnaire were added and then it was divided by the total number of candidates. This gave an overall average. Such averages were taken out for all the categories such as age, sex, school, city and correlated with variables such as school, age, sex, family income, professional status of parents, educational level of parents, type of family and so on.

Example

Number of boys with mothers educational level as graduates is 79. A total of each boys AIDS awareness score when added up gives 1889. This figure gives us the total awareness score of boys with graduate mothers.

When 1889 is divide by 79 it gives us the average AIDS awareness score of boys with graduate mothers.

1889 divided by 79 = 23.91

In order to find the percentage of awareness in this group, this score is divided by 36 and multiplied by 100. Where 36 is the all correct score of AIDS awareness.

23.91 divided by 36 multiplied by 100 = 66.42 per cent.

Thus the AIDS awareness percentage of boys with graduate mothers is 66.42 per cent.

Similarly calculations were carried out for each category and the comparison of overall AIDS awareness score was possible. This analysis gives us the AIDS awareness profile of the target group. Separate analysis has been made of the knowledge of AIDS where independent questions have been analysed.

Demographic Data and AIDS Awareness

It was found that the AIDS awareness profile of the metropolitan students (69.5%) was better than the satellite town students (53.25%). The girls in the metropolis scored the best with 75.9 per cent. The metropolis boys stood next with 63.6 per cent. The satellite town girls had a higher figure (59.8%) as compared to the satellite town boys (46.7%). This clearly shows that metropolitan students are better aware than the satellite town students although both of them exhibit similar media profile. The girls in the metropolis have scored the best and even the girls in the satellite town have scored better than their male counterparts proving better health consciousness amongst the girls.

The public school boys had the best awareness score with 66.9 per cent and the public school girls stood next with 63.44 per cent. The government school boys scored 57.8 per cent and girls 54.98 per cent. This goes to prove that boys and girls in public schools are certainly better informed than the boys and girls in the government schools (Refer Fig. 5.28).

When comparisons were made as to the occupation of the mother with AIDS awareness percentages it was found that AIDS awareness scores in the category 'Any other' was the maximum (75.7%) but this finding loses its significance if one considers that the total number of candidates in this category was only 3. Maximum number of students had housewife mothers and their awareness score was 60.5 per cent. Similarly the largest group of students had fathers in government service and their awareness score was 59.4 per cent (Refer Figs. 5.29 and 5.30).

When considering the educational level of the mother, marked difference was shown in the levels of awareness of boys and girls with highly educated and not so educated mothers. Students with post graduate and professional mothers exhibited highest awareness levels whereas students who had middle school passed or matriculate mothers showed low awareness level. The girls who had mothers with low level of education showed least awareness scores (41.78%) (Refer Fig. 5.31).

Similarly, highly educated fathers had children with a greater awareness score. The students whose fathers were not so educationally qualified scored only 48.6 per cent and 41.66 per cent on the awareness level (Refer Fig. 5.32).

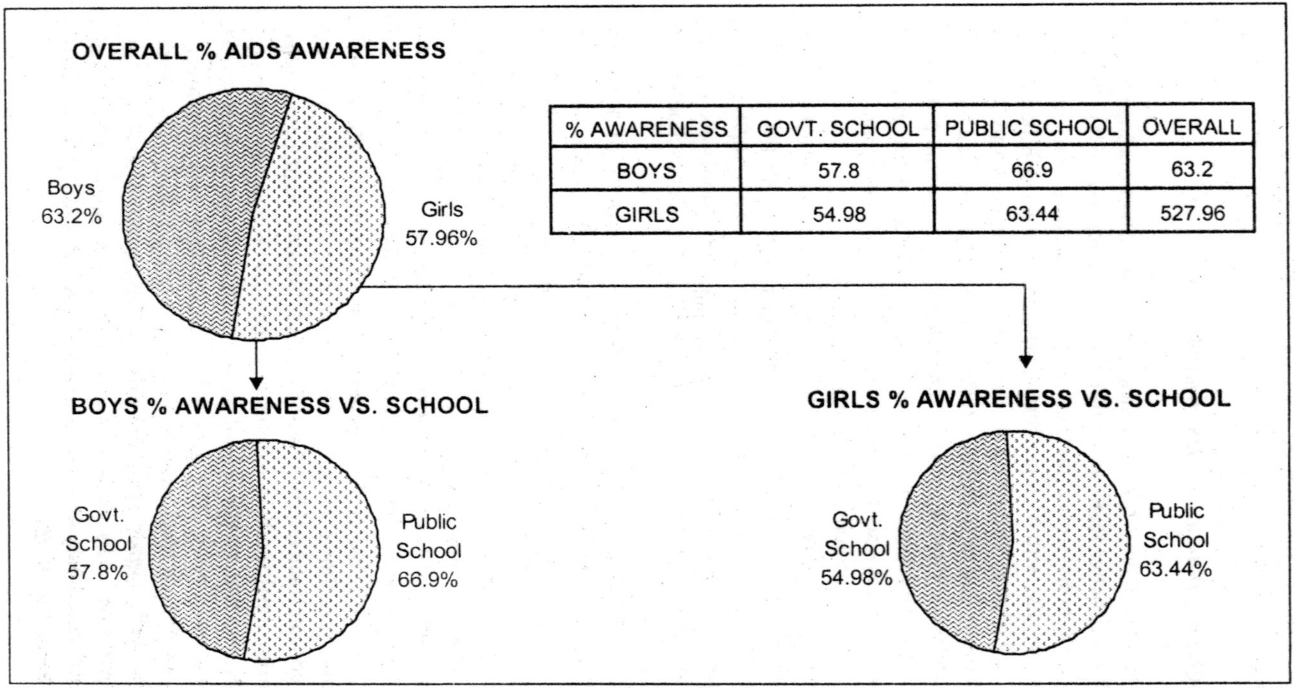

% AWARENESS	GOVT. SCHOOL	PUBLIC SCHOOL	OVERALL
BOYS	57.8	66.9	63.2
GIRLS	54.98	63.44	527.96

Fig. 5.28: AIDS Awareness: % AIDS awareness level as per school and sex

	Boys		Girls	
	No's	% Awareness	No's	% Awareness
House Wife	201	63.19	157	57.69
Teaching	21	59.92	21	58.99
Professional	5	65	3	66.67
Govt. Service	12	64.81	14	56.75
Any Other	2	81.94	1	69.44

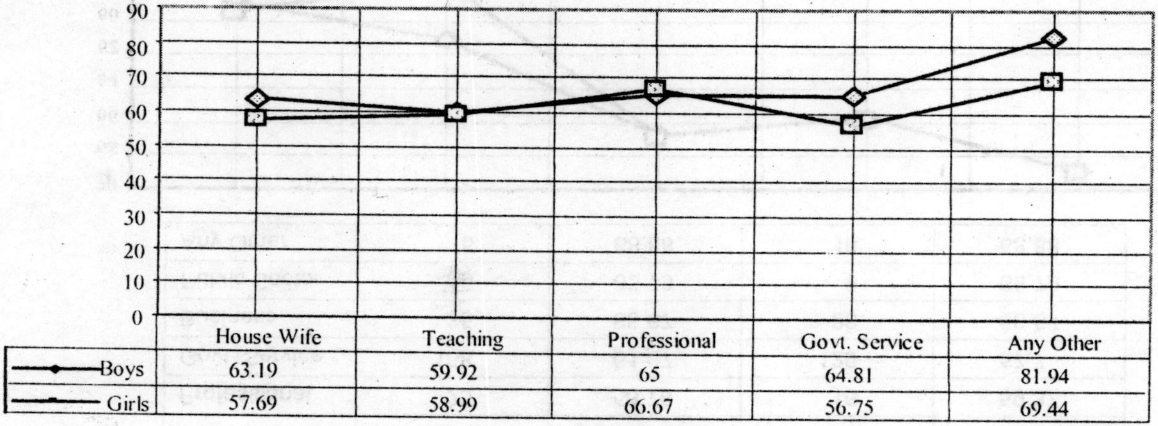

Fig. 5.29: AIDS Awareness: % Awareness as per occupation of mother

	Boys		Girls	
	No's	% Awareness	No's	% Awareness
Professional	25	58.78	16	59.37
Govt. Service	158	61.07	129	57.7
Business	35	66.67	26	66.67
Public Sector	16	65.79	9	65.79
Any Other	5	68.88	10	68.88

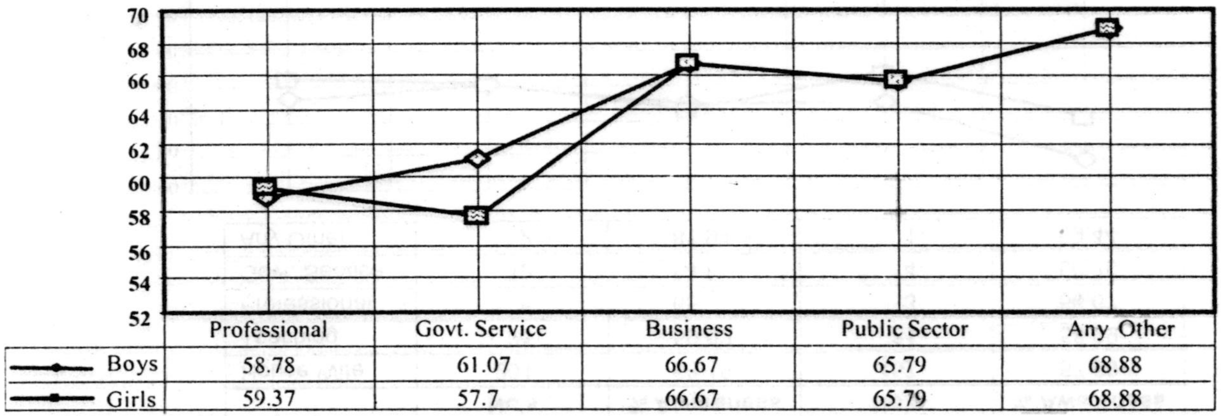

Fig. 5.30: AIDS Awareness: % Awareness as per occupation of father

	Boys		Girls	
	No.	% Awareness	No.	% Awareness
Middle School Passed	56	57.2	23	41.78
Matriculate	57	61.5	59	56.59
Graduate	79	66.42	68	59.92
Post Graduate	35	67.14	28	64.88
Professional	12	67.36	14	65.67

% AIDS AWARENESS – BOYS

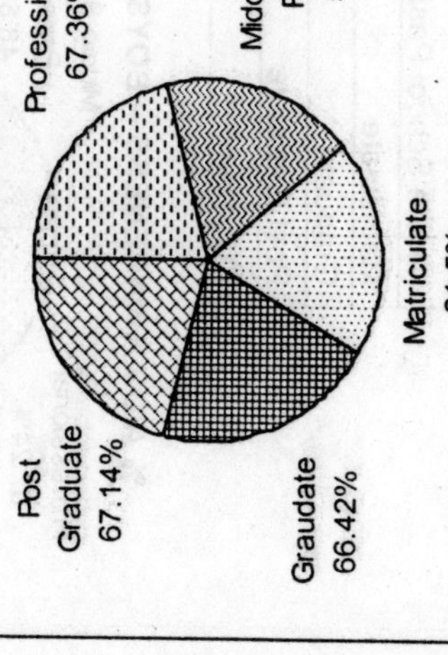

% AIDS AWARENESS – GIRLS

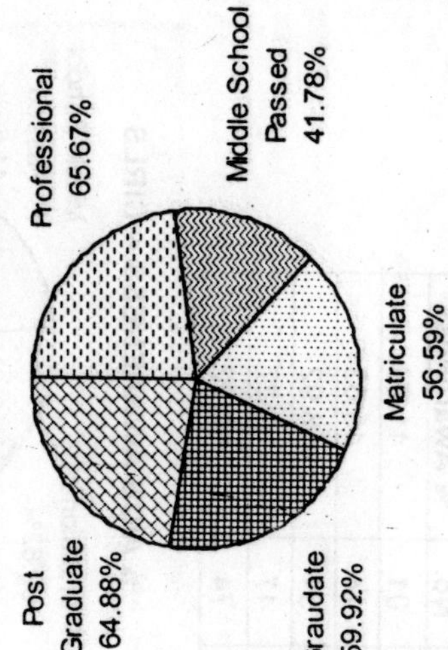

Fig. 5.31: AIDS Awareness: % Aids awareness as per educational level of mother

	Boys		Girls	
	No.	% Awareness	No.	% Awareness
Middle School Passed	6	48.6	01	41.66
Matriculate	36	58.48	14	45.63
Graduate	67	67.13	51	53.92
Post Graduate	56	62.64	47	59.27
Professional	72	67.24	74	62.82

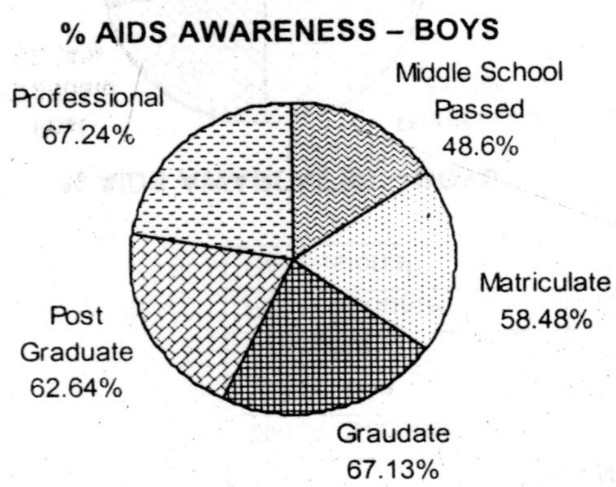

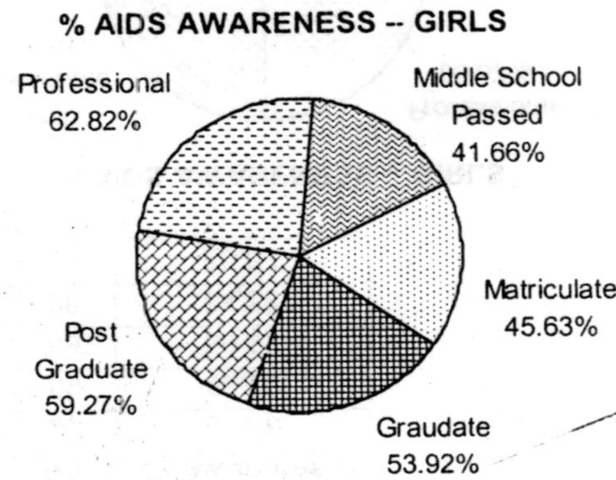

Fig. 5.32: AIDS Awareness: % Aids awareness as per educational level of father

In the age-wise analysis of AIDS awareness scores one finds that maximum awareness is with the maximum age. Students who were 13 years had an awareness score of 57.27 per cent amongst boys and 48.1 per cent amongst girls. Among 14 years old, the boys has 58.68 per cent and girls 57.2 per cent. Among the 15 years old boys scored 67.26 per cent and girls scored 66.1 per cent. If one observes closely one finds that the girls although, initially, rather unaware, slowly catch up with the boys as they grow older. Amongst the 16 years old boys scored 72.47 per cent and girls 69.7 per cent. The 17 years old boys are left behind with 77.31 per cent score by the 17 years old girls who scored 78.2 per cent. This is an interesting finding because it clears two factors:

(a) The overall AIDS awareness score increase with age of the respondent.
(b) The girls continue to learn as they grow older and beat the boys in their AIDS awareness score by the time they are 17 (Refer Fig. 5.33).

An expected finding was the increase in AIDS awareness levels with the increase in family income. The students with lowest income group (500-5000) had the lowest awareness level 57.40 per cent. The highest awareness score was 70.55 per cent which was won by the highest income group category (20,001 and above). Maximum number of students belonged to the 5,001-10,000 income bracket and their AIDS awareness score was found to be 62.34 per cent.

The students belonging to nuclear families showed better AIDS awareness score (61.55%) as compared to the students from the joint families (57.67 %). This finding was rather unexpected as joint families are traditionally expected to provide a more wholesome atmosphere to the child where all the questions find answers with favourite uncles or aunts (Refer Fig. 5.34).

Media Habits and AIDS Awareness

The way a medium is being used by the target group may depict the interests of the people but it may lead a researcher to assume that the respondent is also learning and deriving information from that particular medium. Since television wins hands down in the media popularity race it is not surprising to note that maximum students heard their first AIDS message on the television. Most of them cite the Shabana Azmi or Amitabh Bachchan campaign as their introduction to the topic of AIDS.

AGE WISE DISTRIBUTION

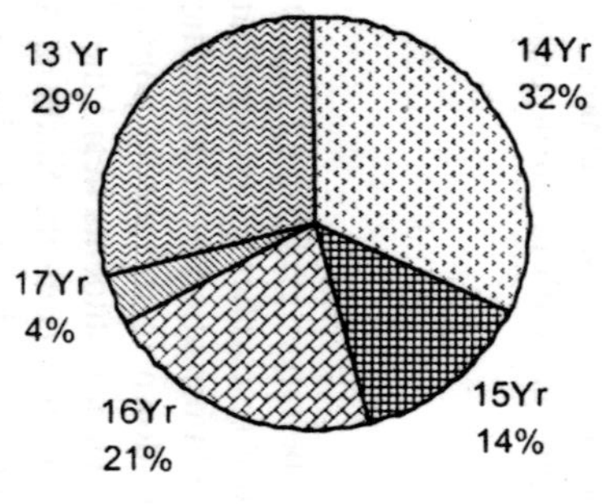

AGE % AWARENESS	13	14	15	16	17
BOYS	57.27	58.68	67.28	72.47	77.31
GIRLS	48.1	57.2	66.1	69.7	78.2

AGE WISE % AWARENESS – BOYS

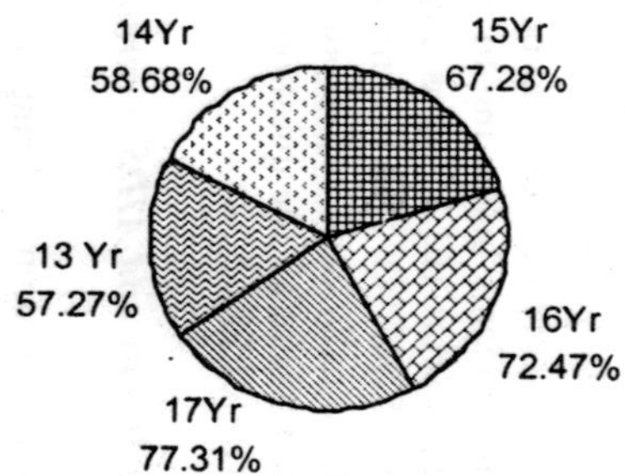

AGE WISE % AWARENESS – GIRLS

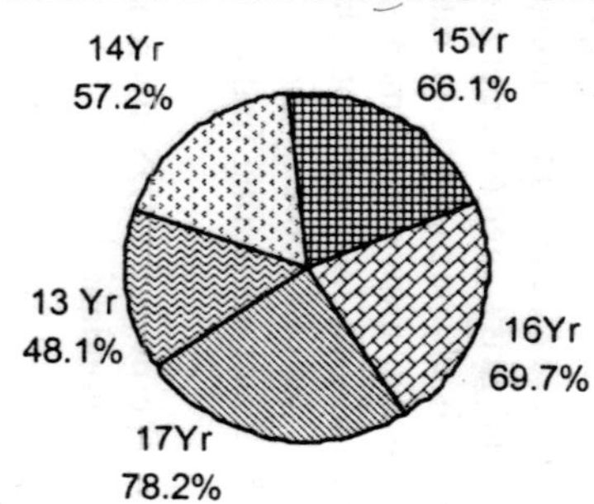

Fig. 5.33: AIDS Awareness: Age-wise % AIDS awareness level

Family Type	Nos.	% Awareness
Joint	89	57.67
Nuclear	348	61.55
Any Other	2	73.61

Population distribution based on type of family

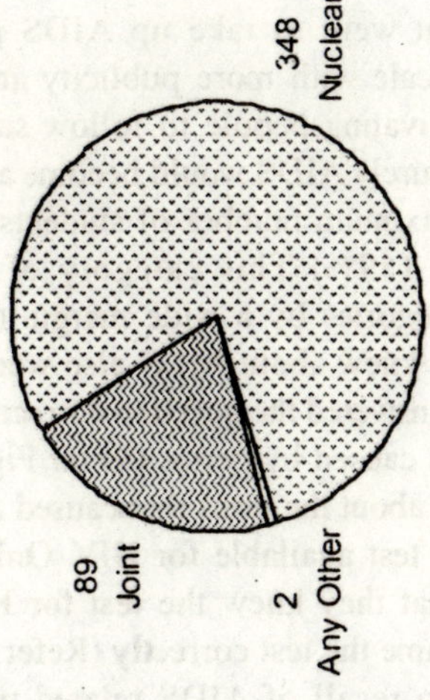

% Awareness

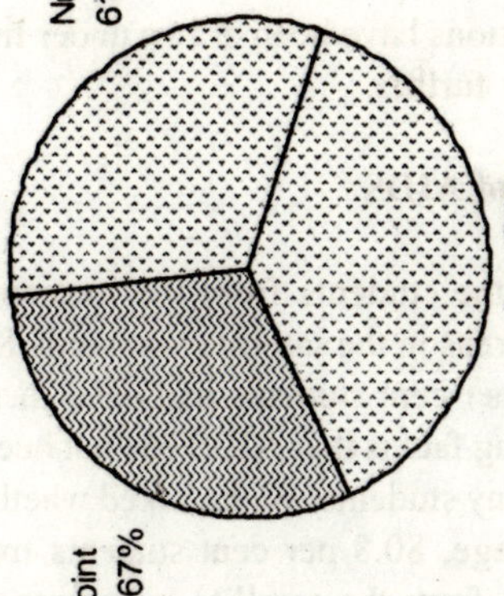

Fig. 5.34: AIDS Awareness: % AIDS awareness based on type of family

However, the group that is more media friendly is also better aware of the scourge of AIDS. Thus, one can safely assume that exposure to media does increase awareness levels as cross check questions have been added in the questionnaire to test the unaided recall of AIDS related message in different media.

Correlations have been drawn under Inferential Analysis to explain this category further.

Knowledge of AIDS

Majority of the students from the metropolis had heard about AIDS (97.7%) whereas in the satellite town only 84.5 per cent had heard about AIDS. 14.6 per cent students had never heard about AIDS.

Surprising fact is that AIDS has not been counted as a health related matter by many students. When asked whether they had heard any health related message, 80.8 per cent students from metropolis and 76.9 per cent students from the satellite town responded that they had heard a health related message but in the very next question a higher percentage of them answered that they had not heard about AIDS. It implies that students consider AIDS as an independent issue in itself and do not club it together with other health related messages that they come across (Refer Fig. 5.35).

Many students respond to the health drives taken up by the government from time to time as the health message that they have heard. Leprosy and polio were most commonly sited examples. This implies that if the government were to take up AIDS prevention programme on a nation wide scale with more publicity and lead the drive for AIDS prevention motivating people to follow safe sex and other preventive measures then surely AIDS would become a household word and not a taboo topic. Maximum number of students had heard about AIDS from Television. (59%) This category of source of information leads the other categories by a wide margin (Refer Fig. 5.36). Most of the students who knew about AIDS also were aware of the cause of AIDS 67.7 per cent answered the question correctly although 11.2 per cent thought that it was caused by germs (Refer Fig. 5.37).

Although the students knew about the virus that caused AIDS, they were absolutely unaware of the test available for HIV. Only 10.3 per cent of the students claimed that they knew the test for HIV out of which only 7.3 per cent could name the test correctly (Refer Fig. 5.38).

On the questions related to recall of AIDS related message on different media, maximum number of students could recall the AIDS related message on Television (59%) 34.4 per cent could recall newspaper messages and 15.3 per cent could recall radio messages. The recall was tested by asking the respondents to write the message that they could recall. Only the respondents who have clearly written down the messages that they could recall have been quantified here (Refer Fig. 5.39) The usage of condom revealed an interesting finding. 48.9 per cent respondents were aware that condoms could prevent AIDS and 31.7 per cent knew that they could prevent STD, but only 26.9 per cent were aware of the contraceptive function of the condom. Having heard many AIDS related messages and the stress on use of condoms in those messages have left them ignorant about the primary use of condoms (Refer Fig. 5.40).

Sex Education

Under this category their sex education related behaviours and ideas have been included. Does any one talk to these youngsters and are they interested in hearing about AIDS, if yes by whom would they like to get the information about AIDS etc. such questions have been put under the above heading.

It was found contrary to the researchers belief that 64.6 per cent girls had discussed about AIDS in school as compared to 52.6 per cent boys who had discussed the issue at school. Yet the awareness levels of boys was found to be more (67.5%) than the girls (64.6%). It means that although more girls discuss the issue amongst each other, they are as ignorant as the one with whom they have discussed the issue. The boys on the other hand increase their knowledge with discussions (Refer Fig 5.41). Most of the students had discussed the issue with their friends (28.9% girls and 27.9% boys) or their classmates (Refer Fig. 5.42).

When asked if anyone had informed them about AIDS authoritatively, 31.6 per cent boys 18.4 per cent girls responded that they had been educated by their teacher but only 2.5 per cent boys and 13.3 per cent girls had been told about the disease by their parents (Refer Fig. 5.43).

80.2 per cent boys and 82.7 per cent girls had never attended any seminar, workshop or lecture regarding AIDS awareness. This would imply serious lack of such activities for this particular target group. Organising an interpersonal programme for school going adolescents should not be a difficult task as one can be assured of one hundred per cent attendance as the group can be found collectively in their schools. 63.4 per cent of boys and 63.3 per cent of the girls would like to attend any programme related to AIDS (Refer Fig. 5.44).

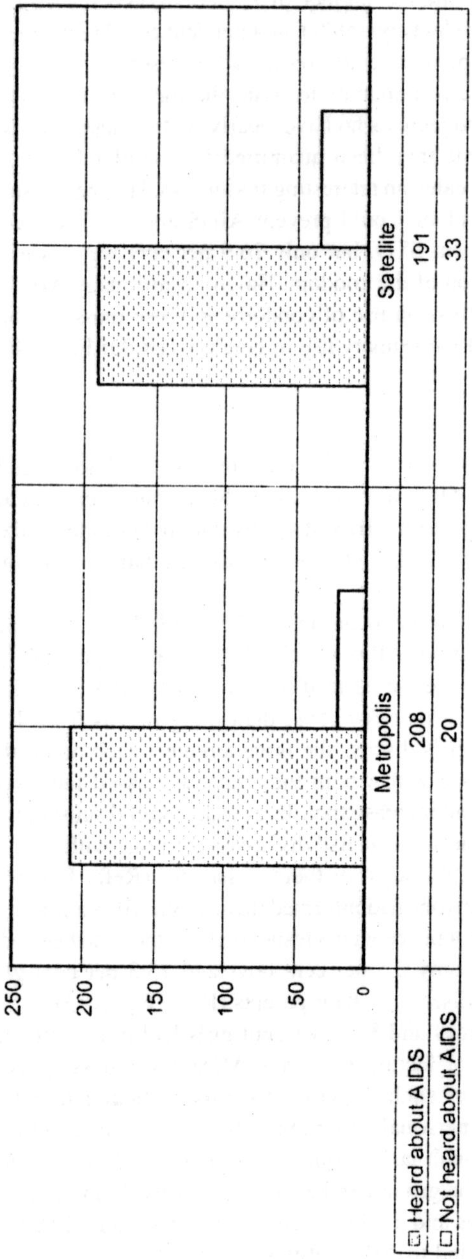

Fig. 5.35: Knowledge of AIDS : Heard about AIDS

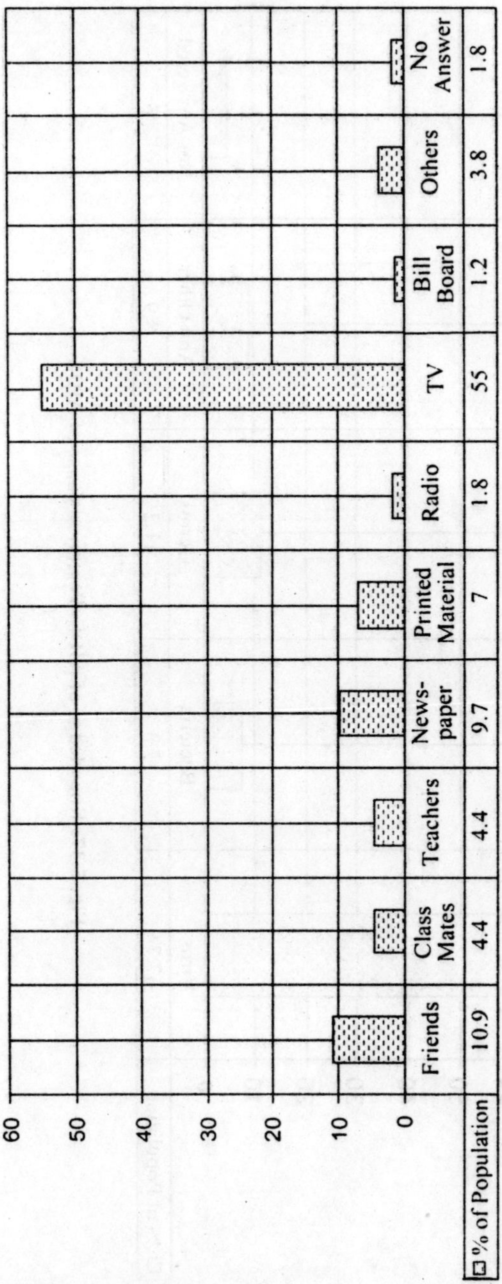

Fig. 5.36: Knowledge of AIDS: Source of information about AIDS

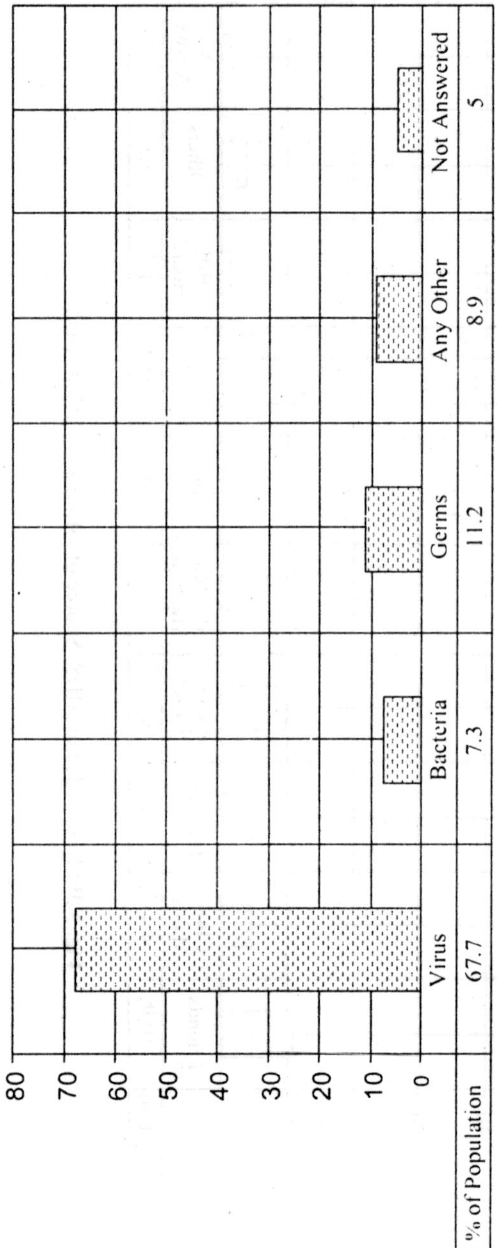

Fig. 5.37: Knowledge of AIDS: Perceived cause of AIDS

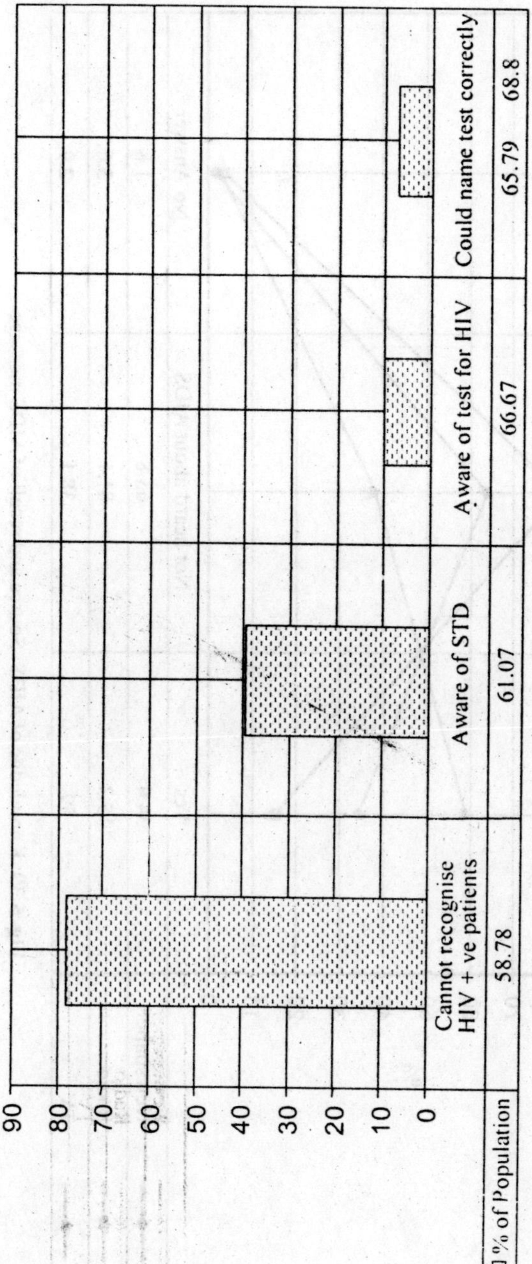

Fig. 5.38: Knowledge of AIDS: Information about AIDS

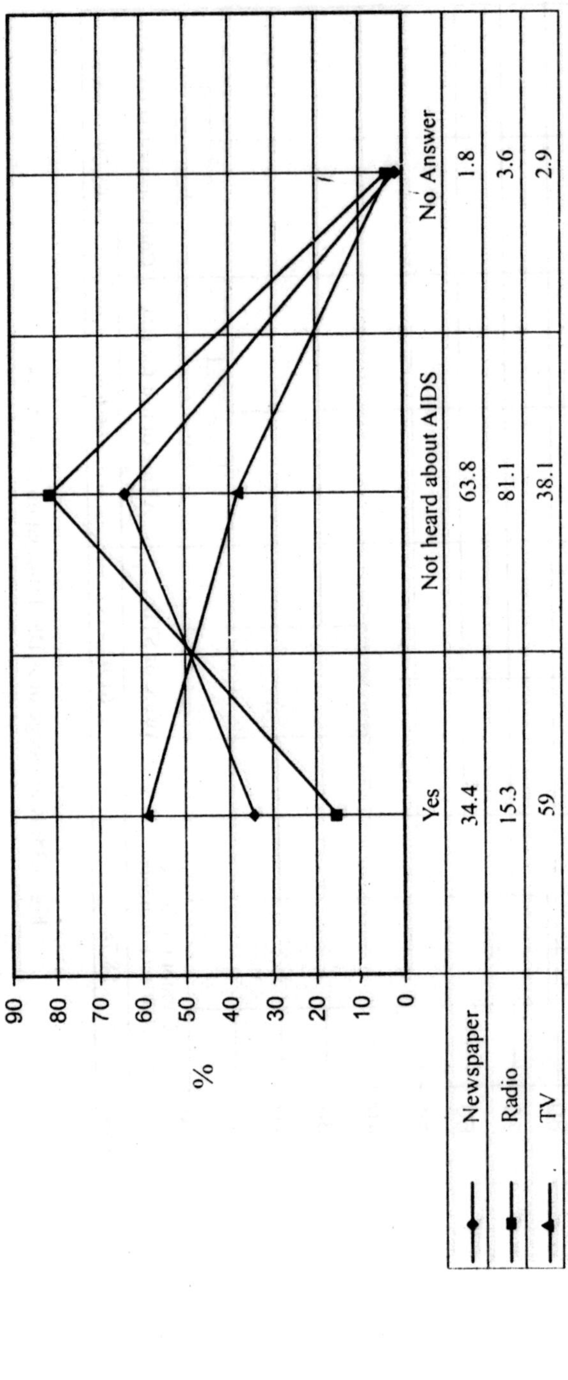

	Yes	Not heard about AIDS	No Answer
Newspaper	34.4	63.8	1.8
Radio	15.3	81.1	3.6
TV	59	38.1	2.9

Fig. 5.39: Knowledge of AIDS: Source and recall of AIDS message

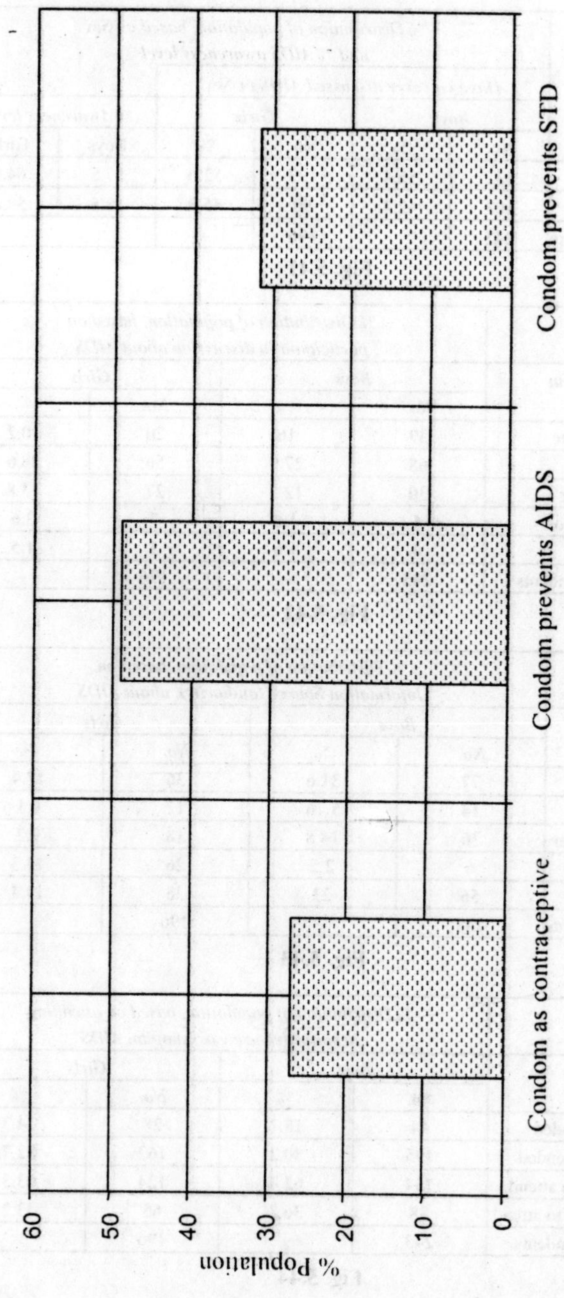

Fig. 5.40: Knowledge of AIDS: Knowledge of condom usage

	% Distribution of population, based on Sex and % AIDS awareness level					
	Have you ever discussed AIDS or Sex					
	Boys		Girls		% Awareness level	
	No.	%	No.	%	Boys	Girls
Yes	137	56.4	103	52.6	67.5	64.6
No	103	42.4	90	45.9	58.5	50.6
No. of respondents	243	–	196	–		

Fig. 5.41

	% Distribution of population, based on participant in discussion about AIDS			
Participant	Boys		Girls	
	No.	%	No.	%
Classmate	39	16	20	10.2
Friend	68	27.9	56	28.6
Teacher	30	12.3	27	13.8
Councellor	4	1.6	7	3.6
Other	4	1.6	3	1.5
No. of respondents	243	–	196	–

Fig. 5.42

	% Distribution of population, based on Information Source (authority), about AIDS			
Source	Boys		Girls	
	No.	%	No.	%
Teacher	77	31.6	36	18.4
Counsellor	14	5.76	12	6.1
Visiting Lecturer	36	14.8	18	9.2
Parent	6	2.5	26	13.3
Others	56	23	38	19.4
No. of respondents	243	–	196	–

Fig. 5.43

	% Distribution of population, based on attending Seminar/lecture/workshop on AIDS			
	Boys		Girls	
	No.	%	No.	%
Have attended	44	18.1	28	14.3
Have not attended	195	80.2	162	82.7
Would like to attend	154	62.4	124	63.3
Would not like to attend	88	36.2	65	33.2
No. of respondents	243	–	196	–

Fig. 5.44

The most preferred source of information regarding AIDS was medical professionals. This was a surprise finding because so far television was the most popular medium but here it follows as the second most preferred source of AIDS related information. This would mean that the students consider AIDS as a serious issue and would like to get their information from someone in authority (Refer Fig 5.45).

Source	*% Distribution of population, based on most preferred source of information about AIDS*			
	Boys		*Girls*	
	No.	*%*	*No.*	*%*
Teacher	48	19.8	39	19.9
Friend	30	12.3	26	13.3
Parent	10	4.1	19	9.7
Counsellor	7	2.9	6	3.1
Medical Professional	73	30	48	24.5
Television	54	22.2	32	16.3
Film	5	2.1	4	2
No. of respondents	243	–	196	–

Fig. 5.45

Correlational Analysis

Correlational analysis between variables was conducted to find out the relationships between, AIDS awareness scores, socio-economic status and mass media reach and access among the target population.

It has already been observed that the media profile of this group is very high. However, *neither age of the respondent nor the sex of the respondent has any direct correlation with media profile*. This would mean that the mass media reach and exposure is not affected by the age and sex of the respondent (Refer Figs. 5.46 and 5.47). In Fig. 5.46 a correlation between media profile index and age has been carried out. Keeping p = 0.05 and for a degree of freedom 6, the critical value of chi square is 12.59 and the chi square value here is 9.87. Since the chi square value is much more than derived here, one has to agree with the null hypothesis. Therefore, there is no correlation between the two variables. Similarly, the chi square value found here is much less than the critical value in Fig. 5.47 and hence no significant correlations are found in this case. The common myth that younger children watch more TV and that by the time they are in 10th class, they are more serious about their studies is not true. Whether girl or boy, younger or older, they are all media savvy and nothing affects their relationship with the mass media.

Cross tab count		*Age of the respondent*				*Total*
		13	14	15	16	
Media profile index	1	11	9	5	3	28
	2	33	25	11	17	86
	3	83	102	49	91	325
Total		127	136	65	111	439

p = 0.05

Chi-Square Tests	*Value*	*Degree of Freedom*	*Asymp. Sig. (2-sided)*
Pearson Chi-Square	9.8732531	6	0.13009374
Likelihood Ratio	10.2840754	6	0.11318755
Linear-by-Linear Association	7.8796169	1	0.00499951

N of Valid Cases	439

1 cells (8.3%) have expected count less than 5. The minimum expected count is 4.15.

Fig. 5.46

Cross tab count		*Sex of the respondent*		*Total*
		Boys	*Girls*	
Media profile index	1	18	10	28
	2	47	39	86
	3	178	147	325
Total		243	196	439

p = 0.05

Chi-Square Tests	*Value*	*Degrees of Freedom*	*Asymp. Sig. (2-sided)*
Pearson Chi-Square	0.966005261	2	0.616928201
Likelihood Ratio	0.983013278	2	0.611704082
Linear-by-Linear Association	0.513656746	1	0.473560149

N of Valid Cases	439

0 cells (.0%) have expected count less than 5. The minimum expected count is 12.50.

Fig. 5.47

When correlations were drawn between media profile and AIDS awareness scores it was found that there is a definite relationship between the two variables. For degree of freedom 6, the critical chi square value is 12.59. Since the chi square value is higher than critical chi square null hypothesis can be rejected. *This directly implies that media profile does effect the AIDS awareness scores.* Since the group has a very high media profile it can be safely assumed that much of their awareness is through the mass media. We have already seen that they rate TV as the provider of maximum information about AIDS (Refer Fig. 5.48).

Cross tab count		***AIDS awareness scores***				***Total***
		1	2	3	4	
Media profile index	1	6	4	17	1	28
	2	7	20	48	11	86
	3	12	60	184	69	325
Total		25	84	249	81	439

$p = 0.05$

Chi-Square Tests	*Value*	*Degree of Freedom*	*Asymp. Sig. (2-sided)*
Pearson Chi-Square	22.8531332	6	0.00084719
Likelihood Ratio	19.7835215	6	0.00302604
Linear-by-Linear Association	14.3199036	1	0.00015423

N of Valid Cases	439

2 cells (16.7%) have expected count less than 5. The minimum expected count is 1.59.

Fig. 5.48

Correlation between media Profile and the Socio-economic Status Indicator show that there is a definite relationship between the SES and the Media Profile. For df = 6, critical chi square = 12.59 which is lower than the chi square value arrived here. Thus null hypothesis stands rejected (Refer Fig. 5.49).

This proves the researchers Hypothesis No. 2 which says that 'It is expected that there will be a positive correlation between the socio-economic status of the respondent and his media access and exposure levels.'

Cross tab count		Socio-economic status index				Total
		1	2	3	4	
Media profile index	1	2	16	8	2	28
	2	2	57	24	3	86
	3	3	151	140	31	325
Total		7	224	172	36	439

p = 0.05

Chi-Square Tests	*Value*	*Degrees of Freedom*	*Asymp. Sig. (2-sided)*
Pearson Chi-Square	19.9961286	6	0.00277379
Likelihood Ratio	18.2763333	6	0.00557749
Linear-by-Linear Association	12.12982	1	0.00049622
N of Valid Cases	439		

3 cells (25.0%) have expected count less than 5. The minimum expected count is .45.

Fig. 5.49

Further correlations were drawn on media profile with the city of residence. Once again a definite relation ship was found between the city of residence and the media profile. We have seen this in the descriptive statistics also that the students living in metropolitan cities are better exposed to a variety of messages whereas those in smaller town lag behind (Refer Fig. 5.50). For df = 2, the chi square derived is very high compared to the critical chi of 5.99. Thus null hypothesis has been rejected.

Cross tab count		*City*		*Total*
		Ghaziabad	*Delhi*	
Media profile index	1	22	6	28
	2	55	31	86
	3	149	176	325
Total		226	213	439

p = 0.05

Chi-Square Tests	*Value*	*Degrees of Freedom*	*Asymp. Sig. (2-sided)*
Pearson Chi-Square	17.71417649	2	0.000142369
Likelihood Ratio	18.36785043	2	0.000102677
Linear-by-Linear Association	17.61681054	1	2.70189E-05
N of Valid Cases	439		

0 cells (.0%) have expected count less than 5. The minimum expected count is 13.59.

Fig. 5.50

This proves the researchers first hypothesis H1 which says 'The interaction level with mass media is significantly greater in a cosmopolitan city as compared to a smaller city.

The correlation between media profile and the type of school also show that there is a definite relationship. For df = 2, critical chi square value is 5.99 which is slightly larger than the chi square value derived here. Hence null hypothesis has been rejected. This would mean that the type of school where a child studies has a definite effect on his interaction with media, it will also effect his/her choice of media (Refer Fig. 5.51). This leads us to believe that mass media interaction is not something one decides out of own free will. Our circumstances, our surroundings, peers, all decide our mass media interaction level. The society effects media interaction. Just as it effects all our conscious and subconscious actions. This finding makes one realize one's helplessness in the face of a force that is the society. Then again the very same society gets effected by the mass media messages. The age old debate that whether the mass media is a mirror of society or moulder of society remains un resolved.

Cross tab count	***Type***	***Govt. school***	***Public school***	***Total***
Media profile index	1	16	12	28
	2	52	34	86
	3	150	175	325
Total		218	221	439

p = 0.05

Chi-Square Tests	***Value***	***Dreeges of freedom***	***Asymp. Sig. (2-sided)***
Pearson Chi-Square	6.241737703	2	0.044118819
Likelihood Ratio	6.273307408	2	0.043427878
Linear-by-Linear Association	4.772714318	1	0.028914205

N of Valid Cases	439

0 cells (.0%) have expected count less than 5. The minimum expected count is 13.90.

Fig. 5.51

Correlations were drawn of various variable with the AIDS awareness profile. In the first of the series a correlation between AIDS awareness profile and the first information about AIDS is taken out. There seems to be no relationship between the two variables. This implies that when and how a child hears about AIDS for the first time does not effect his/her later quest for information. For df=12, the critical chi is found to be 21.03. The chi square value here is very low so null hypothesis cannot be rejected. Thus, it is safe to say that *there is no relationship between first source of information and subsequent AIDS awareness* (Refer Fig. 5.52).

Cross tab count		*Sex*		*Total*
		Boy	*Girl*	
AIDS awareness profile	1	9	16	25
	2	42	42	84
	3	136	113	249
	4	56	25	81
Total		243	196	439

p = 0.05

Chi-Square Tests	*Value*	*Degree of Freedom*	*Asymp. Sig. (2-sided)*
Pearson Chi-Square	11.04338598	3	0.01149357
Likelihood Ratio	11.24469178	3	0.010473713
Linear-by-Linear Association	10.02213628	1	0.0015467

No. of Valid Cases	439

0 cells (.0%) have expected count less than 5. The minimum expected count is 11.16.

Fig. 5.52

Since in this case the first source of information happens to be television in maximum number of cases, this finding only points out towards the short term effect of the medium. This would also mean that television cannot lead to sustained behaviour change or even to behaviour modification. Some other inputs have been planted into the knowledge levels of the respondents that have given their AIDS awareness score.

In Fig. 5.55, the correlation shows a definite relationship between recall of AIDS message on newspapers and the AIDS awareness profile, similarly in Fig. 5.56, a *definite relationship has been found between recall of message on radio and the AIDS awareness profile*. In Fig. 5.57, *definite relationship has been found between the recall of message on Television and AIDS awareness profile*. This clearly shows that consistent messages by the mass media do have some retention in the minds of the audiences. Since our target group is of a very impressionable age messages have a high retention value and they do add to the overall increase in knowledge.

Cross tab count		*Age*				*Total*
		13	14	15	16	
AIDS awareness Profile	1	17	4	2	2	25
	2	29	41	9	5	84
	3	80	75	35	59	249
	4	1	16	19	45	81
Total		127	136	65	111	439

p = 0.05

Chi-Square Tests	*Value*	*Degree of Freedom*	*Asymp. Sig. (2-sided)*
Pearson Chi-Square	101.136401	9	9.2668E-18
Likelihood Ratio	112.833148	9	3.8919E-20
Linear-by-Linear Association	74.4173038	1	0

No of Valid Cases	439

1 cells (6.3%) have expected count less than 5. The minimum expected count is 3.70.

Fig. 5.53

Cross tab count		*First heard about AIDS*					*Total*
		Others	*Newspaper*	*Radio*	*TV*	*Billboards +*	
AIDS awareness profile	1	6	4	1	12	2	25
	2	26	6		47	5	84
	3	58	20	5	148	18	249
	4	20	10	2	38	11	81
Total		110	40	8	245	36	439

p = 0.05

Chi-Square Tests	*Value*	*Degree of Freedom*	*Asymp. Sig. (2-sided)*
Pearson Chi-Square	12.4853675	12	0.4075273
Likelihood Ratio	13.1194829	12	0.3604163
Linear-by-Linear Association	0.62856231	1	0.4278832

N of Valid Cases	439

6 cells (30.0%) have expected count less than 5. The minimum expected count is .46.

Fig. 5.54

Cross tab count		*Recall AIDS message in NP*		*Total*
		Yes	*No*	
AIDS awareness profile	1	6	19	25
	2	15	69	84
	3	80	169	249
	4	47	34	81
Total		148	291	439

p = 0.05

Chi-Square Tests	*Value*	*Degree of Freedom*	*Asymp. Sig. (2-sided)*
Pearson Chi-Square	32.20863903	3	4.72968E-07
Likelihood Ratio	31.90260714	3	5.48689E-07
Linear-by-Linear Association	24.75683547	1	6.50427E-07
N of Valid Cases	439		

0 cells (.0%) have expected count less than 5. The minimum expected count is 8.43.

Fig. 5.55

Cross tab count		*Recall on Radio*		*Total*
		Yes	*No*	
AIDS awareness profile	1	1	24	25
	2	8	76	84
	3	37	212	249
	4	21	60	81
Total		67	372	439

p = 0.05

Chi-Square Tests	*Value*	*Degree of Freedom*	*Asymp. Sig. (2-sided)*
Pearson Chi-Square	11.74410911	3	0.008313172
Likelihood Ratio	11.87223925	3	0.007833878
Linear-by-Linear Association	10.8704887	1	0.000977087
No of Valid Cases	439		

1 cells (12.5%) have expected count less than 5. The minimum expected count is 3.82.

Fig. 5.56

Cross tab count		*Recall on TV*		*Total*
		Yes	*No*	
AIDS awareness Profile	1	7	18	25
	2	38	46	84
	3	151	98	249
	4	60	21	81
Total		256	183	439

p = 0.05

Chi-Square Tests	*Value*	*Degree of Freedom*	*Asymp. Sig. (2-sided)*
Pearson Chi-Square	24.19076264	3	2.27907E-05
Likelihood Ratio	24.5254906	3	1.94017E-05
Linear-by-Linear Association	24.02500308	1	9.50857E-07

N of Valid Cases	439

0 cells (.0%) have expected count less than 5. The minimum expected count is 10.42.

Fig. 5.57

In Fig. 5.58, correlations have been made between the AIDS awareness profile and Media Profile. For df = 6, critical chi was found to be 12.59, while the chi square value here is 22.85, which is much higher the critical chi. Hence the null hypothesis has been rejected.

This proves the researchers hypothesis H5 which says 'It is expected that mass media has contributed largely to the AIDS awareness levels of the respondents.'

When correlations were drawn between the AIDS awareness levels and location, type of school and SES levels (Refer Figs. 5.59, 5.60, 5.61) definite relationships were found through out. This goes on to say that AIDS awareness is a result of not just good interaction with the mass media but also the place of stay, the socio economic status, the type of school and such demographics. The relationship between HIV and poverty has been much talked about. This finding reiterated the need to act fast and try to reach all sections of the society. Since ignorance is the only factor that can decide life or death for a person, it should not be a persons fault that he/she remained ignorant because of the economic strata he/she belonged to or the type of school he/she attended. The messages have to cross the socio economic barriers and reach the nooks and corners of the country.

With direct relationship between SES and AIDS awareness levels the researchers hypothesis H3 is proved. H3 says 'The socio economic status of the respondent will correlate directly with the AIDS awareness levels.'

Cross tab count		*Media Profile*			*Total*
		1	2	3	
AIDS awareness Profile	1	6	7	12	25
	2	4	20	60	84
	3	17	48	184	249
	4	1	11	69	81
Total		28	86	325	439

p = 0.05

Chi-Square Tests	*Value*	*Degree of Freedom*	*Asymp. Sig. (2-sided)*
Pearson Chi-Square	22.8531332	6	0.00084719
Likelihood Ratio	19.78352149	6	0.00302604
Linear-by-Linear Association	14.31990362	1	0.000154226

No of Valid Cases	439

2 cells (16.7%) have expected count less than 5. The minimum expected count is 1.59.

Fig. 5.58

Cross tab count		*Location*		*Total*
		Ghaziabad	*Delhi*	
AIDS awareness Profile	1	19	6	25
	2	59	25	84
	3	120	129	249
	4	28	53	81
Total		226	213	439

p = 0.05

Chi-Square Tests	*Value*	*Degree of Freedom*	*Asymp. Sig. (2-sided)*
Pearson Chi-Square	28.20302118	3	3.29258E-06
Likelihood Ratio	29.05190193	3	2.18392E-06
Linear-by-Linear Association	26.87879052	1	2.16635E-07

N of Valid Cases	439

0 cells (.0%) have expected count less than 5. The minimum expected count is 12.13.

Fig. 5.59

Cross tab course		***Type of School***		***Total***
		Government	*Public*	
AIDS awareness Profile	1	7	18	25
	2	38	46	84
	3	145	104	249
	4	28	53	81
Total		218	221	439

p = 0.05

Chi-Square Tests	*Value*	*Degree of Freedom*	*Asymp. Sig. (2-sided)*
Pearson Chi-Square	20.04939332	3	0.000165788
Likelihood Ratio	20.377574	3	0.000141746
Linear-by-Linear Association	0.082989962	1	0.773285668

No of Valid Cases	439

0 cells (.0%) have expected count less than 5. The minimum expected count is 12.41.

Fig. 5.60

Cross tab count		***Socio economic Status Index***				***Total***
		1	2	3	4	
AIDS awareness Profile	1		18	6	1	25
	2	3	46	32	3	84
	3	4	132	91	22	249
	4		28	43	10	81
Total		7	224	172	36	439

p = 0.05

Chi-Square Tests	*Value*	*Degree of Freedom*	*Asymp. Sig. (2-sided)*
Pearson Chi-Square	21.1137282	9	0.01215491
Likelihood Ratio	22.8962044	9	0.00643368
Linear-by-Linear Association	14.3224378	1	0.00015402

No of Valid Cases	439

5 cells (31.3%) have expected count less than 5. The minimum expected count is .40.

Fig. 5.61

In correlations between AIDS awareness and age, (Refer Fig. 5.53) a very definite relationship has been found between the respondents age and the awareness levels. This implies that as the respondent grows in age his/her knowledge level increases.

This proves the researcher's hypotheses H 7 which says 'There will be a significant difference in AIDS awareness levels and the age of the respondent.'

Similarly a definite relationship was found between the sex of the respondent and the AIDS awareness levels (Refer Fig. 5.52) proving the next hypothesis of this researcher.

Researchers hypothesis H 8 is proved which says 'there will be a significant difference between the AIDS awareness levels of boys and girls'.

Although the correlation between the Recall of AIDS message and recall of health related message (Fig. 5.62) shows that there is a definite relationship between the two we have seen in the previous analysis that many of them did not include AIDS as a health problem. If there is a relationship then the health aspect of AIDS may not be totally lost on them.

Cross tab count		*Heard about AIDS*			*Total*
		Not Ans.	*Yes*	*No*	
Heard health message	Not Ans.	0	10	0	10
	Yes	1	320	20	341
	No	2	70	15	87
	Don't know	0	1	0	1
Total		3	401	35	439

p = 0.05

Chi-Square Tests	*Value*	*Degree of Freedom*	*Asymp. Sig. (2-sided)*
Pearson Chi-Square	17.75998922	6	0.006860839
Likelihood Ratio	15.51367668	6	0.016616499
Linear-by-Linear Association	6.30552312	1	0.012036239

No of Valid Cases	439

7 cells (58.3%) have expected count less than 5. The minimum expected count is .01.

Fig. 5.62

Various correlations were also drawn on the basis of Socio-economic Index and variables such as age, sex, message recall on radio, message recall on television (Refer Figs. 5.63, 5.64, 5.67, 5.68) and no relationship was found between any of the variables. This was an obvious finding. However a definite relationship was found between Socio-economic Index and first information about AIDS and this means that since mass media reach is effected by the SES so is the first information. More often than not the first information has been received though the mass media, therefore, the finding (Refer Fig. 5.65). Similar correlations between SES and type of school and location showed no relationship (Refer Figs. 5.69, 5.70).

Cross tab count		*Age*				*Total*
		13	14	15	16	
Socio-economic Status	1	1	4	1	1	7
	2	64	71	33	56	224
	3	49	48	29	46	172
	4	13	13	2	8	36
Total		127	136	65	111	439

p = 0.05

Chi-Square Tests	*Value*	*Degree of Freedom*	*Asymp. Sig. (2-sided)*
Pearson Chi-Square	6.78972639	9	0.65900135
Likelihood Ratio	7.25684248	9	0.61039764
Linear-by-Linear Association	0.15813146	1	0.6908827

No of Valid Cases	439

4 cells (25.0%) have expected count less than 5. The minimum expected count is 1.04.

Fig. 5.63

Most of the researchers hypothesis have been proved in this section but researchers Hypothesis H6 was rejected in the descriptive analysis section itself. The fact that students wanted to get their AIDS awareness information from medical professionals rejected the researchers hypothesis, H6 (Refer Fig. 5.45 in the descriptive analysis).

H6 says 'It is expected that respondents would prefer to receive AIDS related information from the mass media.' The hypothesis stands rejected.

Cross tab count		*Sex*		*Total*
		Boy	*Girl*	
Socio-economic Status	1	4	3	7
	2	142	82	224
	3	85	87	172
	4	12	24	36
Total		243	196	439

p = 0.05

Chi-Square Tests	*Value*	*Degree of Freedom*	*Asymp. Sig. (2-sided)*
Pearson Chi-Square	15.38196146	3	0.001517689
Likelihood Ratio	15.47197912	3	0.001454668
Linear-by-Linear Association	14.19349913	1	0.000164939

No of Valid Cases	439

2 cells (25.0%) have expected count less than 5. The minimum expected count is 3.13.

Fig. 5.64

Cross tab count		*Mode of information about AIDS*					*Total*
		Other	*NP*	*Radio*	*TV*	*Billboards+*	
Socio-economic Status	1	3			2	2	7
	2	63	16	7	125	13	224
	3	36	21	1	100	14	172
	4	8	3		18	7	36
Total		110	40	8	245	36	439

p = 0.05

Chi-Square Tests	*Value*	*Degree of Freedom*	*Asymp. Sig. (2-sided)*
Pearson Chi-Square	22.738137	12	0.030033149
Likelihood Ratio	21.5361972	12	0.043058864
Linear-by-Linear Association	2.38138934	1	0.122788301

No of Valid Cases	439

10 cells (50.0%) have expected count less than 5. The minimum expected count is 13.

Fig. 5.65

Cross tab count		*Recall message on NP*		*Total*
		Yes	*No*	
Socio-economic Status	1	5	2	7
	2	73	151	224
	3	59	113	172
	4	11	25	36
Total		148	291	439

p = 0.05

Chi-Square Tests	*Value*	*Degree of Freedom*	*Asymp. Sig. (2-sided)*
Pearson Chi-Square	4.769580495	3	0.189468314
Likelihood Ratio	4.458982869	3	0.215978231
Linear-by-Linear Association	0.348105693	1	0.555187415

No of Valid Cases	439

2 cells (25.0%) have expected count less than 5. The minimum expected count is 2.36.

Fig. 5.66

Cross tab count		*Recall message on Radio*		*Total*
		Yes	*No*	
Socio-economic Status	1	3	4	7
	2	33	191	224
	3	23	149	172
	4	8	28	36
Total		67	372	439

p = 0.05

Chi-Square Tests	*Value*	*Degree of Freedom*	*Asymp. Sig. (2-sided)*
Pearson Chi-Square	5.993868008	3	0.111908941
Likelihood Ratio	4.796236725	3	0.187340365
Linear-by-Linear Association	0.001154418	1	0.972895709

No of Valid Cases	439

1 cells (12.5%) have expected count less than 5. The minimum expected count is 1.07.

Fig. 5.67

Cross tab count		***Recall messages on TV***		***Total***
		Yes	*No*	
Socio-economic Status	1	6	1	7
	2	123	101	224
	3	102	70	172
	4	25	11	36
Total		256	183	439

p = 0.05

Chi-Square Tests	*Value*	*Degree of Freedom*	*Asymp. Sig. (2-sided)*
Pearson Chi-Square	5.13305965	3	0.162309156
Likelihood Ratio	5.510148752	3	0.138032868
Linear-by-Linear Association	1.278578112	1	0.258163579

No of Valid Cases	439

2 cells (25.0%) have expected count less than 5. The minimum expected count is 2.92.

Fig. 5.68

Cross tab count		***Location***		***Total***
		Ghaziabad	*Delhi*	
Socio-economic Status	1	4	3	7
	2	110	114	224
	3	89	83	172
	4	23	13	36
Total		226	213	439

p = 0.05

Chi-Square Tests	*Value*	*Degree of Freedom*	*Asymp. Sig. (2-sided)*
Pearson Chi-Square	2.818871898	3	0.420402682
Likelihood Ratio	2.853752769	3	0.414727524
Linear-by-Linear Association	1.655405982	1	0.198224742

No of Valid Cases	439

2 cells (25.0%) have expceted count less than 5. The minimum expected count is 3.40.

Fig. 5.69

Cross tab count		*Type of school*		*Total*
		Government	*Public*	
Socio-economic Status	1	1	6	7
	2	104	120	224
	3	90	82	172
	4	23	13	36
Total		218	221	439

p = 0.05

Chi-Square Tests	*Value*	*Degree of Freedom*	*Asymp. Sig. (2-sided)*
Pearson Chi-Square	7.844021689	3	0.049347734
Likelihood Ratio	8.27263968	3	0.040700633
Linear-by-Linear Association	6.130874581	1	0.013284114

No of Valid Cases	439

2 cells (25.0%) have expected count less than 5. The minimum expected count is 3.48.

Fig. 5.70

Only one out of researcher's seven hypotheses has been disproved. Some salient findings from the above survey are:

(1) Television has emerged as the most powerful medium:
   (a) Maximum number of students own it.
   (b) Most have got their AIDS related information from TV.
   (c) Most of the respondents could recall the AIDS related message appearing on TV.

(2) Newspaper reading was found to lag behind TV and cinema. Students from the satellite town were found to have yet to develop the habit of newspaper reading.

(3) Music programmes on radio and TV wins hands down as most popular programme.

(4) Cinema is the most popular medium and most films are watched on TV.

(5) AIDS awareness profile of metropolitan students was better than satellite town. Girls in metropolis as well as in the satellite town have better AIDS awareness profile.

(6) In the overall analysis, boys from the Public Schools had the best awareness profile and the girls from the public schools followed a close second.

(7) Music programmes on television were the most watched, followed by serials and feature films.

(8) The AIDS awareness profile of metropolitan students was better than the satellite town students. Although the media access profile was similar the metropolitan students certainly had more information.

(9) Girls exhibited better awareness profile as compared to boys in both the categories.

(10) While comparing public schools and government schools, public school boys and girls scored better than government schools.

(11) Media availability or access could not be the sole cause of high or low AIDS awareness.

(12) 97.7 per cent students had heard about AIDS, but they did not count it as a health problem. Polio and leprosy were most frequently counted as health issues.

(13) Television was cited as the most efficient source of AIDS related information. Most students could recall messages from TV 67.7 per cent were aware of the cause of AIDS, however, they were ignorant about the tests needed for HIV detection.

(14) Condom was cited as a method of preventing AIDS but only 26.6 per cent were aware of its use as a contraceptive.

(15) More girls had discussed AIDS in school yet boys have better awareness.

(16) Most students had never attended any seminar, workshop orlecture regarding AIDS awareness but more than half the number of students were keen to attend a programme related to AIDS.

(17) Most preferred source of information regarding AIDS was medical professionals. Although the students receive all their information from TV, they would like to receive it from qualified medical professional.

Focus Group Discussions

The quantitative data has shown that awareness levels are high in:

(a) older boys and girls,
(b) public school students.
(c) metropolis students,
(d) Boys as compared to girls.

At the same time it was found that the level of misinformation is also very high with only 7.3 per cent of the entire sample could name the test for the detection of HIV. Only 39.4 per cent were aware of any sexually transmitted disease and although 67.7 per cent of the respondents knew that virus causes AIDS, 11.2 per cent named germs, 7.3 per cent named bacteria and 8.9 per cent were not clear about the cause of AIDS. Only 26.9 per cent of the population knew that condoms could also be used as contraception's, while 48.9 per cent knew that it prevents AIDS.

While conducting the FGDs the researcher was well aware of the quantitative data. The schedule had been designed in order to help in the interpretation of the quantitative data.

A Section-wise Analysis Has Been Conducted.

Use of Free Time

These questions acted as ice breakers. Young people love their free time and like to talk about it. The respondents in all the schools were eager to discuss their hobbies. Most common past times were reading books, listening to music, watching films and also sleeping. Students from public schools in Delhi specifically mentioned net surfing, going out with friends as a group to watch films or to go to the disco was common. At the mention of dates, some girls refused to discuss but they were quick to add that "other" classmates did go out for dates mostly to the fast food restaurants or discotheques. The boys and girls in Ghaziabad seem to hesitate to discuss this aspect. Socialising among sexes was not common here. Boys and girls went out in all boys or all girls groups. They knew people who had girl friends/boy friends but it was still considered a taboo activity.

Media Seeking Habits

Radio

Radio listener ship was common among the Delhi students more than Ghaziabad students. Most of them listened to the radio while travelling by car or only listened to one or two favourite programmes on FM radio, while in Ghaziabad some people did not even know if they owned a radio. Some knew that it came together with their music system but they had never really paid attention to this medium. Girls from government school in Ghaziabad mentioned that they did listen to the radio in the mornings or in the afternoons. No regularity was found in the use of this medium. Its best use was sited as a mobile medium best suited for cars. It is considered as a non serious medium by the boys and girls. Even in the smaller town, TV viewing is 98 per cent in Government school, Ghaziabad (according to the survey) and 100 per cent in public school (survey), whereas radio listener ship was only 71.6 per cent in government schools and 68.2 per cent in public school. (Survey report) The focus group substantiates this finding. The FGD revealed that:

(1) Boys and girls belonging to Public school in Delhi listen to the radio more than any other counterparts.
(2) This target group switches on the radio only for music.
(3) They like to play the radio while doing something else. Active listener ship was minimal.
(4) Some of them could recall AIDS related messages on radio.
(5) They knew that there was a help line for AIDS where their questions could be answered.
(6) They had no difficulty in comprehending the message but since they were not radio enthusiasts, they were indifferent to the idea of more messages being presented on the radio.
(7) Not a single candidate could recall any advertisement or message broadcast on the radio.

The findings were a surprise as radio as a medium has achieved 100 per cent reach. Amongst this target group, only those who owned cars, lived in metropolitan cities and were adept at English language, listened to the radio. The potentiality of a medium was not being tapped to its full. Youngsters in the satellite town, failed to appreciate the youth programmes that were broadcast on other channels while not being able to identify with the FM radio broadcasts targeted at young persons. The youngsters of today are moving on from one medium to others and in the process radio seems to have taken the toll. If steps are not taken to improve the messaging on radio, coming generations will completely loose touch with it.

Television

Television is a very popular medium amongst this group. The FGD only validates the high scores achieved by this medium in the survey.

Most of the young people watched Television for 2-3 hours a day and much more on holidays. Girls in Ghaziabad government school watched television more in the afternoons, whereas all other groups preferred evenings or night. Television viewing is not a solitary activity and they all watched television in a family setting. It was found that:

(1) They can vividly recall AIDS related messages appearing on television.
(2) The celebrity endorsement messages (Madhuri Dixit, Shahrukh Khan) had a high recall rate.
(3) They could understand the message but some of them were embarrassed while watching them.
(4) Some girls in Ghaziabad Public school specifically mentioned that they walked out of the room when such advertisements appeared.
(5) Boys and girls in Delhi felt that the condoms advertisements appearing on television were so blatant that AIDS awareness messages were not at all embarrassing. They suggested that condom manufacturers should include AIDS protection as one of the advantages of condom use.
(6) Most of them would not mind more advertisements about AIDS on television but boys in Public school at Delhi wanted to watch English feature films with AIDS as a theme.

Television as a medium wins hands down as far as reach and accessibility is concerned. It is popular amongst all the groups in this study. Recall value of advertisements appearing on television is much more than radio as the visuals contribute a lot to the recall. Celebrity endorsements have always had higher recall value and although the students may not follow the message, they certainly remember it. Since, in our country, television viewing is a family activity, with TV sets occupying prime locations in drawing rooms across the country, explicit AIDS related messages may sometimes evoke embarrassment. The smaller towns boys and girls need more interpersonal interaction to make them come out of their inhibitions.

Delhi boys and girls are more comfortable while discussing the issue. They find AIDS messages very mundane when they compare them to the condom and sanitary napkin advertisements. The age group of the target audience also matters in this case. With increasing age the acceptance of television messages also increased. In the final analysis, it was found that messages on television have high level of recall and viewer ship and they are also accepted better as the audience gets more knowledge.

Newspaper

Newspaper readership was found to be very high amongst all the groups. All the members claimed to read newspapers everyday. They liked the supplements, the cartoons and the Sunday magazines. Some of them mentioned that newspaper reading formed a part of their class activity. Most commonly read newspapers were *The Times of India* and *Hindustan Times*. Some also read Hindi newspapers. Following are the salient findings:

(1) Not many of the members could recall reading about AIDS. Actually, cognitive dissonance plays a major role in interaction with media. AIDS as an issue is not a part of the audience agenda and so when they come face to face with AIDS related messages they just look through them. Messages will have to be designed not only to set the AIDS awareness agenda but also to find a place in the audience agenda.
(2) The full page AIDS messages inserted by NACO every year seemed to have missed this target group altogether.
(3) Human interest stories had high recall with girl students especially when a child was somehow involved.
(4) However, no one could particularly recall any specific message.
(5) Some were aware of a body called NACO, but were not sure where and how they had heard about it.
(6) The target group would prefer to read more about AIDS in the newspapers. Some girls said that since newspaper reading is a solitary activity and not public activity, they could read articles about AIDS without feeling embarrassed.

Cinema

Cinema viewing is a common pastime in this group. They go out with a group of friends after every exam, to celebrate each other's birthdays, on holidays. Some go out for dates to cinema halls. Some members recalled having seen the slides in cinema halls but most of them were of the view that slides do not have high visibility. They would prefer it if

AIDS as an issue could be incorporated in the story. They would not mind the protagonist having AIDS. They felt that the message would reach a wider audience.

Internet

It would be a lapse in judgment if Internet surfing is not included as media habit at this stage. During the survey, Internet had not spread so much but by the time the FGDs were conducted it was found that teenagers are moving on towards this medium. Since this is by far the most interactive medium and caters to the demand almost immediately the possibilities of using this as an appropriate medium should also be tapped. Findings of the FGD were as follows:

(1) Boys and girls in Delhi surfed the net more than the students in Ghaziabad.
(2) The number of net savvy boys was more than the girls.
(3) Those students who owned computers at home and had Internet connections were obviously more net savvy.
(4) Some even mentioned going to one of the cybercafes for using the net.
(5) Some boys mentioned having visited the pornographic sites on the Internet.
(6) Some even mentioned the word cyber sex but were shy to elaborate on it.
(7) No one had hit any AIDS related web site on the Internet.

When asked during the discussion if they knew about any AIDS web sites, they responded that it had not even crossed their minds to check out any AIDS related information on the net.

This clearly implies that people still believe that AIDS is not an issue they should be worried about. Media has a limited role here. Mass media efforts have to be supplemented by the efforts at interpersonal level in order to sensitise people about the disease.

Knowledge about AIDS

They had heard of AIDS and they knew that AIDS had no cure. Public school students from both the cities knew about the Elisa test for AIDS, but only one boy could correctly identify the Western Blot. Girls were as knowledgeable about AIDS except the girls of government school in Ghaziabad. The girls there were very hesitant to speak up in front of the boys and refused to participate in the discussion. They knew that people with AIDS cannot be identified by looks. About methods of AIDS prevention there seemed a lot of confusion. They had all heard about condoms and some has also seen them, although no one mentioned having used them. They showed no fear from AIDS as Ghaziabad girls claimed, that they were 'good' girls. Delhi boys claimed that they were knowledgeable. They were not very forthcoming when asked if they had met anyone of their age who indulges in sex. They were ready to discuss generalities but when it came to specific information, they looked to each other to speak.

Sex Education

Most of the teenagers have discussed sex in school. Although the researcher found that the mode of discussion was very different among boys and girls and also among various age groups. While the younger set (13-14) had just begun to understand sex, they discussed it in hushed tones only among close friends. AIDS could be discussed as a disease, a medical problem more openly. Older boys and girls had a more mature outlook and they had discussed AIDS not only in their peer group but also with older people such as aunts, teacher, mother, and so on. Girls as they grow older show more maturity, as compared to the boys while responding to questions about AIDS/Sex. While VIII class girls in Ghaziabad burst into giggles, VIII class girls in Public school in Delhi maintained composure and treated the issue academically. No one had really discussed the issue with them officially. Most of them had not attended any seminar or workshop.

The students showed keen enthusiasm to learn about the subject. This population already knows quite a lot about the subject as the survey has shown, and the same was visible here too. In VIII class, they are still hesitant but by the time they reach X, XI class, they do not even need to be prompted. They can have intellectual discussions and form their own opinions on the subject. They are open to discussions with teachers, only if moralizing is not made a part of the message. History has also shown that moralizing never works.

This is the age group that needs to be targeted by policy makers. If the threat of an epidemic has to be thwarted, young adults are the people who can do it. They can walk into the adult world armed with information that they need and cultivate behaviours and lifestyle that would lead them to a healthy and informed life. This is possible only if the action is taken immediately.

In the absence of medical defences against AIDS, public education is the only weapon in the fight to limit the spread of HIV infection. With no cure in sight, the only way to combat the spread of AIDS is 'prevention' and this is possible only through information, education and communication, which is a planned effort aimed at creating informed and educated public. Efforts through mass media result in generating awareness and creating a positive ambiance. The press sets the agenda in the minds of the public. This could be the first step towards creating an educated public.

Discussion

The demographic profile reveals that the sample has been distributed amongst all strata of society, with majority belonging to the middle income group. When the Socio-economic Status Indicator was drawn, it was found that maximum number (227) of the students were from the group 2, which is the second last group in the SES order. This would mean that most students were from the middle income group and not the higher or the elite groups. Such a division, arrived at through random sampling, clearly points out towards the population that is there. Since the middle class is the largest class in the society this finding is only appropriate.

The media profile also revealed certain interesting factors—newspaper readership is very low while television viewership is reasonably high. This is a startling finding as all the students come from educated families. The respect that the daily newspaper commands in urban homes across the country seems threatened with this behaviour of future citizens. With the inclusion of children section in the newspapers, perhaps there must have been some improvement in the readership percentage, but the point to worry about is that the sample population is not children population. These are young people who should be reading the regular newspaper. If the *status quo* is maintained, newspapers will have to work harder to cultivate a generation of readers who are as loyal to the medium as their grandfathers had been.

Another medium that seems to be losing ground is the radio. Two decades ago radio listeners could be found across the country with transistors glued to their ears for cricket commentaries or a family collected around the radio set for Binaca Geetmala or Inspector Eagle. Only 79 per cent of the population in the satellite town owns radio sets, while Delhi with the onset of FM radio has a better percentage. The popularity of the radio although on a downhill can be improved with better programming. Nothing can beat this medium with its special quality of mobility. As for the AIDS awareness messages, youngsters of today rate television as the medium that has given them some information. Television with its visuals can provide a clear picture and hence an effective message. Moreover with its extensive reach in this particular group it can spread the message really far. Cinema although popular as a medium has not contributed to AIDS awareness at all. The students also liked to watch films on the television itself making cinema take a back seat.

Media profile of a group as such was quite high and this implies that there is a lot of scope for mass media to use its potential with the target group. Definite relationships have been found between the media profile and socio-economic status and AIDS awareness profile and the city of residence. Keeping in mind these findings messages can be designed for different locations and for various classes of audience. Télevision messages hold special significance as they have shown highest recall in this study, with the best received messages being the celebrity endorsements.

Whatever they have imbibed from various media does not seem enough to give them a clear picture of the situation. While 97.7 per cent students in the metropolis and 84.5 per cent students in the satellite town have heard about AIDS, only 80.8 per cent in the metropolis and 76.9 per cent in the satellite town seemed to have heard any health related message. It is rather puzzling to see that our youngsters do not consider AIDS a health problem. For them the implications of sex and sexual matters related to AIDS stand out. Other implications of AIDS have not yet registered in their minds. The denial stage is very evident in this group. They seem almost certain that they are not at all susceptible to this disease.

The obvious finding here is that metropolitan students have better AIDS awareness profile. Since most interpersonal programmes are carried out in these cities, students hear a lot about AIDS from sundry other sources and not just from television. More discussions in schools, well publicized health melas, international conferences, more hoardings on the main roads, transit messages, messages on bus stops, all this has had an impact on the group, whereas the students in the satellite town are deprived of this type of message onslaught. They seldom discuss AIDS in schools, are wary of talking about AIDS to their parents, are embarrassed when AIDS messages appear on television. This difference in the reach of the messages can prove to be disastrous for the country. India does not reside in the metropolitan cities alone. For all those who live in the far-flung areas, away from any capital cities the situation can be worse. One can safely assume this, just looking at the AIDS awareness profile of the satellite town students (53.25%), who are only a stone's throw away from the capital of India.

Students belonging to public schools and higher socio-economic strata with educated parents have a better AIDS awareness profile. AIDS, however, does not discriminate. HIV can infect anybody and the uninformed are more susceptible. These findings reiterate the need for the messages to be taken to smaller towns, among the lower economic groups and among the uneducated.

The data also reveals that as the students reach higher classes, they are better informed, while it also shows that there is no relationship between media profile and age. This would mean that the increase in awareness about AIDS is not a result of better interaction with media. There are other sources of information at play. A direct implication of this finding would be that younger girls who have the least awareness are the ones who need to be informed. Being thirteen and fourteen is a difficult time for girls. They need much more than just a mass media message. For them, the sex education messages become imperative because they are the most vulnerable group. The myth of a moralistic Indian society already lies shattered and cases of sexual abuse of young girls are on the rise. In such a scenario, this group of young people should be armed with enough knowledge to be able to tackle any unforeseen circumstances. An additional benefit of sex education classes is that the mysterious changes in the body at puberty can be explained to these confused teenagers by an expert whom they can trust. They have revealed in the survey that they want to get more AIDS related information from medical professionals. The girls as they grow show better awareness levels, so much so that they surpass the boys in awareness. This fact has been proved in Delhi as well as Ghaziabad. The young boys, who are going to grow up to be husbands and fathers, need to be shown a direction which they can follow. Young people are gregarious by nature, the need of the hour is to channellise their energies towards the direction of safe sex and no use of drugs. This is not an easy task. Besides, any one agency cannot take up a responsibility as serious as this one. The ambiance of information created by the mass media can be supplemented with more focused inter-personal communication. The students have exhibited a desire to attend seminars, workshops or lectures regarding AIDS. This is a group that is keen to get information. They have been oscillating between peer and porn to get their sex education. The time is ripe to target this group.

Conclusion

Mass Media has changed its form every few years. Change is not something most people look forward to or are particularly good at predicting. Even for inventors and innovators who stimulate technological and social changes, visualizing the future presents an enigmatic problem. The technological changes that are brought about in the media world, have forced the communicologists to rethink their mass media theories. Roger Fidler (1997) calls this process as 'Mediamorphosis' which he defines as 'The transformation of communication media, usually brought about by the interplay of perceived needs, competitive and political pressures, and the social and technological innovations.' New media does not arise on its own but they emerge gradually from the metamorphosis of the old media. When newer forms of communication media emerge, the older forms continue to evolve and adapt. The example of FM's success which transformed radio from a mass audience medium to a niche audience medium can be used to illustrate this principle. The rapid diffusion of TV also brought about significant transformations within the newspaper, magazine and film industries. This also leads us to the concept of mass media convergence, where diverse technologies of media come together. Nicholas Negroponte at MIT was the first to recognize this phenomenon. He predicted that media industries and digital technologies would ultimately lead to new forms of multimedia communication. We are now witness to the phenomenon.

The changes in media are a direct reflection of the changes in the society or *vice versa* is yet to be decided. Media on one hand moulds the society's needs as per its messaging, and on the other hand also reflects the needs of the society through its content. Whatever the case may be, one aspect is certain that mass media gets affected and in turn affects the society through its messages. Mass society theory of media (Mills, 1951, Kornhauser, 1959, Bell, 1961, Bramson, 1961, Giner, 1976,

Beniger, 1986 and Neuman, 1991) emphasises the interdependence of institutions that exercise power and thus the integration of media into sources of social power and authority. Mass society gives a primacy to the media as a causal factor. As, C. Wright Mills (1951) puts it, 'Between consciousness and existence, stand communications, which influence such consciousness as men have of their existence.' How far do our young audience from the target group studied in this work, get affected by media is not certain but it has been proved beyond doubt that they are very media friendly and spend a lot of time with one or the other medium. The young people, are wary of discussing sensitive issues with their parents, but are open to discussion amongst peers. They prefer to have a society of their own.

The invention of the Internet has given rise to a new community. Stephen Doheny-Farina (1996) in 'the wired neighbourhood' expressed it well 'A community is bound by place, which always includes complex social and environmental necessities. It is not something you can easily join. You can subscribe to a community as you subscribe to a discussion group on the net. It must be lived. It is entwined, contradictory, and involves all our senses.' The new generation lives in a dual community. They have online lives and off-line lives. Never before an interaction with the media was so intense as it is now. The convergence of various media has created a generation of youngsters that are not only media savvy but also 'dependent' on a form of media for their interpersonal needs. There should be no mistake about the appreciative 'realness' of the reality encountered online-Internet users have strong emotional attachments to their on line activities. As our horizons have expanded, have they also collapsed on us with a weight that forces us inward on ourselves ? What are the very meanings of 'public' and 'private' in a world where media and events and personalized media coexist? Or to put it in another way, Nguyen and Alexander (1996) claimed that. 'The old mass media were unifying media; they assembled and sustained nations with real time theatre. In cyberspace, there is no centre stage, however, immense, cyberspace time is intensely decentralizing.' The generation that we are talking about in the previous chapters is a generation that cannot imagine life without the Internet. This new medium is as much a part of their lives as television was in the previous generation.

They have grown up seeing the computer. Internet is a medium where mass and interpersonal get intermingled as new societies are formed and new lives are led online. New communities and relationships take shape in front of the computer screen. Net dating, which is fast becoming fashionable provides many routes to emotional satisfaction among the participants, especially the teen aged girls get an opportunity to experiment with and claim power within heterosexual relationships. Internet dating provides an illustration of the pure relationship in its contemporary form. The self-gratification of dating on the net can be seen as a natural outgrowth of current cultural conditions (Jones, G. Steven, 1998).

In the scenario that we face today, with the AIDS threat looming large, relationships amongst youngsters need to be tackled with immense caution. Internet dating provides a safe outlet wherein, no risk is involved. This is the generation that has grown up with AIDS. Just as they have never seen a world without multimedia convergence, they have not seen a world without AIDS. The outcome of this form of self-gratification, is yet to be seen. Will it produce a generation of young people who will not be able to adjust in the 'real' world ? Will they be able to tackle real relationships after the cyber relationships which offer anonymity and no commitment at all ? The need in the present times is to make the youngsters self-reliant, able to take sensible and responsible decisions. In the present survey, adolescents were found to be media savvy, net savvy and considerably knowledgeable about AIDS. They have also acquired their AIDS related information from the media. However, they have also revealed that they want to get more information from medical professionals and other people in authority. This raises the question as to the credibility of the media in the minds of these young people. Do they not trust the media messages with serious information? As it is, the survey found that the newspaper readership was on a decline and television and cinema viewing was high only for entertainment purposes. Does this mean that mass media are utilized only for superficial purposes and not intellectual pursuits? Does it also imply that mass media are taken lightly and are not considered authoritative enough? Considering, the fact that all the groups have come across AIDS related messages in the media and recall them rather vividly, would mean that even if conscience attention was not being paid to the messages they were being registered and remembered. The audience exercise selectivity in not only media and message selection but also in the amount of information imbibed and remembered. Media as is said, provides the frame of reference, for the audience. Westley and Maclean (1957) suggest that some additional elements are needed for a frame of reference. Mass media only act as one of the factors for the creation of a frame of reference while society and its various structures act as contributing factors.

As has already been observed, through the content analysis, that mass media have not yet begun to beam AIDS related messages in a planned manner. Sporadic messages, lacking continuity and regularity are placed in our newspapers and on TV and radio channels with no regard to the readership habits or the viewing habits of the targets. These messages although well designed, lose half their impact because of lack of planning. Golding (1981) in his study of campaigns, helps to distinguish between the concepts of news and its effects. He argued that, intended short term effects, may be considered as 'bias'; unintended short term effects fall under the heading of 'unwitting bias'; intended long term effects indicate 'policy'. The planned diffusion of innovations for the long term development using a series of campaigns and other means of influence, especially the interpersonal network has been seen to spread knowledge over a period of time. Shifts in overall pattern of values, behaviours especially among young people has been observed. Possible weakening of cultural identity may also be an example of this effect. However, the effectiveness of a campaign will depend on the match between planned effects and those achieved. Campaigns also depend on the relationships between the sender and the receiver. Especially important are the moral or effective ties between the audiences and the media, and the audience belief in the media. This makes it imperative for the mass media to plan, campaigns for suitable target groups keeping the knowledge levels, media reach and accessibility in mind. Besides, the interest level of the audience in obtaining that information has also to be considered.

In the study of mass media effects the concept of 'personal influence' has acquired a very high status. The underlying idea of personal influence is a simple one; its originators expressed it in the course of their research in 1940 US Presidential Elections (Lazarsfeld, *et al.*, 1944) as follows: Ideas often flow from radio and print to the opinion leaders and from them to the less active sections of the population. In the context of this study, the two-step flow theory seems just too appropriate. The trust in peer group, and the use of the peer group as source of information has proved beyond doubt that, the two step flow theory is being followed and could be used effectively, in a planned manner, in this case. Direct effects of media can and do occur and the personal influence has the power to reinforce those effects or to counteract them.

AIDS Prevention Campaigns

- AIDS prevention campaigns are mostly a part of a broader education effort designed to accomplish the following objectives.
- Increase general public awareness and knowledge about AIDS, its transmission and risk reduction strategies.
- Reduce general public fears and correct misinformation about the dangers of casual contagion and ordinary social contact with the HIV infected individuals.
- Create support for constructive action by increasing general public understanding of the severity of the crisis, its complexity and costs.
- Reduce the role of HIV transmission/infection by changing the behaviours of at risk individuals.

To meet the above objectives the mass media channels can help in various ways:

1. *Media advertising*: These are paid or public service advertising placed in print, transit, billboards and television and radio.
2. *Press Management*: Most information about AIDS comes from news stories. Finding ways to use news formats to correct misinformation or impart new information is extremely valuable.
3. *Use of feature and other non-news media formats*: Columns, feature stories and electronic talk show formats can often be used to disseminate risk reduction information and other general educational messages.
4. *Pamphlets, videos and collateral materials*: These are materials developed for distribution via mail, for public health care facilities (Mahadevan, K.,1992).

While using mass media for AIDS awareness campaigns, it has to be kept in mind that mass media are not the most effective channels of communication for affecting behaviour change. As we have seen in the present study, young people want to get AIDS related information from authoritative persons. They want to learn about it from people not from machines. They also like to get their knowledge from peers. According to Everett M. Rogers, 'most individuals evaluate an innovation, not on the basis of scientific research by experts but on the basis of subjective evaluation of near peers who have already adopted the innovation.' These peers serve as models whose behaviour is imitated by others in the social system. Thus imitation and social modelling are essential elements in diffusion process. Everett Rogers has described this as the process of social diffusion in terms of 'communication of innovative ideas of practices through certain channels over time among members of a social system.'

Rogers believes that mass media channels of communication are more effective in increasing knowledge of innovations, while interpersonal channels are more effective in changing attitudes and behaviours. This contention has been proved by the present study. While the students do not mind getting information from television specifically, they would want to get their doubts cleared by medical professionals (Rogers, M., 1993). However, studies have shown that television probably exerts a greater influence over adolescent sexual behaviour than sex education programmes, parents and perhaps even the peer group (Strauss and Fabes, 1985).

The task of AIDS prevention, is to access the informal peer group of all target populations. If diffusion theorists are right in asserting that interpersonal communication is the best way to accomplish behaviour change, it follows that AIDS prevention campaigns will be able to accelerate the process of change by providing opportunities for large numbers of, at risk individuals to communicate with one another about AIDS.

One way of configuring the communication is through the use of small groups. Small group processes have been used in almost every conceivable setting over the past few decades to accomplish attitude and behaviour change. If significant number of individuals can be motivated to make a commitment to AIDS risk reduction and to communicate this intention to others, it may be possible to accelerate this process of change. Diffusion theorists believe that once an innovation is accepted by 15-20 per cent of a population it cannot be stopped. At a certain point the process becomes self-generating. This is true because when opinion leaders adopt innovations they influence the opinions of others in their peer network. These newly influenced individuals then diffuse the innovations through their networks, and so on (Lewin, K., 1947). Adolescents deserve special attention because patterns of risk taking behaviours are often established during teenage by targeting this population, protection will be granted not only to youth but future adult population.

Despite the obvious benefits associated with reaching adolescents, less is known about effective interventions for this group than for adults. The programmes designed for adults require modification to accommodate the behavioural, social and developmental diversity found in the adolescent population.

Reaching Adolescents

The earliest messages have relied on threatening messages that evoke high levels of fear. No studies have been conducted to study the impact of such messages. Research suggests, however, that usefulness of frightening and uninformative messages has particular limitations. Ideally, health promotion messages should heighten an individual's perception of threat and his or her capacity to respond to that threat, thus modulating the level of fear. Long term commitment to prevention efforts for adolescents is the need of the hour. It is highly unlikely that one lecture, one public service announcement or exposure to a few brochures will be sufficient to induce and sustain the behavioural changes needed to reduce the risk of HIV transmission among adolescents. AIDS prevention programmes should take advantage of multiple venues and formats of communication to deliver clear, consistent messages about behaviour that risk HIV transmission and the ways in which these risks may be reduced or eliminated.

In addition to information, adolescents may require new skills to apply in conversation, resisting peer pressures to have unprotected sex or to use drugs, and negotiating less risky activities may be more difficult than learning facts about transmission routes of HIV. In the present study the researcher observed certain reservations the students from Ghaziabad displayed during the FGDs. They had never seen a condom, never discussed it, were never told by anyone about sex. Ignorance about the use of condoms as a contraceptive is common to all teenagers that were surveyed. This theoretical knowledge will not help the youngsters in facing the situations that can arise in a young person's life. Sex education programmes in schools should include skill training such as dealing with pressures, a sample of situations that might arise, how to handle sexual overtones in daily transactions, how to use a contraceptive if need arises. They should be demonstrated the situations that can lead to drug use, the kind of peer pressure they might be faced with, most of all how to say no to drugs and use of sterilised needles whenever necessary. Since, young people follow group norms, the task before the communicator is to identify the social or group norms existing in the society and to try and find the opinion leaders from amongst these groups. All programmes that seek to change the behaviour must inevitably confront the diverse and complex social forces that motivate and shape the behaviours for that particular issue. Another benefit of peer led strategy is that it is possible, as demonstrated by the study at hand that teenagers will be more comfortable discussing sensitive issues with peers rather than with adults. In the Indian context, the family is a social group that all youngsters look to when they are ill, it is a source of insurance or money for medical help, but this group cannot be relied exclusively for information about AIDS and related topics.

First, in many cases less parent child communication takes place than is commonly assumed; second, such communication, whether to provide information or to prescribe behaviour, may not be fully heard by the child; and third, communication about sexual matters frequently does not occur until after initiation of sexual activity. Mother's role in sex education is rather minor, especially the more traditionally oriented mothers are, on matters of sexual morality, sex roles etc. the less likely they are to initiate discussions of these topics with their children. During the FGDs the students asked the researcher if such FGDs could be conducted with their parents to 'check out' their information levels. The students wanted the parents to be better informed and more open about the subject. Such findings, may indicate a need for interventions to motivate and assist parents in the difficult and important task of educating their children about the dangers of HIV transmission.

As demonstrated in the survey, teenagers want to get their information from medical professionals, which is a group that has an authoritative standing in the community. It would also not be difficult for the schools to have a doctor coming in once or twice a week for information dissemination and assistance of the youngsters. Adolescent AIDS prevention programmes should be given sufficient class room time and should be viewed as part of an ongoing educational activity rather than a one time event. If school based programmes are to reach and educate students effectively, an informed and supportive group of adults must be developed in adult communities to implement these programmes. Many of today's twenty year olds lack the motivation to change behaviour. They are not terrified of HIV/AIDS (AIDS at 20, Newsweek, June, 2001). In a new survey of six American cities, researchers found that the new face of HIV is young and female. Among 13-19 years old, 64 per cent of HIV positives are women (AIDS at 20, Newsweek, June, 2001).

Efforts to reach young people need to go beyond the schools. Community based organisations can make an effort to reach the out of school youth. Such organisations have credibility within the community, knowledge of local cultural values and beliefs, and knowledge of local channels of communication. Further, inter-personal channels can work best in these groups due to lack of education. The medical professionals at the primary health centres can act as educators. The interventions necessary for this group have to be designed keeping in view the need of the target group. Since these youth have not been studied by this researcher, suggestions for interventions are beyond the scope of this work. For many years the disease was confined mostly to drug users and prostitutes, which made it easier for the rest of the country to pretend that it did not exist. Currently 0.7 per cent of all adults carry the virus in India; health officials consider 1 per cent an epidemic. If the infections are allowed to climb beyond 5 per cent of the adult population, it would be difficult to control the disease later (Mackinnon Ian, Piore Adam, Newsweek, 2001). The youngsters are the target group that needs to be tapped now. The future belongs to the young, who are healthy and strong.

Sex Education

Sex education as a part of population education has greatly received the attention of social and biological scientists for the last three to four decades. The United Nations as part of its activities has instituted the UNFPA (United Nations Fund for Population Activities) funding country projects on school education for imparting population education. Besides, the International Planned Parenthood Federation (IPPF) located in London was the first in the world to initiate population education activities in schools and colleges. Lately, it is concentrating on creating awareness on sex amongst schools, and college students.

In India, the concept of sex education is rather recent. Whenever the decision was taken to include sex education in the curriculum, it was faced with opposition from not only the school system but also from the concerned teachers who had to teach the courses. In the FGDs conducted in the schools the students categorically stated that biology teachers who are assigned the task of sex education just overlook the portion and concentrated only on the theory that comprises the syllabus for the examinations. With renewed efforts from NCERT and NACO, one can look forward to a better informed teenager in the future. NACO had taken up the sex education challenge in its resolution for the year 2001. The success of this programme is yet to be seen.

Sex Education: Historical Perspective

As an educational concern, the subject can be traced back about a century. Carrerra (1971) points out that as early as the 1880s, groups such as American Purity Alliance, the YMCA, the YWCA and the child study association sponsored lectures and panels on sex related topics. He also indicates that the National Educational Association and the National Congress of Parents and Teachers discussed sex education in schools in the early 1890s.

Provision for sex instruction in schools was stimulated by the 1919 White House Conference on Child Welfare, at which it was stated that 'the problem of sex instruction becomes most properly the task of the school'. Two publications were also brought out in the same year by the US government printing office:

1. A high school course in physiology
2. Problems of sex education in schools

Many studies were conducted in the coming decades on the teaching methods, hygiene and health behaviours, and so on. In 1940 the US Public Health Service produced a pamphlet titled 'High schools and sex education', that broadly covered methods, materials, planning, organisation and integration of sex education in many fields. By the 1960s groups were formed both for and against sex education. Such opposition proved to be a hurdle in smooth functioning of the sex education programmes but the Sex Information and Education Council of the United States and the American Association of Sex Educators, Counsellors and Therapists remained strong in their contribution to sex education (Bruess E. Clint, Greenberg S. Jerrod, 1987). Today there is a trend toward more total approach to sex education. This has meant broadening of programme objectives and an obvious emphasis on such things such as 'total person' and decision making as opposed to earlier educational efforts aimed mainly at acquisition of knowledge.

Adolescents: As a Target Group

Derived from the Latin word 'adolescere', the literal meaning of adolescence is apparent. 'To grow to maturity'. The concept of adolescence as a period of life distinct from childhood and adulthood has some rootings in the writings from the distant past. Plato wrote that males under the age of 18 should not be permitted to drink, because 'fire must not be poured on fire'. Likewise, Aristotle conceived of the young as distinct from their elders 'of bodily desires, it is the sexual to which they (young) are most disposed to give way and in regard to sexual desire they exercise no self-restraint'. However, the concept of a period of lifecycle known as adolescence seems to have developed only during the 19th century (Demos and Demos, 1979). Moreover, it is only in the recent decades that both the social significance and the psychological development of adolescents have assumed their present importance. One factor contributing to the dramatic changes affecting adolescents and our evolving views of this developmental period is the transformation that has occurred in size and composition of elementary and secondary schools during the past three decades (Elder, 1980). Not only is the development of the concept of adolescence relatively recent, but the researchers have adopted different theoretical perspectives with regard to the study of adolescent behaviour. These can be categorised as biological, psycho-analytical, cognitive developmental, sociological-anthropological and social learning or behavioural (Mussen, 1970).

The present study can be included as a **behavioural study** of this particular group of people. For the purpose of this study, adolescents have been defined as '**young people between the age of 13 and 17**'. They have been randomly chosen from different settings. No discrimination has been made amongst boys and girls. Media too, needs to tackle gender specific issues carefully. The roles that are socialised in to the public during childhood, as part of the tradition, are perpetuated by the media. These are ways of stereotyping to ensure limited experience and growth. Communication campaigns need to change this *status quo*, and focus on developing media that include women at all levels.

Objectives of this Study

The general objective of the study was to review the role of mass media in AIDS prevention and Control by assessing the AIDS awareness levels and media exposure amongst the target group of school going adolescents. With the help of the survey and the focus group discussions the objective has been fulfilled. The media habits of the target group and the AIDS awareness levels have been discovered and the relationships amongst various variables has also been deducted. The specific objectives of the study, have been fulfilled with a detailed study of the socio-economic and the psychological factors that are associated with the disease and the IEC methods that can be employed to counter the various problems faced by the people with AIDS and their carers. Use of mass media for the purpose of disseminating the message of AIDS has been studied with the help of the time series content analysis of national English daily newspapers. The audio visual media messages have been studied over the period of time through observation method to find out the role played by the media in AIDS prevention.

The media used most favourably for acquiring information about AIDS forms a part of the findings of the survey and the most preferred media for the purpose of getting informed further about AIDS has also been found. Ironically, both the media are different not only in terms of their character but also in their method of dissemination. The findings of the survey have been substantiated by the focus group discussions which have been conducted after the results of the survey were computed. The focus group discussions have provided a deeper insight into the preferences of the target group and individual characteristics of the various groups used for the discussions have added to the information about the target group as a whole.

The study was successful in finding out the most suitable medium and method for AIDS awareness messages for the target group of adolescents.

The Need of the Hour

Responding to HIV/AIDS requires good information. This is particularly important because of the dynamic nature of the disease and the absence of policies on prevention and care programmes that can respond quickly and appropriately to felt needs. The Indian government has already increased its efforts substantially. In 1999, India began the second phase of its programme, tripling the budget to more than US $300 million. In the second phase, public health officials will open hundreds of new clinics and will run TV and radio advertisements. The goal now is to forestall the worst: to keep HIV from reaching 5 per cent of India's adults. When Sub Saharan Africa reached this threshold, the infection rate took off: the graph of new cases was almost vertical (*Newsweek*, June, 2001).

It is hard to imagine how the epidemic will be stopped.The obstacles are legion: illiteracy, poverty, social stigma. In Karnataka, locals have erected a shrine to India's only AIDS Goddess-Aidsamma—at a temple near Mysore (Mackinnon, Ian, Piore, Adam, The other AIDS crisis, *Newsweek*, 2001). In a scenario such as this, information is vital. The drugs cannot be seen as the ultimate solution. The nature of the virus is such that susceptible strains mutate into drug resistant strains. Besides, people who take drugs feel better. They see a decrease in their viral load, become confident that the drug works and then become sexually active. That is the time they may not practice safe sex (Micheal Merson, *Newsweek*, 2001). In order to meet this grim reality in the face and to take up the challange of controlling the spread of, HIV/ AIDS, all sectors of the society will have to respond. The government can help by framing plans and policies favourable for AIDS prevention programmes, the society at large can be more understanding to people with AIDS and be sympathetic to their predicament. On their part the members of the general public, should come out of the denial stage and face the truth, that AIDS does not discriminate. The educators can design suitable syllabus for sex education and help the future generations to lead healthy and informed lives. In the back drop, one institution, will have to work round the clock to bring about all of the above. This institution is the mass media. Mass media products such as Television, Radio, newspapers, magazines and billboards will have to be developed in such a way as to provide access to well defined audiences. Research is used to analyse the size of the audience and to find their profile. This information can be utilised for the telecast or broadcast of the target specific messages.

The study has clarified the importance of mass communication not only as a means of obtaining information but also of sustaining the audience interest in a particular topic. Communication strategies for mass communication range from IEC strategies adopted by the government, various non-government organisations and voluntary agencies to the audience specific programmes such as Universities Talk AIDS, AIDS and sex education in schools, Community Action Network programmes for commercial sex workers and special programmes by various agencies for men who have sex with men (MSMs), drug users, truck drivers and so on. Interwoven amongst all these specialised measures runs a fine thread of communication that reaches all the sections of the society, some more than others. Mass media, with its various means, adaptable to suit any specific target group, caters to all and sundry without restrictions. In its own utilitarian manner, it remains in everyone's selective memory and at least some percentage of these messages are retained by the audience. How far reaching are the effects of this method of communication? Can mass media messages find a place in the public mind? Can the messages related to AIDS compete with other types of programming? Which of the various media is most effective for imparting information related to such a sensitive topic? Do the people get their AIDS related information from the mass media? Do they want to get their AIDS related information from these media? Numerous questions can be raised. These questions need to be answered. The study has attempted to answer some of these questions in relation to one particular target group. For the specific target group of adolescents, who are found to be media friendly, the mass communication messages can create a natural atmosphere for AIDS communication without sensationalising it. Mass media messages have the ability to erase the stigma attached to topics such as AIDS and sex. Communication through the mass media can make AIDS a regular word, sex a non taboo topic and this can encourage healthy discussions about the topic at home and at school.

7

Scope and Limitations of the Study

This study provides relevant information regarding the gravity of AIDS situation in the world as well as in our country. The review and content analysis of the media, provides an insight into the quality and quantity of media messages about AIDS. The IEC strategies outlined in this study can help in designing interventions for HIV/AIDS. An attempt has been made to study the role played by the Indian media in disseminating information regarding AIDS and whether the message is within the reach of the target audiences in physical and psychological terms.

The information regarding the media and AIDS awareness profile is very useful for not only further study in this area but also in a better understanding of the particular target group. This shall help in designing interventions for this group and sending the right message across to the right people through the right medium.

The comparisons between

(a) Metropolis and satellite towns
(b) Public and government schools
(c) Males and females

gives this study a three dimensional perspective. One problem has been looked at from many directions before any conclusions are drawn.

This study can be used as a base for many further researches as the data is available with the researcher in print as well as on floppy. Only the data which was relevant to the objectives of this research was used by this researcher. A veritable data bank is available for further research.

This research is an original one person study. There can be no doubt about the authenticity of this work. A survey of 439 questionnaires, conducted honestly with appropriate research tools enhances the usefulness of the research manifold. Simple statistics of mean and percentages have been used to illustrate the data with correlation's amongst variables where ever necessary, have been used to prove the researcher's hypotheses. This makes the study interesting, reader friendly and easy to understand.

While there is a lot of scope limitations are also present. No study can be flawless. Inadvertently, errors must have slipped into the content analysis or even in the survey. Some amount of bias is also inherent in any study. Presence of artifacts cannot be denied altogether. The researcher has tried her level best to keep the study free of error and bias.

Inherent Disadvantages of Survey Research May Also be Present in this Study

- Variables cannot be manipulated as in laboratory research. Without control over the independent variables, the researcher cannot be sure of the relationship between the dependent and the independent variables.
  A survey may establish that A is related to B but it is impossible to determine from a survey that A is the cause of B. Causality is difficult to establish because of many intervening and extraneous variables involved.
- Wording of questions and their placement in the questionnaire can have biasing effect on survey results.
- A survey is largely dependent on sampling technique.

Other Limitations Could be

- FGD could not be transcribed on tape as the researcher had difficulty in comprehending the contents of the tape.
- Content analysis was limited to one month in each year due to lack of resources.

Suggestions for Further Research

1. The content analysis of the news items can be conducted for a longer duration of time in order to evolve trends in reporting.
2. The audio visual media analysis can be more comprehensive and video tape recorders can be used to record the AIDS related messages and this will lead to better authoritative analysis.

3. Non-school going adolescents also form a very susceptible target group. This group can be used as the sample for study.
4. Little media plays a big role in AIDS awareness. A study can be designed using pamphlets, fliers, bill boards, hoardings etc.
5. Vernacular press plays an important role in reaching people. The AIDS related messages appearing in the vernacular press can be analysed for content analysis.
7. In order to make the questionnaire clearer to Hindi speaking audiences, questions can be added in Hindi also making the questionnaire bilingual.

ANNEXURES

ANNEXURE-I

AIDS Awareness Among Adolescents: An Exploratory Study

Gita Bamezai
Archana R. Singh

Abstract

A Ugandan man aged 32 was asked last year if he had changed his sexual behaviour in the light of information about AIDS. 'Yes', he replied, he had. "I stopped playing sex with prostitutes. I now use schoolgirls."[1] This answer underlines the risk faced by young people in the age of AIDS.

The following study was carried out in Ghaziabad, a neighbouring town of Delhi. Respondents were chosen from 3 English medium schools and from the slum localities of the city. Ghaziabad, being an industrial town employs a large number of young people in the factories. Adolescents who are out in the adult world are more at risk of contacting HIV than those who are cacooned in the security of their families. However, the teenagers who are more at risk were found to be totally ignorant about the disease, having never even heard about AIDS. Mass media exposure of the respondents was also determined. Mass media should take up the social responsibility to spread the AIDS message as it has a vast network and can reach the remotest corners of the country. This study reveals the shocking lack of information about AIDS among adolescents and also emphasizes the use of mass media as a tool to spread the AIDS message.

The Grim Reality

The relentless spread of AIDS in the past few years has dramatically underscored its multi-dimensional socio-economic and health impact.

As of November 1992, over 500,000 AIDS cases had been reported to WHO from over 164 countries. It is, however, estimated that the actual global figure is close to 1.7 million. In addition over 500,000 children are reported to have AIDS. By the year 2000, WHO projections place the cumulative total of HIV infections between 30 and 40 million, while the total of AIDS cases is expected to be between 12 to 18 million.[2] What, in fact, causes deep concern is the explosive increase in the HIV infection rates. By the year 2000, India, which is often referred to as the "sleeping giant" of AIDS will have more AIDS cases than any other nation in the world : about 10 million according to modest estimates.[3]

Socio-economic Impact of HIV/AIDS

AIDS threatens the very fabric of society. It affects people in their productive age, resulting in several direct and indirect costs. Because AIDS incapacitates people at ages when they are most needed for the support of the young and the elderly, the impact on families and the society is enormous. Studies have shown that people in the age group of 20-30 constitute the largest population of HIV infection. The impact of AIDS on society would include enormous health care costs, decimation of work force and loss of skilled labour and educated workforce.

AIDS Education for Adolescents

Since HIV attacks people in the age group of 20-30, and two-thirds of all HIV infections today are due to heterosexual transmission, the importance of AIDS education among adolescents gets highlighted. As adolescents step into their productive age, they should be well armed with the knowledge of HIV and AIDS as well as its mode of transmission. If AIDS education should start in school, sex education has to play an important role in the course curriculum.

HIV is a challenge that requires each of us to reconsider our traditions, morals and values and to respond positively to the pandemic. Rarely is this more evident than when considering the question of how to provide the young people of a community with the knowledge and skills required to protect themselves from HIV infection.

As many families find it difficult to discuss sexual matters at home- and AIDS as a subject on which many parents are not well informed—

the importance of AIDS education in schools and through mass media can scarcely be exaggerated. In many developing countries, more than two thirds of adolescents between the ages of 15 and 19 have had sexual intercourse. At least one fifth of all people with AIDS are in their 20s and the long latency period of the disease means that most of them were infected as adolescents.[4]

In the light of the seriousness of the problem, a need was felt to assess the role of mass media in AIDS awareness amongst the adolescents.

A study was designed with the following objectives:

- To determine the reach of mass media among the adolescents.
- To study mass media exposure amount school going and non-school going adolescents.
- To assess the level of AIDS awareness among teenagers, through sex education and mass communication.

Research Design

With the above objectives in mind, an exploratory study was designed to generate data on the subject. An interview schedule was designed in which open ended questions were asked. The interview covered 50 respondents selected at random from three English medium schools in Ghaziabad and from a slum colony.

To find out about the socio-demographic profile of the respondents, questions relating to their age, marital status, monthly family income, profession and parent's education levels were asked. Mass media reach was measured in terms of their access to television, radio, newspaper, cinema and video. Media exposure was measured on a four point scale ranging from, "Never", "Sometimes", "Often" to "Very Often".

Questions relating to media asked whether media informed them about the problem of AIDS. The study confined itself to the awareness generation as studies have shown that media works as a catalyst for change and gives support to development (Development Support Theory).

Mass Media: A Profile

Print Media : Modern mass media serves functions very similar to those fulfilled by the traditional media in primitive societies. Harold Lasswell has defined three major functions of mass media : Information, Consensus and Entertainment. Newspapers today perform the three functions and a new dimension of agenda setting was added in 1970s. The basic idea of agenda setting — the ability of media to influence the salience to events in the public minds. This impact of the print media as also of the others, the ability to effect cognitive change among individuals, to structure their thinking can be effectively used to prepare public minds for certain issues. Since the mass media provide many facts that make up the cognitive world of each individual, it can play up certain issues and they become significant in the public mind.

In a world full of prejudice and discrimination, a better understanding of how people's attitudes, beliefs and behaviour could be modified in socially approved ways through carefully designed persuasive communication is important. In the learning of new attitudes Carl Hovland and his associates found three variables as important : attention, comprehension and acceptance. The theoretical approach to this could be studies under the stimulus response theory.

In India, the regional and vernacular press has the largest circulation — 42 per cent of the total circulation of newspapers. At least 6-10 per cent of the newspapers trickle into rural areas, particularly where literacy levels are high.[5] In the urban areas, the readership is definitely on the rise despite the onslaught of television and cable networks. Newspapers are still the major source for information and can be used effectively.

Radio

Broadcasting in India has always been considered as a social service, dedicated to the development of the country. Radio broadcasts now reach 90 per cent of homes in India.[5] Simple and repetitive messages can effectively influence the public mind.

Television

Virtually all social scientists have acknowledged that attitudes, values and behaviour of any individual may be developed, at least in part, through observational learning. Television portrayals can both create and reinforce attitudes, values and behaviour. Television with its enthralling visual immediacy gives its audience a feeling of participation far more powerful than any other medium. However, excess of a particular message may have the narcotysing dysfunctional effect as had happened to the serials on Doordarshan based on Punjab. It is hence, important that a proper balance be maintained in telecasting.

Findings

The findings of the study can be divided into two parts viz. (1) The socio-economic data, (2) The mediawise breakup of mass media reach, media exposure of the respondents and the level of AIDS awareness amongst the respondents.

Socio-Demographic Profile

The sample consisted of 50 respondents. Of these 0 per cent were from the schools and 50 per cent were from the slum locality, who were either primary school drop outs of totally illiterate. Table 1.1 shows the complete data.

Mass Media Reach and Exposure

The study reveals that mass media has a fairly good reach among the school going adolescents. With access to channels of communication, literacy and educated set of parent, the school going adolescent is obviously more informed than his less privileged counterpart. Figs. 2.1 and 2.2 depict the exact position of mass media reach and exposure of the respondents. Radio has a good reach — 70 per cent, however it has only 30 per cent of exposure. It is disheartening that a medium with such high availability was not being utilized to its full potential. Cinema, remarkably has 80 per cent reach among the audience. Every teenager, barring 20 per cent who never watched films, used cinema as a mode of recreation.

Television viewing, was concentrated on the urban elite. Only the school going teenagers were regular viewers of television. The slum dwellers collect in front of the singly television set in their locality to watch television entertainment programmes. Only about 10 per cent watch it 'often' and 5 per cent 'sometimes'.

Newspapers were read only by 40 per cent of the respondents and only 20 per cent read them 'often'.

AIDS Awareness Through Media

AIDS awareness is directly related to media exposure and literacy level. It was found that only 10 per cent of the respondents were fully aware of the pandemic and its implications. However, 38 per cent had heard about the disease, as compared to 52 per cent who had never heard about AIDS. 40 per cent of these were from the slums where knowledge of AIDS is negligible.

It was found that the students with educated parents, particularly educated mothers (in case of girls) were more aware of the disease.

Factors associated with high level awareness

School Education + Good media Exposure + Educated Parents → High level of Awareness

Factors associated with low level awareness

Illiteracy + Limited Media Exposure + Low level Parental Education → Low level of Awareness

Discussion

Studies have shown that **AIDS** travels from a small high risk group to a larger low risk group of people. Adolescents constitute a portion of the larger low risk group that is likely to get infected with HIV.

Movement of AIDS

Rapidly developing but small epidemic .... Small high Risk group .... Sex workers, intra-venous drug users with high — Risk group	———→	.... Clients of sex workers housewives, youth adolescents LARGER LOW RISK GROUP Slowly developing persons Risk behaviour but large epidemic.

If adolescents step into their youth with no information about AIDS, the results would be disastrous. Heterosexual activities among the teenagers are on the rise and this is also the time that they can get addicted to drugs. Education about AIDS becomes imperative at this stage.

The strategy for AIDS communication would be through three ways:

1. Sex Education in schools
2. Mass media
3. Interpersonal communication with opinion leaders and health educators.

Sex Education in Schools

Often the challenge of providing AIDS education in schools has been great, because of the sensitive nature of the subject matter. In a report presented by Graham Collier and Kevin Donnelly[6] 5 the following objectives were outlined:

Students passing out of schools should be able to

- Understand the nature of AIDS and its transmission.
- Make informed decisions about behaviour that protects them from AIDS.
- Understand the symptoms of AIDS and seek appropriate medical care when needed.
- Value their own health and relationships free from AIDS.
- Behave personally and socially in ways that eliminate the risk of spreading HIV infections.
- Reject biased information and myths relating to HIV.
- Develop positive attitudes towards those who are infected with HIV.

The results of the experiment show a possible shift in attitude from blaming certain groups for the disease to acceptance of HIV as a virus threatening everyone's life. Sex education could be made a part of a broader programme such as personal development or health education. Teachers have to be trained specially for sex education, because teaching strategies employed in this area are often very different from those used in traditional areas.

It is important that AIDS education in schools be aimed particularly at students younger than the age group likely to have risk behaviour, presenting the subject for the first time at an early age and returning to it in greater detail as the pupils reach sexual maturity. It has been proved that early sex education does not encourage early sexual experimentation as some parents may fear.

The 'Sami Sobie' (Ourselves for Ourselves) experiment in Poland, where female students of midwifery aged 18 and 19 talk about AIDS to school children 11 years upwards, has started a welcome trend in AIDS education. With nursing and midwifery students one can make an army of health educators[7].

As Dr. Mariella Baldo from WHO's Global Programme on AIDS says, "It is a crime to deny information on AIDS to young people. In the age of AIDS, sex is no longer a private matter."

Mass Media

Newspapers

Since mass media has its reach even in the remotest comers of the country, efforts should be made to use it effectively for AIDS education. An exploratory content analysis study conducted by Operations Research Group, Arvind Singhal and Anjali Ram during 1989-90 revealed inadequacy of print media coverage on AIDS in India. The limited coverage was focussed more on clinical diagnostic research on AIDS in western countries, and little on the impending AIDS problem in India. In 1992, the coverage was relatively higher, newspapers were still 'reactive' and not "proactive". Coverage on AIDS can be categorized as apathetic, superficial and generally dismal. (3) Cinema : India is a country where films are watched with passion and involvement and the stars are larger than life. If films starring prominent film stars with a theme on AIDS, were to be produces, AIDS could become the subject of public discussion. With its reach among both the categories of teenagers, this medium should be well exploited in India.

Television

The public in general has a "philosophy of denial" as they believe that any catastrophic illness could never attack one's own family. A powerful medium like television can use its vast influence to perpetuate this myth. One study, indicated that television is thought to be an important source of health information[8] 50 per cent of the teenagers surveyed for this study said that most of what they knew about AIDS had been learnt from television. The best way to introduce AIDS campaign on television is to place it in between prime time programmes of heavy viewer ship.

Interpersonal Communication

As the survey has shown that most of the teenagers who do not go to school, also have no media options open to them. Such teenagers are also largely ignorant and more likely to contact HIV.

Any communication strategy geared to bring about AIDS awareness needs to be articulated at the level of mass as well as interpersonal communication. These channels should compliment as well as supplement one another. It is necessary to channelise public health campaigns *via* existing interpersonal communication networks. Peer Counselling system can be used. For instance, the Sami Sobie system of Poland can be improvised in India with health workers spreading the AIDS message in slums and under-privileged areas. Bright young boys and girls from the slums could be trained to impart knowledge among their peer group and act as Opinion Leaders.

Conclusion

The inadequate knowledge about AIDS amongst our teenagers leads us to believe that mass media should take up the cudgels of AIDS campaign. As cinema reaches teenagers of both the categories, this medium should be exploited. Inter-personal methods are necessary to reach the less privileged section of the society. Sex education has to be imparted at secondary school level.

AIDS pandemic threatens everybody in the world. It does not discriminate between strata of society. Integrated multi media marketing is required to combat the disease. As long as there is no vaccine or remedy for this disease, prevention is the only cure.

REFERENCES

1. World AIDS day features ; WHO No. 2, 1992.
2. Dr. U. Ko Ko, Regional Director, WHO South-East Asia Region, World AIDS Day, 1992.
3. Arvind Singhal and Anjali Ram, *Can the media do more ?* Critique Vol 1 No. 5.
4. WHO programme on AIDS.
5. Keval J. Kumar, *Mass Communication in India*, Jaico Books.
6. Graham Collier and Kevin Donnelly, Introducing AIDS education in schools, AIDS prevention through health promotion: Facing sensitive issues; WHO and Royal Tropical Institute, Amsterdam.
7. AIDS : In the Schoolroom; World AIDS Day Features No. 2 1992.
8. P.V. Miller, A.J. Morrison and F.G. Kline, "Approaches to characterizing Information Environments." Paper presented at the meeting of international Communication Association; New Orleans, 1974.

SOCIO DEMOGRAPHIC DATA T = 50

Status Variable		*% age*	*Number*
Category	School going	50	25
	Non-school going	50	25
Age (In Years)	13-14	8	4
	15-16	60	30
	17-18	30	15
Profession	Student	50	25
	Labour	34	17
	Housewife	8	4
	Own business	8	4
Family Income (monthly)	Upto 500	6	3
	Between		
	500-1000	40	20
	1001-2000	4	2
	2001-3000	10	5
	3001-4000	30	15
	Above 4000	10	5
Parent's Education			
Father	Post-Graduate	40	20
	Graduate	10	5
	High School	8	4
	Below High School	42	21
Mother	Post Graduate	12	6
	Graduate	20	10
	High School	18	9
	Below High School	50	25

AIDS AWARENESS

Status Variable	*Aware*	*Heard About*	*Don't Know*
School Going	5	17	3
Non-school Going	-	2	23

QUESTIONNAIRE.

1. Age:
2. Class:
3. School:
4. Monthly family income:
5. Media Exposure:
   (a) How much average time do you spend with TV per day ?
   (b) Which programme(s) do you watch on TV?
   (c) Which channel do you prefer?
   (d) How much time do you spend with radio?
   (e) Do you read newspapers?
   (f) Have you ever seen an advertisement for AIDS or drug abuse?
   (g) Have you seen any billboard or poster on AIDS or drug abuse ?
   (h) Have you ever seen or read a sex magazine?
   (i) Have you ever watched a blue film?
   (j) How much time do you spend with the VCR in a week?
   (k) Have you seen the advertisements on AIDS on DTC buses?
   (1) Have you ever discussed AIDS or drugs with your friends?
6. AIDS awareness:
   (a) What do you understand by AIDS ?
   (b) How is AIDS transmitted ?
   (c) How is AIDS not transmitted ?
   (d) Can you differentiate between HIV+ and AIDS ?
   (e) How can AIDS be prevented ?
   (f) Have you ever indulged in any type of sexual behaviour ?
7. Drug abuse:
   (a) Can you name any drugs commonly used by drug addicts ?
   (b) Have you ever seen a drug addict ?
   (c) Have you ever seen a 'drug' ?
   (d) Have you ever met a drug vendor ?
   (e) Do any of your friends take drugs ?

8. Sex Education
   - (a) Do you have a class on sex education in school ?
   - (b) Has any teacher talked to you about correct sexual behaviour ?
   - (c) Have your parents talked to you about sexual behaviour ?
   - (d) Have you discussed sexual behaviour with your friends ?

ANNEXURE-II

Pre-Test Questionnaire

The Questionnaire consists of both close-ended and open-ended questions. In order to collect qualitative data Focus Group Discussion will be conducted.

The Questionnaire consists of 4 categories. The first category will seek to elicit personal information about the respondent (Age, Income etc.). The second category will elicit information about the media seeking habits of the respondents. The third will gather information regarding knowledge and awareness about AIDS/HIV.

Thus the questionnaire will be divided into following criteria:

1. Demographic levels
2. Exposure to media:
   (a) Radio
   (b) Television
   (c) Print Media
   (d) Personal media
3. Knowledge of AIDS/HIV

Reference:

1. Draft Survey Questionnaire for assessing the knowledge, attitude and practice of students, involved in the Universities Talk AIDS project in India, 1994.
2. A study of AIDS awareness among adolescents in the city of Madras – An MCRC study.
3. Study of AIDS knowledge awareness and behaviour among college students in Bihar, Madhya Pradesh and Rajasthan – A UTA-MCRC study. All the questions included in the questionnaire have been tested on similar large groups in various parts of the country.

QUESTIONNAIRE

I. Demographic Data

1. Age
   1. 14 yrs. 2. 15 yrs. 3. 16 yrs.
2. Sex
   1. Male 2. Female
3. Which class do you read in ?
4. Your religion
   1. Hindu 2. Muslim
   3. Christian 4. Any other
5. Mother tongue
6. Educational level of mother:
   1. Middle 2. Matric
   3. Graduate 4. Post-graduate
7. Professional Degree
8. Educational level of father:
   1. Middle 2. Matric
   3. Graduate 4. Post-graduate
9. Professional Degree
10. Father's occupation
11. Mother's occupation
12. Place of residence
13. Family Income (per month)
    1. Up to Rs. 1500 2. Rs. 1501 to 3000
    3. Rs. 3001 to 5000 4. Rs. 5001 to 8000
    5. Rs. 8001 to 10,000 6. Rs. 10,000 and above
14. Type of family:
    1. Joint 2. Nuclear

II. Media Seeking Habits

15. Do you own/subscribe at home (Tick all the applicable options)

News-paper	Magazine	T.V.	Radio	V.C.R./V.C.P	Audio Cassette Recorder

16. Do you listen to the radio ?
    1. Yes 2. No
17. Where do you listen to the radio ?
    1. Home 2. Friend's House
    3. Neighbour 4. Shops
    5. Buses 6. Any other
18. When do you listen to the radio and for how much time?

	Less than 1 Hour	1-2 hours	2-3 hours	3 & above hours
(i) Morning				
(ii) Afternoon				
(iii) Evening (5 to 8 p.m.)				
(iv) Night (8 and above)				

19. Which programmes do you listen to on radio and on which channel? Give order of preference for each.

Programmes	*Channels*
(1) Hindi film music	(1) Vividh Bharti
(2) Film based programme	(2) FM Radio
(3) Radio drama/serials	(3) B.B.C.
(4) News	(4) Any other
(5) English music	
(6) Youth programmes	
(7) Any other	

20. Which is your most favoured radio programme and why?
21. Do you watch T.V.?
    1. Yes 2. No
22. When do you watch T.V. and for how much time?

	Less than 1	1-2	2-3	3hrs above
(i) Morning				
(ii) Afternoon				
(iii) Evening (5 to 8 p.m.)				
(iv) Night (8 and above)				

23. On which channel do you mostly watch programmes?
    1. National Network 2. Metro 3. Any other
24. Do you watch programmes on cable?
    1. Yes 2. No

25. Which programmes do you watch on which channel (Give the order of preference for each)

Programme	*Channels*
(1) Films Songs	(1) Star
(2) Serials	(2) BBC
(3) Feature films	(3) MTV
(4) Film based programme	(4) Prime Sports
(5) Talk shows	(5) CNN
(6) Interviews	(6) Video
(7) Any other	(7) Zee T.V.
	(8) Any other

26. Which is your most favoured T.V. programme and why?
27. Do you read the daily newspaper?
    1. Yes   2. No
28. If yes, which paper do you read and in what language?
    1. Name of the paper   2. Language
29. What type of articles do you read in the newspaper?
    1. News   2. Metro page   3. Sport
    4. Sunday magazine   5. Cartoons
    6. Features/Stories   7. Advertisements
30. Do you read any magazine or journal?
    1. Yes   2. No
31. If yes, kindly name them in your order of preference:
    (1)   (2)   (3)   (4)
32. What type of articles do you read in the magazines?
    1. Stories   2. Features   3. News
    4. Film   5. Interviews   6. Any other
33. How much time do you spend with the newspaper everyday?
    1. Less than ½ hour   2. ½ hour   3. 1 hour
    4. 2 hours   5. More than 2 hours
34. Do you watch films?
    1. Yes   2. No
35. Do you go to the cinema hall?
    1. Yes   2. No
36. How often do you go to the cinema hall?
    1. Once a month   2. Twice a month
    3. Thrice a month   4. Four times a month
    5. Once in 2 months   5. Once in 3 months
37. Who is your favourite? Name them.
    1. Actor   2. Actress

38. How many times do you watch the video?
    1. Once a month   2. Twice a month
    3. Thrice a month   4. More than thrice a month
39. Do not watch video.
40. How much time do you spend listening to audiocassettes?
    1. Less than one hour   2. 1-3 hours
    3. More than three hours   4. Do not listen everyday

III. Knowledge About AIDS

41. Have you ever come across a health related message on any media?
    1. Yes   2. No
42. If yes, what was the health problem?
43. Did any message pertaining to health recommend a change in any behaviour to avoid a health problem?
    1. Yes   2. No
44. Have you heard about AIDS?
    1. Yes   2. No
45. If yes, how did you first hear about AIDS?
    1. From Friend   2. From class fellows   3. Teacher
    4. Newspaper   5. Printed Material   6. Radio
    7. Television   8. Billboards
    9. Other sources (define)
46. AIDS is caused by:
    1. Virus   2. Bacteria
    3. Germs   4. Any other
47. Which statement is true:

	True	False	Don't know
1. AIDS affects Mean only	☐	☐	☐
2. AIDS affects Women only	☐	☐	☐
3. AIDS only affects Non-Indians	☐	☐	☐
4. AIDS only Effects prostitutes	☐	☐	☐
5. AIDS can affect Children	☐	☐	☐
6. AIDS can affect Men, women & children	☐	☐	☐

48. How is AIDS transmitted

	True	False	Don't know
1. AIDS can be contracted by touching the body of the person who has AIDS	☐	☐	☐
2. By sharing food and drinks with a person who has AIDS	☐	☐	☐
3. By kissing a person who has AIDS	☐	☐	☐
4. A pregnant woman with HIV/AIDS can pass the virus to her unborn child	☐	☐	☐
5. By sharing syringes for injecting drugs with person who has HIV/AIDS	☐	☐	☐
6. By wearing clothes of the infected person	☐	☐	☐
7. By having protected sex with a prostitute	☐	☐	☐
8. By having unprotected sex with a person who is infected with AIDS	☐	☐	☐
9. By being bitten by a mosquito or other blood sucking insect	☐	☐	☐
10. Through blood transfusion	☐	☐	☐
11. By receiving blood from HIV +ve person	☐	☐	☐
12. An HIV infected mother can pass the virus to her infant through breast-feeding	☐	☐	☐
13. Through the use of common toilet			
14. By sharing utensils			
15. One can get HIV/AIDS			

even if he/she has under gone sterilisation

16. By men having unprotected sex with men
17. By having unprotected sex with many partners
18. Have you heard about HIV?
    1. Yes 2. No
19. Can you tell a HIV +ve person by the way he/she looks?
    1. Yes 2. No
20. AIDS is
    1. Curable 2. Non-curable
    3. Preventable 4. Non-preventable
21. Are you aware of any test to detect HIV infection?
    1. Yes 2. No
22. If yes, which of the following is a test for HIV?
    1. Elisa 2. Barium Milk
    3. Western Blot 4. Biopsy
    5. Cat-scan
23. I am afraid of getting AIDS
    1. Yes 2. No 3. Don't know
24. I am not the kind of person who can get AIDS
    1. Yes 2. No 3. Don't know
25. What do you know about condom?

	Yes	No	Don't know
(a) Have you seen a condom			
(b) Have you used a condom			
(c) Condom is a family planning method			
(d) Condom reduces sexual pleasure			
(e) Condoms are very costly			
(f) Condoms can prevent AIDS			

IV. Sex Education

49. Have you ever-discussed sex or AIDS in the classroom.
50. With whom?

51. Have you ever been told about sex or AIDS by
    1. Teachers 2. Counsellors
    3. Visiting Lecturer
52. Have you ever attended a seminar, lecture or workshop on AIDS?.
53. Would you like to attend a AIDS related programme?
54. From whom would you prefer to get information about AIDS (Rank in order of preference)
    1. Teachers 2. Friends 3. Parents
    4. Counsellors 5. Medical Professionals
    6. Television 7. Film 8. Radio
    9. Newspaper

ANNEXURE-III

Final Questionnaire

Dear Respondent,

I am a student of Mass Communication Research Centre, Jamia Millia Islamia. This survey is being conducted as part of my Ph.D. programme. The information provided in this questionnaire will only be used for research purpose and will not be disclosed to anybody for any other purpose.

Your frank responses to the questions will be highly appreciated.

Thanking you for your cooperation.

Yours sincerely,

(Archana R. Singh)

Questionnaire No.: ☐ ☐ ☐
Place of Survey: ☐
Date of Survey:

QUESTIONNAIRE
ON
STUDY OF AIDS AWARENESS AND MASS MEDIA REACH AMONGST ADOLESCENTS IN DELHI AND GHAZIABAD

Note: Option numbers given below the questions may be treated as code Numbers, unless instructed otherwise.

I. Demographic Data/Profile

1. Age (as on last birthday) ☐ ☐

Enter the real age in years in corresponding boxes.

2. Sex:
   1. Male 2. Female
3. Which class do you read in ?
   Enter the class in real numbers in corresponding boxes.
4. Which religion do you belong to ?
   1. Hindu 2. Muslim
   3. Christian 4. Sikh
   5. Any other
5. Mother tongue:
   1. Hindi 2. English
   3. Punjabi 4. Urdu
   5. Marathi/Gujrati
   6. Tamil/Telugu/Kannada/Malayalam
6. Educational level of mother:
   1. Middle 2. Matric
   3. Graduate 4. Post-graduate
   5. Professional Degree
7. Educational level of father:
   1. Middle 2. Matric
   3. Graduate 4. Post-graduate
   5. Professional Degree
8. Mother's occupation:
   1. Housewife 2. Teaching
   3. Professional 4. Govt. Service
   5. Any Other (Please Specify)
9. Father's occupation:
   1. Professional 2. Govt. Service
   3. Business 4. Public Sector
   5. Any other (Please Specify)
10. Family Income (per month in Rupees)
    Enter the Figure in the corresponding boxes
11. Type of family:
    1. Joint 2. Nuclear
    3. Any other (Please Specify)

II. Media Seeking Habits

12. Do you own/subscribe at home (Tick all the Applicable options)

News-Paper	Magazine	T.V.	Radio	V.C.R./ V.C.P.	Audio Cassette Recorder
☐	☐	☐	☐	☐	☐

13. Do you listen to the radio ?
    1. Yes   2. No
14. (a) If yes, when do you listen to the radio and for how much time ?
    Mention numbers of minutes in corresponding boxes.
    1. Hour = 60 Minutes, 1.5 Hours = 90 Min., 2 Hours = 120 Min.
    2.5 Hours = 150 Min., 3 Hours = 180 Min.
    (In case you do not listen to the radio in a specific session fill 0,0,0 in the corresponding boxes.
    (i) Morning ☐ ☐ ☐
    (ii) Afternoon ☐ ☐ ☐
    (iii) Evening 5 to 8 p.m. ☐ ☐ ☐
    (iv) Night 8 and above ☐ ☐ ☐
14. (b) Total number of minutes of radio listening ☐ ☐ ☐
15. (a) Which programmes do you listen to on radio ?   (b) Which channel do you prefer ?
    Kindly give order of preference (1 for most preferred item, 2 for next and so on.)

Programmes		*Channels*	
(1) Hindi film music	☐	(1) Vividh Bharti	☐
(2) Film based programme	☐	(2) FM Radio	☐
(3) Radio drama/serials	☐	(3) Foreign Channel	☐
(4) News	☐	(4) Any other	☐
(5) English music	☐		
(6) Youth programmes	☐		
(7) Any other	☐		

16. Which is your most favoured radio programme and why ?

17. Do you watch T.V. ?
    1. Yes 2. No ☐
18. (a) If yes, when do you watch the Television and for how much time ?
    Mention numbers of minutes in corresponding boxes.
    .5 Hr=30 Min, 1 Hr=60 Min., 1.5 Hrs.=90 Min., 2 Hrs.=120 Min.
    2.5 Hrs=150 Min., 3 Hrs. = 180 Min.
    (In case you do not watch the T.V. in a specific session fill 0,0,0 in the corresponding boxes).
    (i) Morning ☐ ☐ ☐
    (ii) Afternoon ☐ ☐ ☐
    (iii) Evening
    5 to 8 p.m.
    (iv) Night ☐ ☐ ☐
    8 and above
    (b) Total number of T.V. viewing hrs. ☐ ☐ ☐
19. On which channel do you mostly watch programmes ?
    1. National Network
    2. Metro
    3. Any other
    (please specify) ☐
20. Do you watch programmes on cable ?
    1. Yes 2. No ☐
21. Which programmes do you watch (a) on Television — Which channel do you (b) prefer
    (Please give order of preference, 1 for most preferred item 2 for next and so on.)

Programme		*Channels*	
Films Songs	☐	Star	☐
Serials	☐	BBC	☐
Feature Films	☐	MTV	☐
Film based programme	☐	Sports channels	☐
Talk shows	☐	CNN	☐
Interviews	☐	Movie channels	☐
Any other	☐	Zee T.V.	☐
(Please specify)		Metro	☐
National Network	☐	Sony	☐

22. Which is your favourite T.V. programme and why ?
23. Do you read the newspaper ?
    1. Daily 2. Occasionaly 3. Never ☐
    (a) If yes, which paper do you read and in what language ?
        1. Name of the paper
        2. Language
    (b) What type of articles do you read in the newspaper ?
        News ☐
        Metro page ☐
        Sport ☐
        Sunday magazine ☐
        Cartoons ☐
        Features/Stories ☐
        Advertisements ☐
24. How much time do you spend with the newspaper everyday ? (Give answer in minutes in the corresponding boxes.)
    2.5 Hrs. = 150 Min., 3 Hrs=180 Min.
25. Do you read any magazine or journal ?
    1. Yes 2. No ☐
26. If yes, which language do you prefer ?
    1. English
    2. Hindi
    3. Any other ☐
       (Please specify)
27. Please name the magazine in your order of preference:
    (1) (2) (3) (4)
28. What type of articles do you read in the magazines ?
    Stories ☐
    Features ☐
    News ☐
    Film ☐
    Interviews ☐
    Any other ☐
    (Please specify)
29. Do you watch films ?
    1. Yes 2. No ☐
30. Where do you prefer to watch films ?
    1. Cinema Halls 2. Video ☐
    3. Television
    (Why, please explain)

31. How often do you go to the cinema hall ? ☐
    1. Once a month — 2. Twice a month
    3. Thrice a month — 4. Four times a month
    5. Once in 2 months — 6. Once in 3 months
    7. Never
32. How many times do you watch films on the video ? ☐
    1. Once a month — 2. Twice a month
    3. Thrice a month — 4. More than thrice a month
    5. Do not watch video
33. How much time do you spend listening to audio cassettes ? ☐
    1. Less than 1 hour daily — 2. 1-2 hours daily
    3. 2-3 hours daily — 4. Occasionally
    5. Do not listen

III. Knowledge about AIDS

34. Have you ever come across a health related message on any media ?
    1. Yes — 2. No ☐
35. If yes, what was the health topic ?
36. Did any message pertaining to health recommend a change in any behaviour to avoid a health risk ?
    1. Yes — 2. No ☐
37. Have you heard about AIDS ?
    1. Yes — 2. No ☐
38. If yes, how did you first ' ear about AIDS ?
    1. From friend — 2. From class fellows
    3. Teacher — 4. Newspaper
    5. Printed Material — 6. Radio
    7. Television — 8. Billboards
    9. Other sources (define)
39. Can you recall an AIDS related message in the newspaper ?
    1. Yes — 2. No ☐
40. If yes, please describe the message.
41. Can you recall an AIDS related message on the radio ?
    1. Yes — 2. No ☐
42. If yes, please describe the message.
43. Can you recall an AIDS related message on television ?
    1. Yes — 2. No ☐
44. If yes, please describe the message.

45. AIDS is caused by:

1. Virus	2. Bacteria	☐
3. Germs	4. Any other (Please specify)	

46. Which statement is true:

	True	False	Don't know
1. AIDS affects men only	☐	☐	☐
2. AIDS affects women only	☐	☐	☐
3. AIDS only affects Non-Indians	☐	☐	☐
4. AIDS only affects prostitutes	☐	☐	☐
5. AIDS can affect Children	☐	☐	☐
6. AIDS can affect men, women & children	☐	☐	☐

47. How is AIDS transmitted

	True	False	Don't know
1. AIDS can be contracted by touching the body of the person who has AIDS	☐	☐	☐
2. By sharing food and drinks with a person who has AIDS	☐	☐	☐
3. By kissing a person who has AIDS	☐	☐	☐
4. A pregnant woman with HIV/AIDS can pass the virus to her unborn child			
5. By sharing syringes for injecting drugs with person who has HIV/AIDS	☐	☐	☐
6. By wearing clothes of the infected person.	☐	☐	☐

7. By having unprotected sex with multiple partners. ☐ ☐ ☐
8. By having protected sex with a person who is infected with AIDS ☐ ☐ ☐
9. By having unprotected sex with a person who is infected with AIDS ☐ ☐ ☐
10. By homosexual relations amongst men. ☐ ☐ ☐
11. By being bitten by a mosquito or other blood sucking insect ☐ ☐ ☐
12. Through blood from an HIV+ person. ☐ ☐ ☐
13. By receiving blood from an HIV+ person ☐ ☐ ☐
14. An HIV infected mother can pass the virus to her infant through breast feeding. ☐ ☐ ☐
15. Through the use of common toilet. ☐ ☐ ☐
16. By sharing utensils ☐ ☐ ☐
17. You can get HIV/AIDS even after sterilisation ☐ ☐ ☐

48. Can you tell a HIV +ve person by the way he/she looks. ☐
1. Yes 2. No

49. AIDS is ☐
1. Curable 2. Non-curable
3. Preventable 4. Non-preventable

50. Are you aware of any test to detect HIV infection ? ☐
1. Yes 2. No

51. If yes, which of the following is a test for HIV ?
1. Elisa 2. Barium Milk
3. Western Blot 4. Biopsy
5. Cat-scan ☐

52. I am afraid of getting AIDS
1. Yes 2. No 3. Don't know ☐

53. I am not the kind of person who can get AIDS
    1. Yes 2. No 3. Don't know
54. Have you heard of sexually transmitted diseases ?
    1. Yes 2. No 3. Don't know
55. In your opinion school going adolescents indulge in sex
    1. Yes 2. No 3. Don't know
    If yes, please mention
    1. Regularly 2. Frequently 3. Rarely
56. Adolescents are aware of the purpose of condoms
    (Tick the right answer)
    1. As contraceptive
    2. Used to prevent AIDS
    3. Used to prevent sexually transmitted disease.
    4. Any other (please specify)
    Are adolescents aware of the concept of safer sex ?
    1. Yes 2. No 3. Don't know

IV. Sex Education

57. Have you ever discussed sex or AIDS in the school ?
    1. Yes 2. No
58. If yes, with whom ?
    1. Classmates 2. Friends
    3. Teacher 4. Counsellor
    5. Any other (please specify)
59. Have you ever been told about sex or AIDS by any of the following:
    1. Teachers 2. Counsellors
    3. Visiting Lecturer 4. Parents
    5. Any other (please specify)
60. Have you ever attended a seminar, lecture or workshop on AIDS ?
    1. Yes 2. No
61. Would you like to attend an AIDS related programme?
    1. Yes 2. No
62. From whom would you prefer to get information about AIDS (Rank in order of preference, 1 for the most preferred source, 2 for the next and so on.)
    Teachers
    Friends
    Parents

Counsellors ☐
Medical Professionals ☐
Television ☐
Film ☐
Radio ☐
Newspaper ☐

Thank you for your co-operation.

ANNEXURE-IV

Schedule for FGD

Focus Group Discussion on AIDS awareness and mass media exposure among school going adolescents in Delhi and Ghaziabad.

I. Introduction

(a) What do you do in your free time ?
(b) Do you go out with your friends ?
(c) Where do you usually go with your friends ?
(d) Do your friends go out for dates?

II. Media Seeking Habits

SECTION ONE

(a) Do you listen to the radio?
(b) If yes, how many hours and when?
(c) What type of programmes do you like ?
(d) Have you ever heard any AIDS related message ?
(e) Could you understand /comprehend the message ?
(f) Do you want to hear more about AIDS on radio?
(g) Can you recall any specific advertisement on the radio ?

SECTION TWO

(a) Do you watch TV ?
(b) When do you watch TV ?
(c) How many hours of TV do you watch ?
(d) Which is your favourite TV programme?
(e) Have you ever watched any AIDS message on TV ?
(f) Can you recall the message.

(g) Could you understand the message?
(h) Would you like to hear more about AIDS on TV ?

SECTION THREE

(a) Do you read the newspapers ?
(b) Which papers do you like to read ?
(c) Have you ever read about AIDS in your newspaper ?
(d) Do you remember the message ?
(e) Would you like to see more messages about AIDS in the newspapers ?

SECTION FOUR

(a) Do you watch films?
(b) At home or in the theatre?
(c) Have you ever seen AIDS related messages in the cinema hall ?
(d) Can you recall the message ?
(e) What if the hero or the heroine had AIDS in the film ? What would be your reaction ?

SECTION FIVE

(a) Do you surf the net?
(b) How much time do you spend surfing the net ?
(c) Have you ever hit an AIDS related web site ?
(d) Did you get sufficient information ?
(e) Would you like to know more?

III. Knowledge about AIDS

(a) Have you heard about AIDS ?
(b) Is it curable ?
(c) Can you identify a person with AIDS just by looking at him or her ?
(d) Is there a test for AIDS ?
(e) Can you name one ?
(f) Can AIDS be prevented?
(g) How can AIDS be prevented ?
(h) Do you know how AIDS is transmitted ?

(i) Are you afraid of getting AIDS ?
(j) Have you ever met a teenager who indulges in sex ?
(k) Do you know what is a condom ?

IV. Sex Education

(a) Have you ever discussed sex/AIDS in school ?
(b) With whom have you discussed sex/AIDS in school ?
(c) Has anyone ever told you about AIDS ?
(d) Have you ever attended a seminar, lecture, workshop regarding the subject ? Would you like to attend one ?
(e) From whom would they like to receive information about AIDS ?

Chi Square Tables

df	0.10	0.05	0.025	0.01	0.005	0.001
1.	2.71	3.84	5.02	6.63	7.88	10.83
2.	4.61	5.99	7.38	9.21	10.60	13.82
3.	6.25	7.81	9.35	11.34	12.84	16.27
4.	7.78	9.49	11.14	13.28	14.86	18.47
5.	9.24	11.07	12.83	15.09	16.75	20.51
6.	10.64	12.59	14.45	16.81	18.55	22.46
7.	12.02	14.07	16.01	18.48	20.28	24.32
8.	13.36	15.51	17.53	20.09	21.95	26.12
9.	14.68	16.92	19.02	21.67	23.59	27.88
10.	15.99	18.31	20.48	23.21	25.19	29.59
11.	17.28	19.68	21.92	24.73	26.76	31.26
12.	18.55	21.03	23.34	26.22	28.30	32.91
13.	19.81	22.36	24.74	27.69	29.82	34.53
14.	21.06	23.68	26.12	29.14	31.32	36.12
15.	22.31	25.00	27.49	30.80	32.80	37.70
16.	23.54	26.30	28.85	32.00	34.27	39.25
17.	24.77	27.59	30.19	33.41	35.72	40.79
18.	25.99	28.87	31.53	34.81	37.16	42.31
19.	27.20	30.14	32.85	36.19	38.58	43.82
20.	28.41	31.41	34.17	37.57	40.00	45.31
21.	29.62	32.67	35.48	38.93	41.40	46.80
22.	30.81	33.92	36.78	40.29	42.80	48.27
23.	32.01	35.17	38.08	41.64	44.18	49.73
24.	33.20	36.42	39.36	42.98	45.56	51.18
25.	34.38	37.65	40.65	44.31	46.93	52.62
26.	35.56	38.89	41.92	45.64	48.29	54.05
27.	36.74	40.11	43.19	46.96	49.65	55.48
28.	37.92	41.34	44.46	48.28	50.99	56.89
29.	39.09	42.56	45.72	49.59	52.34	58.30
30.	40.26	43.77	46.98	50.89	53.67	59.70
40.	51.81	55.76	59.34	63.69	66.77	73.40
50.	63.17	67.50	71.42	76.15	79.49	86.66
60.	74.40	79.08	83.30	88.38	91.95	99.61
70.	85.53	90.53	95.02	100.43	104.21	112.32
80.	96.58	101.88	106.63	112.33	116.32	124.84
90.	107.57	113.15	118.14	124.12	128.30	137.21
100.	118.50	124.34	129.56	138.81	140.17	149.45

*** Table generated in Excel using = CHIINV (alpha, *df*).**

Bibliography

Agee, Warren K., Ault, Phillip H., Emery, Edwin, (1985). *Introduction to Mass Communications*, New York, Harper & Row.

Ahmad, S. I., (November, 1992). "Truck drivers as vulnerable group in north east India", Second International Congress on AIDS in Asia and the Pacific, New Delhi (abstract no. D624).

AIDS Division, Ministry of Public Health (2000). "HIV/AIDS in Thailand up to April 30, 2000". AIDS Education and Prevention 9 (2):147-160.

AIDS at 20,(June11, 2001). *Newsweek, the International Newsmagazine*, 251 West 57th Street, New York.

Akarasewi, Khanchit Limpakarnjanarat, Phillip Nieburg, and Timothy Mastro (1996). "Rapid increase in HIV-related tuberculosis, Chiang Rai, Thailand, 1990-94". *AIDS* 10 (5) : 527-531.

Alexander, C., S., Kim Y., J. Ensminger, M., Johnson K., E., Smith, B., J. and Dolan, L., J., (1990) A measure of risk taking for the young adolescents: reliability and validity assessments. *Journal of Youth and Adolescence*,19 (6), 559-569.

Altschull, J.H., Weaver, M., Benedict, T.E. (1984). *Agents of Power: The Role of News Media in Human Affairs*. New York: Longman.

Apuuli Kihumuro, David N., (2001). *Uganda HIV/AIDS*, Uganda AIDS Commision, The Republic of Uganda, Project ID UGPE 72482.

Asia Harm Reduction Network. Country Reports: Thailand. August 25, 1999.

Balmer, D.H., (1994). The phenomenon of adolescence. An ethnographic inquiry NARESA Monogram No. 4, Nairobi.

Bamezai, G., Singh, R.A., (1993). "AIDS awareness among adolescents: An exploratory study," Paper presented at the Regional Conference on Adolescent Health, AIIMS, New Delhi 1993.

Bamezai, G., Shukla, A., (1998). The impact of enter educate radio broadcasts in promoting AIDS awareness among the youth: A case study of FM radio's broadcasts to promote AIDS awareness among the youth in New Delhi, in Youth and the global media; papers from the 29th University of Manchester Broadcasting Symposium, 1998. (Sue Ralph, J, Langham Brown, Tim Lees, Marjorie Burton, Edward Burton, eds.); University of Luten Press, U.K.

Bandura, A. (1992). A social cognitive approach to the exercise of control over AIDS infection. R.J. DiClemente (ed.), *Adolescents and AIDS*, (pp. 89-116) Newbury Park, CA: Sage.

Basch, C. E., (1987). Focus Group Interview: An underutilised research technique for improving theory and practice in health education, in *Health Education Quarterly*, Vol 14: 4, pp. 411-448.

Behrens, G.M., M. Stoll and R.E. Schmidt (2000). "Lipodystrophy syndrome in HIV infection: what is it, what causes it and how can it be managed?" *Drug Safety* 23 (1): 57-76.

Bell Douglas, Feraios Andrew, Bryan Tanis, (1990). 'Adolescent Males, knowledge and attitudes about AIDS in the context of their social world,' *Journal of Applied Social Psychology*: 424-448.

Berelson, B. (1949). 'What missing the newspaper means' in P.F. Lazarsfeld and F.M.Stanton (eds), *Communication Research 1948-49*, New York: Duell, Sloan and Pearce.

Besharov, D.J., (1993). Risk and realism: teen sex. *The American Enterprise*, March/April 52-59.

Besharov, D.J. and Gardner K.N., (1993). Truth and consequences; teen sex. *The American Enterprise*, Jan-Feb, 52-59.

Bidwai Prafulla (2001). Death Warrant for four million, Article appeared on the edit page, *Hindustan Times*, 17th August.

Bien, Darl D. (2000). "Thai Red Cross Program to prevent transmission of HIV from mother to infant: Cost-effectiveness and sensitivity analysis". Unpublished manuscript, University of Denver, USA.

Black R. Thomas (1990). *Doing quantitative research in the social sciences*, London, Sage.

Blix, O. and L. Gronbladh (1988). "AIDS and IV Heroin Addicts: The preventive effect of methadone maintenance in Sweden". Paper presented at the Fourth International Conference on AIDS, Stockholm.

Brown, P., (1992). AIDS in the media. In: Mann, J., Tarantola, D.,(eds). AIDS in the World. Cambridge, Harvard University Press.

Brown, W.J., Singhal, A., Rogers, E.M., (1989). Prodevelopment soap operas, *Media development*, 4: 43-7.

Brown Jane D., Waszak Cynthia S., Childers Kim Walsh (1989). Family Planning, Abortion and AIDS: Sexuality and Communication Campaigns in: Charles T. Salmon (Ed) *Information Campaigns: Balancing social values and social change*, Sage annual reviews of Communication Research, Vol 18, (Sage Publication).

Bruess, E. Clint, Greenberg S. Jerrod (1981). *Sex Education theory and practice*; Wadsworth Publishing Company, Belmont, California.

Bryman, A., (1993). *Quantity and Quality in Social Research;* London, Sage.

Bunnell, Rebecca E., Somboonsak Yanpaisarn, Peter H. Kilmarx, Phillip H. Rhodes, Khanchit "Overland heroin trafficking routes and HIV-1 spread in south and southeast Asia". *AIDS* 14: 75-83.

Burton Dawn (2000). *Research training for social scientists*, London, Sage.

Carley, M., (1981). *Social measurement and social indicators*; London, George Allen and Unwin.

Carr, W. & Kemmis S. (1986). *Becoming Critical: Education, Knowledge and Action Research*, The Palmer Press, London.

Carl, Greg (1999). Unpublished data on male sex workers, courtesy of Greg Carl, Thai Red Cross.

Chamratrithirong, Aphichat, Varachai Thongthai, Wathinee Boonchalaksi, Philip Guest, Churnrurtai Kanchanachitra, and Anchalee Varangrat (1999). "The success of the 100 per cent condom promotion programme as indicated by the decline of sexually transmitted diseases." *Lancet* 344: 243-45.

Chariyalertsak, Suwat, Thira Sirisanthana, Orapan Saengwonloey, and Kenrad E. Nelson (2000). "Clinical presentation and risk behaviours of AIDS patients in Thailand, 1994-1998: Regional Variation.

Cohen, B. (1963). *The press and foreign policy*, Princeton, NJ: Princeton University Press.

Cohen I, and Manion L. (1989). *Research Methods in Education*, London; Routledge.

Checquer, Pedro (2000). "A strong response to the HIV/AIDS epidemic: The Brazilian Example". Presentation to the XIIIth International Conference on AIDS. Durban, South Africa, July 2000.

Clark, H. (1973). Space, time, semantics and the child. In Moore, T.E. (ed.) *Cognitive development and the acquisition of language*. N.Y.: Academic Press, 287.

Cowan, F.M., & Mindel, A. (1993). Sexually transmitted diseases in children: adolescents. *Genito Urinary Medicine*, 69 (2), 141-147.

Crimp, D. and Rolston A. (1990). *AIDS Demographics*, Bay Press, Seattle.

Dabis, F., V. Leroy, K. Castetbon, R. Spira, M.L. Newell, and R. Salamon (2000). "Preventing mother-to-child transmission of HIV-1 in Africa in the year 2000". *AIDS* 14 (8): 1017-1026.

Dann, B.B. (1992). T.V. or not T.V. *Journal of the American Medical Association*, 268 (8): 1026-7.

Darymple, L. (1992). A Drama Approach to AIDS Education: A report on an AIDS and lifestyle education package implements in rural schools in Kwa Zulu, report compiled for the Department of Health, Pretoria.

Dasgupta P.R. (1993). AIDS Control Programme: the Strategy and the Action, *Swasth Hind*, Nov. Dec.; Vol XXXVII No.11-12: pp. 265-267.

Davies John (1990). Evaluation of a national drug and AIDS education Campaign for Youth; AIDS Health Promotion Exchange, No.1.

Dearing W. James and Rogers M. Everett (1996). *Communication Concepts 6: Agenda Setting*; Sage Publications, 1996; pp. 30-31.

Dearing W. James and Rogers M. Everett, (1992). 'AIDS and the media agenda,' in *AIDS: A communication perspective*, (eds) Edgaar Timothy, Fitzpatrick Anne, Friemuth S.Vicky, Hillsdale, NJ: Lawrence Erlbaum Associates.

Des Jarlais, D.C., H. Hagan, S. R. Friedmann, P. Friedmann, D. Goldberg, M. Frischer, S. Green, K.Tunving, B. Ljungberg, A. Wodak, M. Ross, D. Purchase, M. Milleon and T. Meyers (1995)."Maintaining low HIV seroprevalence in populations of injecting drug users". *JAMA* 274 (15):1226-31.

Demos and Demos (1979). In Linda Neilson's *Adolescent Psychology, A Contemporary view*, Wake Forest University, Hold, Rinehart and Winston Inc. (1987).

Diclement, R.J. and Houston, Hamilton A (1989) Health promotion strategies for prevention of human immonodeficiency virus infection among minority adolescents. *Health Education*, 20 (5), 39-43.

Diclemente, R.J., Brown, L. K., Beausoleil, N. I. and Lodico, M. (1998). Comparison of AIDS Knowledge and HIV related sexual risk behaviours among adolescents in low and high prevalence communities. *Journal of Adolescent Health*, 1998, 14, No.3, pp. 231-236.

Diclemente, R.J., Boyer, C.B. and Morales, E.S., (1988). Minorities and AIDS-Knowledge, attitudes and misconceptions among Blacks and Latino adolescents. *Am.J. Pub. Health Jan.* 1988, Vol.78, No.1.

Diclemente, R.J., Zern, J., Temoshok, L., (1986). Adolescents and AIDS: A survey of knowledge, attitudes and beliefs about AIDS in San Fransisco. *Am. J. Public Health* 1986. 1443-1445.

Diclemente, R.J., (1991). Predictors of HIV–Preventive sexual behaviour in a high risk adolescent population: The influence of perceived peer norms and sexual communication on incarcerated adolescents consistent use of condoms. *Journal of Adolescent Health*, 12, 385-390.

Division of Epidemiology, Ministry of Public Health (2000). Monthly Epidemiological Surveillance Report 31 (Supplement 1), February 2000.

Doheney-Farina, S., (1996). *The Wired Neighbourhood*. New Haven, CT: Yale University Press.

Downs, Anthony, (1972). 'Up and down with ecology-the issue attention cycle,' *The Public Interest* 28:38-50.

Dupree, J.D., Mkwinda, E.N., Kalilani, J.A., (June 20-23, 1990). 'A generation free of AIDS', Developing AIDS Education Materials for Public and Private Schools in Malawi.Int. Conf. AIDS (United States).

Durant, R.H., Sanders, J.M., Jay, S. and Levinson, R. (1988). Analysis of contraceptive behaviour of sexually active female adolescents in the United States. *Journal of Pediatrics*, 113 (5), 930-936.

Editorial (1995). AIDS epidemic catches up with Asia, *AIDS Asia* Vol. III, Issue I (Published by Indian Health Organisation in India).

Eliot, T.S (1945). *Four Quartets*, London; Faber and Faber.

Elder (1987). in Linda Neilson's *Adolescent Psychology, A Contemporary View*, Wake Forest University, Hold, Rinehart and Winston Inc. (1987).

Entz, Achara Thawatwiboonpol, Vipan Prachuabmoh Ruffolo, Vilai Chinveschakitvanich, Varda Soskolne and G.J.P. van Griensven (2000). "HIV-1 prevalence, HIV-1 subtypes and risk factors indicator for the impact of the AIDS epidemic on the Thai population." Bangkok: Institute of Population.

Fielding, N.G. and Fielding, J.C., (1986). *Li... Data*; London; Sage.

Fidler Roger; (1997). *Mediamorphosis; Understanding New Media*; Pine Forge Press.

Fisher, T.D., (1986). An exploratory study of parent child communication about sex and sexual attitudes of early, middle and late adolescents. *Journal of Genetic Psychology*, 147 (4), 543-557.

Fairclough, G., (1995). "Doing the Dirty Work: Asia's brothels thrive on migrant labour". *Far Eastern Economic Review.* December 14, pp. 27-28.

Fiske, J., (1982). *Introduction to Communication Studies*, Metheun, London.

Findahl Olle and Hoijer Briggitta, (1981). 'Studies of news from the perspective of human comprehension,' in *Mass Media Review Yearbook*, Vol.2 (eds) Cleveland G. Wilhoit and Bock, Harold de, Beverly Hills, CA: Sage.

Flora, J.A. and Thoresen, C.E., (1988). Reducing the risk of AIDS in adolescents, *American psychologist*, 43 (11), 965-970.

Francis, P.T., Gill, J.S. and Chowdhary, S., (1994). Knowledge, beliefs and attitudes regarding AIDS, STDs and human sexuality among senior secondary students in Delhi. *Ind. Journal of Community Medicine.* Vol XIX, No.1, 1994. pp. 16-20.

Freeman, P., (1990). Risky business: One days look at the pleasures and pressures of sex at an early age, People 50-60, *Journal of Adolescent Health*, 12, 573-575.

Freire, P., (1996). *Pedagogy of the oppressed, Continuum*, New York.

Garret, Laurie, (1988). The role of media in AIDS epidemic in: Raymond F. Schinazi & Andre J. Nahmias (Eds) *AIDS in children, adolescents and heterosexual adults*, Elsevier Science Publishing Co. Inc.

Gephart, R.P., (1988). *Ethnostatistics: Qualitative Foundations for Quantitative Research*; London: Sage.

Golding, P., (1981). The missing dimensions: News Media and the management of change,' in E. Katz and T. Szecsko (eds), *Mass Media and Social Change.* London and Beverly Hills, CA: Sage Publications.

Goodman, E. and Cohall, A.T., (1989). Acquired immunodeficiency Syndrome and Adolescents: Knowledge, attitudes, beliefs and behaviours in a New York city adolescent minority population. *Pediatrics*, 84 (1), 36-42.

Goulart, M. and Madovar, S., (1991). An AIDS prevention programme for homeless youth. *Journal of Adolescent Health*, 12, 573-575.

Gracious Thomas; *AIDS in India*, Rawat Publications, 1994.

Haffner, D.W., (1988). AIDS and adolescents: school health education must begin now. *Journal of School Health*, 58 (4), 154-155.

Health Policy, (1989). *Economic Impact of AIDS*; Vol. II, No. 2 pp. 101-208.

Health Systems Trust, (1997). South African Health Review, *HST*, Durban.

Herrick, J., (1995). Empowerment practice and social change: The place for new social movement theory, working draft presented for the new social movement and community organizing conference, Seattle, 1995.

Hertog, K., James, Pan, P. David, (1995). The Impact of press coverage on social beliefs: *The case of HIV transmission. Communication Research*, Vol. 22 No. 5 pp. 545-574 (Sage Publications, Inc.).

Hertog, K. James, Finnegan John R., Jr., Kahn, Emily, (1994). Media Coverage of AIDS, Cancer, and sexually transmitted diseases: A test of Public Arenas model, *Journalism Quarterly*, Vol. 71, No. 2, 291-304.

Hiramani, A.B., (1992). Knowledge and attitudes of college students towards AIDS control programme. Intt. Conf. AIDS 1992, 19-24.

Hohenberg, John, (1973). *The professional journalist: a guide to the practices and principles of the new media*, 3rd edition, Columbia University, Holt, Rinehart, Winston, Inc.

Hunt, C.W., Migrant Labour and sexually transmitted diseases (1989). AIDS in Africa; *Journal of Health and Soc. Behaviour*, 30: 353-373.

Hanenberg, R., W. Rojanapithayakorn, P. Kunasol, and D. Sokal (1994). "Impact of Thailand's HIV-Control", *Lancet* 353 (9155): 773-80.

Heineman, S.A., Cowan, F., M., and Mindel, A., (1993). Sexually transmitted diseases in children: adolescents. *Genito Urinary Medicine*, 69 (2), 141-147.

Hilgartner Stephen and Bosk, Charles L., (1988). 'The rise and fall of social problems: a public arena model,' *American Journal of Sociology* 94 (July): 53-78.

IEC (1990). Keys to progress in behaviour change: HIV infection and AIDS; a report to congress on USAID programme for prevention and control; July, USAID, Washington D.C.

Im-em, Wassana (1999). Mortality trends and levels to verify the AIDS epidemic in Thailand: Analysis from death registration statistics, 1984-1997. Bangkok: Institute for Population and Social Research, Mahidol University.

Jackson, P. and Holbrook, B. (1995). Multiple meanings; shopping and cultural politics of identity, *Environment and Planning*, 27: 1913-1930.

Jacob, K.S., Jayakumari Harriot, John, K. Jacob, John, Jacobs T., (1992). Awareness of AIDS in India; effect of public education through mass media; *British Medical Journal*, 99, p. 721.

Jaffe, L.R., Seehaus, M., Wagner, C., and Leadbeater, B.J., (1988). Anal intercourse and knowledge of acquired immunodeficiency syndrome among minority group female adolescents. *Journal of Pediatrics*, 112, 1005-1007.

Jemmott, J.B., Jemmott, L.S. and Fong, G.T., (1997). Reductions in HIV risk associated sexual behaviours among black male adolescents: Effects of an AIDS prevention intervention. *American Journal of Public Health*, March 1997, Vol. 82, No.3, pp. 372-377.

Joffe, A., (1993). Adolescents and Condom Use. *American Journal of Disease of Children*, 147, 746-754.

Johnson A.M., Adler, M.W. and Crown J.M., (1986). The acquired immune deficiency syndrome and epidemic of infection with immunodeficiency virus: Costs of Care and prevention in an inner London district: *Br. Med. J.*; 293/6545 (1986) 489-492.

Johnson, R.L., Douglas, W. and Nelson A., (1992). Sexual behaviour of African-American male college students and the risk of HIV infection. *Journal of National Medical Association*, 84 (10), 864-868.

Joseph, S.C., (1991). AIDS and adolescents: A challenge to both treatment and prevention. *Journal of Adolescent Health*, 12, 614-618.

Kaliyaperumal, K., (1992). Communication in Health Education: Perspectives on methods, in *Health Education for quality of life*, K. Mahadevan. BR Publishing Corporation, Delhi, 1992.

Kasamiya, J., (1991). *Social Environment and HIV seroprevalence in Males in Surat, Preventive and social medicine*, department of Surat Medical College, University Press, Surat.

Katahoire, A., Moodu, R., Kaharuza, F., Balikowa, D., Busuulwa, J., Barten, T., Naamara, W., (Jul 19-24, 1992). W. Int. Conf. AIDS (Netherlands); 8 (20): p. 529 (Abstract no. POD 5843).

Kegeles, S.M., Adler, N., and Irwin, Jr. C.E., (1988). Sexually active adolescents and condoms: changes over one year in knowledge, attitudes and use. *American Journal of Public Health*, 78 (4), 460-461.

Kegeles, S.M., Adler, N.E. and Irwin, C.E., (1989). Adolescents and condoms *America ı Journal of Diseases in Children*, 143, 911-915.

Kelly, R., Konde-Lulu, J.K., Musgrave, S., Sewankambo, N.K., Wawer, M., J., (Jun 6-11, 1993). HIV prevention in Rakai, Uganda. Int. Conf. AIDS (Germany); 9 (2): 791 (Abstract No. PoD 02-3440).

Kennamer, David J., Honnold Julie A., (1995). 'Attitude toward Homosexuality and attention to news about AIDS', *J& MC Quarterly*, Vol.72, No. 2, 322-335.

Khamboonruang (1995). "Same sex behaviour, sexually transmitted diseases, and HIV risks among young northern Thai men". *AIDS* 9:171-176.

Khan, M.E., Anker, M., Patel, B.C., Sadhwani, S., Kohle, R., (1991). The use of focus groups in social and behavioural research—some methodological issues. *World Health Statistical Quarterly*, 44 (1991); pp. 145-149.

Kiamba, J., Kimani, V., Olenja, J., Kanani, S., (July 1994). *Composition on AIDS by primary schools in Kiambu*, Plan International Kiambu.

Kilman, P., Wanlass, R., Sabalis, R. and Sullivan, B., (1981). *Sex education, a review of its effects; Archives of sexual behaviour*.

Kitzinger, J., (1994). The methodology of focus groups: the importance of interaction between research participants; *Sociology of Health and Illness*, 16 (1): 103-121.

Klaidman, S., (1990). How well the media report on health risk. *Deodalus*, 119, pp. 119-132.

Knodel, J., (1993). The design and analysis of focus groups studies; in D.L. Morgan (ed.) *Successful Focus Groups Newbury Park*, CA: Sage.

Krueger, R.A. and Patton, M.Q., (1988). *Focus Groups: A Practical Guide for Applied Research*, Newbury Park, Calif: Sage Publications.

Krueger, E. Leigh, Wood, W. Robert, Diehr, H. Paula, Maxwell, L. Clare (1990). Poverty and HIV Seropositivity; The poor are most likely to be infected; *AIDS* 1990,4:811-814.

Kunawararak, Piyada, Chris, Beyrer, Chawalit, Natpratan *et al.* (1995). "The epidemiology of HIV-1 and mother-to-child HIV transmission prevention program in Thailand". Abstract WeOrC619 and oral presentation, XIIIth International Conference on AIDS, Durban, South Africa, July.

Lazarsfeld, P.F., Berelson, B. and Gaudet, H., (1944). *The Peoples Choice*. New York: Duell, Sloan and Pearce.

Lee, P.R. and Arno, P.S., (1986). The Federal Response to the AIDS Epidemic; *Health Policy*: 6/3 (1986) 259-267.

Lehman, Virginia and Russel Noreen (1998). Psychological and social issues of AIDS and strategies for survival; *Understanding AIDS, a comprehensive guide*, edited by Gong Victor; Syndicate of the University of Cambridge.

Lemert, B. James, (1981). *Does mass communication change public opinion after all* ? Chicago: Nelson Hall.

Lewin, K., (1958). Group decision and social change in Maccaby, E.E., Newcomb, T.M., Hartley, E.L., (eds): *Readings in social psychology*. New York, Holt, Reinhart and Winston, 1958.

Linney, B., (1995). *Pictures, People and Power*, Macmillan, London.

Loibon, D., Lavelle, S., (Jun 20-23, 1990). "Psychological Predictors of Intended Condom Use among Zimbabwean Youth," Int. Conf. AIDS (United States); 6 (1):147 (Abstract No. Th. D. 53).

Long, E., (1991). 'Feminism and Cultural Studies' in R. Avery and D. Eason (eds) *Cultural Perspectives on Media and Society*, pp. 114-125, New York and London, Guillford Press.

Lurie, Peter, Hintzen, Percy, Lowe, Robert A., (1995). Socio-economic obstacles to HIV prevention and treatment in developing countries: the roles of the International Monetary Fund and the World Bank; *AIDS* 1995, 9:539-546

Mackinnon, Ian, Piore, Adam, (June 11, 2001). The other AIDS Crisis, *Newsweek*, 251 West, 57th Street, New York.

Mahadevan, K., (1992). *Health Education for Quality of Life*; BR Publishing Corporation, Delhi, 1992.

Mahalingam, M., (1993). University Talks AIDS Materials Development. Int. Conf. AIDS, 1993 Jun. 6-11; abstrc. no. POD 14-3/95.

Mann, J. and Tarantola, D., (1996). *Health Communication: Lessons from Family Planning and Reproductive Health*, Praeger, Connecticut.

Manual, Carbello and Ronald, Bayer (1990). Social, Cultural and Political Aspects, *AIDS*, 4 (Suppl. 1).

Maticka-Tyndale, E., (1991). Sexual scripts and AIDS prevention: Variations in adherence to safer sex guidelines by heterosexual adolescents. *The Journal of Sex Research*, 28 (1), 45-66.

Mays, V.M., Albee G.W. and Schneider, S.F., (1989). *Primary Prevention of AIDS—Psychological Approaches*. Sage Publications, New Delhi, India.

McKusick, L., Horstman, W., Abrams, D., Coats, T., (1986). The Impact of AIDS on Primary Practice Physicians, Paper presented at II International Conference on AIDS, Paris 23-25 June.

McCombs, M.E. and Shaw, D.L., (1972). 'The agenda setting function of the press', *Public Opinion Quarterly*, 36: 176-87.

McDevitt, M. Teresa, Shehehan, Eugene, R., Lennon Randy, Ambrosio L. Anthony, (1990). 'Correlates of attitudes towards AIDS', *Journal of Social Psychology*,130: 699-701.

Melton, G.B., (1988). Adolescents and the Prevention of AIDS. *Professional Psychology Research and Practice*, 19 (4), 403-408.

Merton, R.K., Fiske, M., Kendall, P.L., (1956). *The Focused Interview*, New York: Free Press.

Metzger, David (1997). "Drug Abuse Treatment as AIDS Prevention". In NIH Consensus Development Conference, Interventions to Prevent HIV Risk Behaviours: Program and Abstracts. Bethesda, MD: N.

Mendelsohn, Harold, (1981). 'Some reasons why information campaigns can succeed,' *Public Opinion Quarterly*, 37: 50-61.

Miller David (1989). HIV and social psychiatry; *British Medical Bulletin* (1988) Vol 44, No.1 pp. 130-148.

Mitra, A., (1994). Condoming Safe Sex in hostels, *The Hindustan Times* (Delhi Edition) September 8, 1994.

Mock, P., Korattana, S. and Mastro, T.D., (2000). "Rapid assessment of sex, drugs, HIV and STDs among adolescents and young adults in northern Thailand using audio-computer interviewing and non-invasive specimen collection. Draft, July. (Thai version in press, *Journal of Health Sciences*).

Mocroft, A., Miller, V., Chiesi, A., Blaxhult, A., Katlama, C., Clotet, B., Barton, S. and Lundgren, J.D., (2000). "Virological failure among patients on HAART from across Europe: results from the Euro SIDA Accounts Development: Lessons from Thailand". Health Policy and Planning 14(4): 342-353.

Moses Stephen, Plummer A. Francis, Ngugi Elizabeth, Nagelkerke J.D. Nico, Anzala O Aggrey, Netinya Achola O Jachomiah (1991). Controlling HIV in Africa: Effectiveness and cost of an intervention in a high frequency STD transmitter group: *AIDS*, Vol. 5, No. 4, April 1991.

Morgan, D.L., (1988). *Focus Groups as Qualitative Research*, Newsbury Park, CA: Sage.

Morgan, D.L., (1993). (ed.) *Successful Focus Groups Newbury Park*, CA: Sage.

Multimedia workshop on AIDS (1994) Educational materials development; Edited By Dr. Bhagban Prakash, Department of Youth Affairs and Sports, GOI.

Mundul, J. and Gilada, I., (1993). Indian Health Organisation; Media Response to AIDS in India; Int. Conference on AIDS.

Murugan, S., Haleelullah, M.C.A. and Mahajan, N., (1997). Knowledge and attitude towards AIDS among medical students. ND. *J. Sex*. Trans. is.

Mussen, P.H., (ed) (1970). *Carmicheal's manual of child psychology* (3rd edition) Vol. I, II, N.Y.: Wiley.

Nangle, D.W. and Hansen, D.J., (1993). Relations between social skills and high risk sexual interactions among adolescents: current issues and future directions. *Behaviour Modification*, 17 (2), 113-135.

Narayan Reddy, D., (1992). Murthy, M.S.R.; *Perspectives on Sex Education*, BR Publishing Corporation, Delhi.

National Commision on AIDS, (1994). Preventing HIV/AIDS in adolescents. *Journal of School Health*, 64 (1), 39-51.

National AIDS Control Programme (India) (1993). Country Scenario Update April 1993, NA. Min. of Health and Family Welfare, Govt. of India.

Napier, R.W. Matli, K. Gershenfeld, (1996). *Groups Theory and Experience*: Temple University, Houghton Mifflin Company.

Neergard, L.D., (1988). *Adolescents—Knowledge, attitude and practice. AIDS Prevention and Control*. WHO: London 26-28 Jan. 1988.

Nelkind, D., (1987). *Selling Science: How the press covers science and technology*. New York, W.H. Freeman.

Nelsen, K.E., Eiumtrakul, S., Celentano, D.D., Beyrer C., Kuntolbutra, S. and Khamboonruang, C., (1998)."HIV infection in young men in northern Thailand, 1991-1997: Increasing role of injection drug use".XIIth International Conference on AIDS, Geneva. [1517/43555]

NESDB Working Group on HIV/AIDS Projections (1994). "Projections for HIV/ AIDS" in Thailand.

News report (3rd December 1995). DD programme on AIDS, (*The Hindustan Times*).

News Report (24th June, 2001). *The Hindu*.

News Report (6th February 2001). New HIV strain found in S. Korea; *The Indian Express*.

News Report (1st December, 1995). AIDS TB epidemic predicted in India, (*The Statesman*).

News Report (2nd December, 1993). Watching AIDS grow from day to day, (*The Times of India*)

News Report (3rd December, 1995). AIDS enters 2nd phase in India: IHO, (*The Times of India*)

News Report (2nd Dec., 1994). AIDS Day? What AIDS Day?, *The Hindu*, 2000.

Newsletter of the National AIDS Control Organisation, (Jun. 1994). AIDS in India: The role of media; points for action and reflection.

Nguyen, T. and Alexander, J., (1996). The coming of cyberspace and the end of the polity. In R. Shields (Ed.) *Cultures of the Internet: Virtual Spaces, real histories, living bodies*. London, Sage.

Nicholas, S.E., (1987). An Overview of the psychological and social reactions to AIDS; Int. Conf. on AIDS; Paris 23-25 June 1986; Paris Elsevier 1987 p. 261.

Nicholi, D.J., (1998). Sex and the modern medical student—the effect of AIDS publicity. *Health Education Journal*, Vol. 48, No. 1, 1998.

Nishino, Y., (1992). Risk perception of AIDS among Japanese graduate students in the United States. Int. Conf. AIDS 1992 Jul. 19-24; 8 (3): 221 (abstr. no. PuD 9135).

Noelle-Neuman, E., (1973). 'Return of the concept of powerful mass media', Studies of broadcasting, 9: 66-112.

Normand, J.D. Vlahov, and L.E. Moses, eds. (1995). Preventing HIV Transmission: The role of sterile needles and bleach. A Report of the Panel on Needle Exchange and Bleach Distribution Programs, Commission on Behavioural and Social Sciences and Education. National Research Council and Institute of Medicine. Washington, D.C. National Academy Press.

Odujinrin, O.M., (1991). Adolescents AIDS knowledge, attitudes and beliefs about preventive practices in Nigeria. Eur. *J. Epidemiol.* 1991 Mar; 7 (2): 127-33.

Orr, D.P. and Langefeld, C.D., (1991). Factors associated with condom use by sexually active male adolescents at risk for sexually transmitted disease. *Pediatrics*, 91 (5), 873-879.

Panos Media Briefing No. 3, Delhi, (1992). AIDS in development; Panos Institute, 9 White Lion Street, London N, 9PDOK.

Pant, K.M. and Singh, K.P., (1993). Indira Gandhi Open University; Analysis of Media Response to an International Conference on AIDS in India.; Int Conference on AIDS.

Parker, W., (1994). The development of community-based media for AIDS education and prevention in South Africa: Towards an action based participatory research model, MA thesis, University of Natal, Durban.

Parker, W., (1997). Action Media – consultation, collaboration and empowerment in health promotion, paper presented at the second international conference on Entertainment education and social change, Athens, Ohio.

Palmer P., *et al.* (1988). The representation of AIDS in entertainment television. A report to the Center for Population Options, 1 November 1988.

Perriens, Jos., (1999). "Compulsory licensing and access to HIV drugs". Conference on Community and Home Care for People with HIV Infection. Paris.

Petosa, R. and Wessinger, J., (1990). The AIDS education needs of adolescents: a theory based approach. *AIDS Education and Prevention*, 2 (2), 127-136.

Phoolcharoen, Wiput, Kumnuan Ungchusak, Werasit Sittitrai, and Tim Brown (1998). "Thailand: 1999, Kuala Lumpur, Malaysia. Director of Disease Prevention and Control, WPRO, WHO, Geneva. abroad", Vol. 1. San Francisco, CA: University of California.

Piercy, F.P., Trepper, T. and Jurich, J., (1993). The role of family therapy in decreasing HIV high-risk behaviours among adolescents. *AIDS Education and Prevention*, 5 (1), 71-86.

Piot P. and Carael, M., (1996). Epidemiological and sociological aspects of HIV infection in developing countries; *AIDS and HIV infections, the wider perspective*; Editors Pinching A.J., Weiss R.A., and Miller D.; Published for the British Council by Churchill Livingstone.

Piotrow, P., Meyer, R.C., Zulu, B.A., (1992). AIDS and mass persuasion. In: Mann, J., Tarantola, D., Netter, T., eds. *AIDS in the World*. Cambridge, Harvard University Press, 733-47.

Pitts, M. and Jackson, H., (1993 a) Press Coverage of AIDS in Zimbabwe: a five year review, *AIDS Care*, Vol.5, No. 2.

Ponnuraj, S. and Shankarapandian (1994). Analysis and assessment of knowledge about AIDS among students of Gandhigram Rural University. Health and Population—Perspectives and Issues 17 (1&2): 45-55.

Ponton, L.E., DiClemente, R.J. and McKenna, S., (1991). An AIDS education and prevention program for Hospitalized adolescents, *Journal of American Academy of Child and Adolescents Psychiatry*, 30 (5),729-734.

Porter, S.B., (1993). Stanford University, Cal USA.: Public knowledge and attitude about AIDS among adults in Calcutta, AIDS Care; Psychological and socio-medical aspects of AIDS/HIV; Volume 5 November 2, 1993; Carfax Publishing Company.

Press Council of India (1998). Norms for journalistic conduct, guidelines on specific issues.

Pujari, S., Walimbe, P., Patwardhan, N., Khatavkar, P., Oak, V., Mulay, S., Mehta, A. and Pense, P., (1992). Impact of health education on knowledge regarding AIDS amongst rural students in Maharashtra, India. Int. Conf. AIDS Jul. 19-24; (abstc. no. PoD 5119).

Porapakkham, Yaowarat, Somjai Pramarnpol, Suparatra Athicbhoddhi and Richard Bernhard (1996)."The evolution of HIV/AIDS Policy in Thailand: 1984-1994". AIDSCAP Policy Working Paper Series, WP5. Family Health International/AIDSCAP/USAID. Project 936-5972.31-4692046.

Pothisiri, Pakdee, Viroj Tangcharoensathien, Jongkol Lertiendumrong, Vijj Kasemsup, and Piya Hanvoravongchai (1999). "Funding Priorities for the HIV/AIDS Crisis in Thailand". UNAIDS Best Practice Collection. UNAIDS: Geneva.

Prescott, Nicholas (1997). "Setting prioirities for government involvement with antiretrovirals", in Eric van Praag, Susan Fernyak, and Alison Martin Katz, eds. *The implications of antiretroviral treatments: Informal Consultation*. Geneva: World Health Organization.

Punnotok, J., Shaffer, N., Naiwatanakul, T., Pumprueg, U., Subhannachart, P., Ittiravivongs, A., *et al.* (2000). "Human immunodeficiency virus-related tuberculosis and primary drug resistance in Bangkok, Thailand". Chapter 20 of Tim Brown, ed., *Sexually Transmitted Diseases in Asia*.

Pyne, Hnin Hnin (1999). Assessing the effects of personal networks on HIV risk sexual behaviours among migrants from Burma in Ranong and Chiang Mai, Thailand. Johns Hopkins University School of Public Health. Unpublised doctoral thesis.

Quraishi, S.R., (1996). Social Marketing of AIDS Awareness, an Indian Experiment, Deptt. of Youth and Sports, Ministry of Human Resource Development, Government of India.

Radway, J., (1987). *Reading the Romance*, London: Verso.

Rae, N., Scechter, K., Kumaresan, G., Nataraj, S., Solomon, W., (1992). Peer educators at no cost; paper presented at the International Conference of AIDS 1992, July 19-24.

Raman, S. Sundara (1992). Positive reinforcement to promote safer sex among clients; AIDS Health Promotion Exchange; KIT Netherlands; No.1.

Reddy, *et al.* (1983). Quoted by Moni Nag: Sexual behaviour and AIDS in India—State-of-the-art. Paper presented at workshop on sexual aspects of AIDS/STD prevention in India. Nov. 23-27, 1993. Tata Instt. of Social Sciences, Bombay. Quoted by Watrsa M.C.: Readings on sexuality and reproductive health. Family Planning Assoc. of India. Bombay, 1993.

Redjimi, G. and Lert, F., (1993). Images of AIDS among teenagers and young adults, *AIDS Care*, Vol 5, No. 4.

Rogers, M., (1983). *Communication Strategies for Family Planning*. New York: The Free Press.

Rogers, E.M., (1993). 'Looking back, looking forward: A century of communication research', in P. Gaunt (ed), *Beyond Agendas: New Directions in Communication Research*, pp.19-40. New Haven, CT: Greenwood Press.

Romer D. and Harnik, R., (1992). HIV education for youth—the importance of social consensus in behaviour change. *AIDS Care*, Vol.4, No. 3, pp. 285-305.

Sahani Ashok, Xirasagar Sudha (1992). *Action Programme against HIV-AIDS, role of various sectors; HIV AIDS in India, Epidemiology, Diagnosis, Prevention and Control*; Health Administrator, Vol. 3 No. 2, December 1992.

Salmon, Charles, T., (1989). (Ed) *Information campaigns: balancing social values and social change*; Sage annual review of communication, research volume 18; Sage publications; 1989.

Samkaram, S. and Samkaram, H., (1993). Economic impact due to AIDS; Int. Conference on AIDS 1993.

Sarkar, Swarup, Das, N., Panda, T., Naik, N., Sarkar, K., Singh, B.C., Ralte, J.M., Aier, S.M. and Tirpathy, S.P., (1993). "Rapid spread of HIV among injecting drug users in North-Eastern States of India". *Bulletin on Narcotics* 45 (1): 91-105.

Savvy, Magna Publication, September 1995.

Schopper, D., (1990). Research on AIDS onterventionsin developing countries—state of the atr. *Soc. Sci. Med.* vol. 30; No. 12, pp. 1265-1272.

Scitovsky, A.A. and Rice D.P., (1987). Estimates of the direct and indirect costs of Acquired Immunodeficiency Syndrome in the United States, 1985-86 and 91; *Public Health Rep.* 102 (1) 5-17.

Scitovsky, A.A., Cline, M. and Lee, P.R., (1986). Medical Care costs of patients with AIDS in San Francisco; *J. Am. Med. Asso.* 256/22, 3103-3106.

Scitovsky Anne A., (1989). The cost of AIDS: an agenda for research: *Health policy* II 197-208.

Schramm, W., Lyle, J. and Parker, E., (1961). *Television in the lives of our children*. Stanford, CA: Stanford University Press.

Seage, G.R., Landers, S. and Barry, M., (1986). Medical Care costs of AIDS in Massachussetts; *J. Am. Med. Asso.* 256 (22) 3107-3109.

Sehgal, P.N. and Singh, K., (1992). Knowledge, practices and beliefs and practices study related to AIDS in Manipur state, India and intervention strategies. Voluntary Health Association of India.

Sehinazi, Raymond K., Nahmias, Andre, J., (1988). *AIDS in children, adolescents and heterosexual adults; An interdisciplinary approach to prevention*; Elsevier Science Publishing Co. Inc.

Seltzer, V.L., Rabin, J. and Benjamin, P., (1999). Teenager's awareness of the acquired immunodeficiency syndrome and the impact on their sexual behaviour. *Obstretr. & Gynaecol.* Vol.74 No. 1, July, pp. 55-59.

Shanmuganandan, S. and Subramanian, P.T., (1989). Department of Geography, Madurai Kamaraja University; Int Conf. AIDS.

Sharma, A.K., *et al.* (1992) KABP study on AIDS in rural female students.Paper presented at the 2nd International Congress on AIDS in Asia and Pacific, New Delhi, 8-12 Nov. (abstr. poster C 10).

Sharma, N.M., (2000). Lecture at Workshop on social and clinical dimensions of HIV/AIDS; ICSSR, Panjab University, Chandigarh, 11th April.

Sharma, R.C., (1992). Awareness of AIDS among final year medical students *Ind. J. of Sex.* Trans. Dis. Dec. 1992, 21-22.

Sherr, L. Long and short-term impact of the U.K. government health education campaign on AIDS. 1998 (unpublished).

Sherr, L., Palmer, C., Goldmeirt, D. and Green, J., (1996). *AIDS Information*: Lancet 1996.

Shilts, R., (1987). *And the band played on: politics, people and AIDS Epidemic*, Penguin, London.

Shyamala Shiveshwarkar (June 24, 2001). Media and the AIDS reality, in *The Hindu*.

Silverman, D., Perakyla, A. and Bore, R. (1992). Discussing safer sex in HIV counselling, assessing three communication formats, *AIDS Care* Vol. 4, No.1.

Silverman, Mervyn F., (9 January 1993). 'Colorado and Amendment 2: Homophobia is a cofactor of AIDS,' *the Am FAR Report*, Special Edition: 7.

Simkins, L. and Kushner, A., (1986). Attitudes towards AIDS, Herpes II and toxic shock syndrome—two years later. *Psycho Rep.*1986;59: 883-891.

Simmonneau, M.Claude Bernard, Regneer P., Vitte Cocq D. *et al.* (1984). *Cost of blood products in AIDS patients: a review of 28 cases followed up in Hospital*; Rev.Fr. Transfer Immuno-Hematol, 27/4 557-560.

Simon, M., Patricia, Morse D. Edward, Balson M. Paul, Osofsky J. Howard, Gaumer Richard H. (1993). Barriers to human immunodeficiency virus related risk reduction among male street prostitutes; *Health Education Quarterly* Vol. 20 No. 2; Wiley Publishers.

Singer, E., (1990). A question of accuracy: How journalists and scientists report research on hazards. *Journal of Communication* 40, pp.102-116.

Siqueira, E., (1992). HIV outreach communication intervention for Brazilian street youth. Int. Conf. AIDS 1992 Jul 19-24; 8 (2): D395 (abstr. no. PoD 5050).

Smith, P.B., Weinman, M. and Mumtord, D.M., (1992). Knowledge, beliefs and behavioural risk factors for HIV infection in the inner city adolescent females. *Sexually Transmitted Diseases*. Jan.-Feb. 1992, Vol. 19, No. 1, pp. 19-24.

Smith, K.W., McGraw, S.A. Crawford, S.L., Costa L.A. and McKinlay, J.B., (1993). HIV risk among Latino adolescents in two New England cities. *American Journal of Public Health*, 83 (10), 1395-1399.

Sreedhar, Jaya, (1995). The vaccine question: the search for a transgenic banana. (India, *Frontline*).

St. Louise Micheal E., (1990). HIV Seroepidemiology Branch, Centre for Infectious Diseases, CDC.

Steinberg, L., Elmen, J.D. and Mounts, N.S., (1989). Authoritative parenting psychosocial maturity, and academic success among adolescents. *Child development*, 60, 1424-1436.

Steven, G.Jones, (1998). *Cybersociety 2.0: Revisiting coputer-mediated communication and community*, Sage Publications, London, New Delhi.

Stevenson, H.C. and Davies, G., (1994). Impact of culturally sensitive AIDS video education on the AIDS risk knowledge of African – American adolescents. *AIDS Education and Prevention*, 6 (1), 40-52.

Stewart, D.W. and Shamdasani, P.N., (1990). *Focus Groups—Theory and Practice*. Newbury Park, Calif: Sage Publications.

St. Louise, Micheal E., (1990). HIV Seroepidemiology Branch, Centre for Infectious Diseases, CDC.

Strauss, J. and Faber, R., (1985). Formal versus informal sources of sex education; *Adolescence*.

Srinivasan, K., (1998). *Basic Demographic Techniques and Applications*; Sage Publications.

'Strunin L., Hingson R., (1987). Acquired Immunodeficiency Syndrome and adolescent knowledge, beliefs, attitudes and behaviours. *Paediatrics* 79: 825-828.

Strunin, L., (1991). Adolescents perceptions of risk for HIV infection-implications for future research. *Soc. Sci. Med.* Vol. 32, no. 2; pp 221-228.

Strunin, L. and Hingson, R., (1992). Alcohol, Drugs and Adolescent Sexual Behaviour. *The International Journal of the Additions*, 27 (2), 129-146.

Sullivan, S., (1993). The media and their limitations, In: Mann, J., Tarantola, D., Netter, T., (eds) *AIDS in the world*. Cambridge, Harvard University Press, 733-47.

Sung Sil Lee Sohng (1995). Participatory Research and Community Organizing, A working paper presented at the new socialk movement and community organizing conference, Seattle.

Swasth Hind: Talking about AIDS-Communicating with youth. Vol. XXXVII no. 11-12; Nov. Dec. 1993.

Suwanvanichikij, Voravit, B.S., Chris Beyrer and Chirasak Khamboonuruang (1996). "Access to Health in Thailand, 2000-2020". Draft. Presented at the Siam City Hotel, Bangkok, June 30, 2000.

Thaineua, V., Sirinirund, P., Kanshana, S., Voramongkol, N., Tanbanjong, A., Natpratan, C., Chinda-abhirakkul, P. and Vinara, P., (2000). "Scaling up: From pilot projects and clinical trials to a nationwide in Thailand: The results of 1995-1999 surveys". *Monthly Epidemiological Surveillance Report* 31 (Supplement 2), February 2000.

Tangcharoensathien, Viroj, Piya Harnvoravongchai, Siriwan Pitayarangsarit and Vijj Kasemsup (2000). "Health impacts of rapid economic changes in Thailand", *Social Science and Medicine* 51 (6): 789-807.

Teokul, Waranya (1998). "Discrepancy between policy and AIDS interventions: Thailand". Paper presented to the 1998 Annual Meeting of the Association for Asian Studies, Washington, D.C.

Tewari, V.K., Bhargava, N.C. and Pandey, V.K., (1990). AIDS-Impact of health education. *Indian J. of Sex*. Transm. Dis. 11; 59-63.

Thai Working Group on HIV/AIDS Projections (2000). "Executive Summary: Projections of HIV/AIDS adolescents and young adults in northern Thailand". The role of same-sex behaviour in the HIV epidemic among northern Thai men. "XIIth International 1987-2020". Bangkok: NESDB. (working group members: Tim Brown, Chirapun Gullaprawit, WerasitSittitrai, Sombat Thanprasertsuk, Aphichat Chamratrithirong).

Thailand Business Coalition on AIDS (TBCA) (2000). "Busines Responds to AIDS. TBCA Working Paper Series. Bangkok, August Thailand, 1998-2000". MOPH, UNICEF, HIV/AIDS Collaboration, US CDC. Oral presentation to the VIIIth International Conference on AIDS, Durban, South Africa, July 2000.

The 1992 Asian Developmant Outlook published by Asian Development Bank.

Thomas, W. Lee, (1999). *Using Qualitative Methods in Organisational Research*; ORM, Sage Publications.

Tomaselli, K. *et al*. (1996). *Comprehensive and integrated HIV/AIDS prevention campaigns*—potentials for South and Southern Africa, in Odasuo Alali, A. (ed) California State University, Berkley (1998).

Turner, C., Anderson, P., Fitzpatrick, R., Fowler, G. and White, R.M., (1992). Sexual behaviour, contraceptive practice and knowledge of AIDS of Oxford University Students. *J. Biosoc. Sci.* 20; pp. 445-451.

Universities talk AIDS —an awareness raising campaign among the student youth in India. Prakash, B. and Larivee, C. presented a paper with the same title at the International Conference of AIDS 1992, July 19-24.

UNAIDS (2000). "HIV and health care reform in Phayao: From crisis to opportunity", UNAIDS Case Study, UNAIDS Best Practice Collection. Geneva, April.

UNAIDS (1999). State of the Global HIV/AIDS Pandemic. Geneva.

UNICEF EAPRO (2000). "Estimating numbers of children affected", Mekong Children and HIV/AIDS, April.

Van Eijeck, C., (1992). Trends in the demand for HIV information.The Netherlands, 1987-92. Int. Conf AIDS Jul. 19-24; (abstrc. no. PoD 5862).

Velasquez, German and Jos Perriens (2000). "WHO/UNAIDS Joint mission: Access to HIV/AIDS-related controlled trial of immediate and deferred zidovudine in symptom-free HIV infection". *Lancet* 343 (8902): 871-81.

Velhal, G.D., Daniel, E.E., Pai, N.P., (1994). What do they know about AIDS? College students of Bombay. *Care Calling*, Vol.7 No. 1, Jan-March, pp. 36-40. Viravaidya, Mechai, Stasia A. Obremskey and Charles Myers (1993). "The economic impact of AIDS on Thailand". Chapter 2 of D.E. Bloom and J.W. Lyons, eds. *Economic implications of AIDS in Asia*. New Wabwire-Mangen, C. Li, F. Nalugoda, N. Kiwanuka, T. Lutalo, R. Brookmeyer, R. Kelley, T.C. Quinn.

Watson, Lashley, J.B., (1928). *Psychological care of infant and child*, N.Y.: Norton.

Walter, H.J., Vaughan, R.D., Gladis, M.M., Ragin, D.F., Kasen, S. and Cohall A.T., (1993). Factors associated with AIDS related behavioural intentions among high school students in an AIDS epicentre. *Health Education Quarterly*, Vol. 20 (3); 409-420 (fall).

Wanta Wayne and Elliot R.William, (1995). Did the 'magic' work ? Knowledge of HIV/AIDS and the knowledge gap hypothesis, *J& MC Quarterly*, Vol.72, No. 2, 312-321.

Westley, B. and Maclean, M., (1957). 'A Conceptual Model for Mass Communication Research', *Journalism Quarterly*, 34: 31-8.

WHO (1991). Initial assessment—Knowledge, attitude, beliefs and practices relating to HIV/AIDS among the general public. WHO AIDS Series No. 5 WHO, Geneva.

Wight, D., (1992). Impediments to safer heterosexual sex: A review of research with young people. *AIDS Care*, Vol. 4, No1, pp. 11-21.

Wilson, D., Greenspan, R. and Wilson, C., (1998). Knowledge about AIDS and self reported behaviour among Zimbabwean secondary school pupils. *Soc. Sci. Med.* Vol.28, no. 9; pp 957-961.

Wilson, David, Paul Cawthorne, Nathan Ford, and Saree Aongsonwang (1999). "Global trade and access to medicines: AIDS treatments in Thailand". *Lancet* 354 (Nov. 27, 1999): 1893-95.

Winsten, J.A., (1995). Science and the media: The boundaries of truth. *Health Affaires*, 4, pp. 5-23.

Wong, T., Chiasson, M.A., Reggy, A., Simonds, R.J., Heffess, J. and Loo, V., (2000). "Antiretroviral therapy and declining AIDS mortality in New York City". *Journal of Urban Health* 77 (3): 492-500.

Wongsena, W., Kunakorn, M., Tanprasert, S. and Petchclai, B., (1997). "Detection of HIV-1 window period infection in blood donors using borderline anti-HIV results, HIV-1 proviral DNA PCR, and HIV-1antigen test". *Journal of the Medical Association of Thailand* 80 (suppl 1): S112-5.

World Bank (1999). *Confronting AIDS: Public Priorities in a Global Epidemic.* Revised edition. New York: Oxford University Press.

World Bank Development Report (1993). *Investing in health*—Oxford University Press. pp. 72-107.

World Health Organisation (1997). AIDS in India: AIDS no time for complacency, AIDS prevention programme.

Wu, Z., Zhang, J., Detels, R., Li, V.C., Cheng, H., Duan, S., *et al.* (1997). "Characteristics of risk-taking behaviours, HIV and AIDS knowledge, and risk perception among young maies in Southwest China." *Journal of Acquired Immune Deficiency.*

Yao, F.K., (1992). Youth and AIDS: A Priority for Prevention Education. AIDS Health Promotion Exchange. No. 2: p.

Yarcheski, A., Mahon, N.E., and Yarcheski, T.J. (1992). Validation of the PRQ85 social support measure for adolescents. *Nursing Research*, 41 (6), 332-227.

Zimet, G.D., Diclemente, R.J., Lazebnik, R., Anglin, T.M., Ellick, E.M. and Williams, P., (1993). Changes in adolescents knowledge and attitudes about AIDS over the course of the AIDS epidemic. *Journal of Adolescent Health*, Vol.14, No.2 pp. 85-90. 11-21.

Index